Morrison of the Bounty

A Scotsman: Famous but Unknown

James Shaw Grant

With all good wishes
Jim Grant
10 · 12 · 57

acair

Permission to reproduce the illustrations which appear in this book are by courtesy of:
National Maritime Museum, Greenwich, London.
National Library of Australia.
National Library of Scotland.
Public Record Office, Kew. Crown copyright material in the Public Record Office is
reproduced with the permission of the Controller of Her Majesty's Stationery Office.

The front cover illustration is a photograph of a plaque of H.M.S. Bounty
discovered in a woodcarver's shop in a small village in the Italian Alps,
two hundred years after the mutiny.

The back cover photograph, the modern day 'Tall Ship Bounty' was supplied and
reproduced with the kind permission of Carl Herzog, Third Mate, 'Tall Ship Bounty'.

The author recieves no royalties from this publication. All royalties have been donated,
as with his previous book, *A Shilling For Your Scowl*, to Acair, to assist with the publication
of Gaelic texts for children.

First published in Scotland in 1997 by Acair Ltd.,
7 James Street, Stornoway, Isle of Lewis.

© 1997 James Shaw Grant.

Designed and typeset by Acair Ltd.

Printed by Redwood Books, Wiltshire.

ISBN 0 86152 197 8

Contents

FOREWORD

I first learned that James Morrison, boatswain's mate on the BOUNTY, was a native of Stornoway sixty years ago, when the film of the mutiny, based on Morrison's Journal, and starring Charles Laughton, was shown in Stornoway Playhouse.

One of my aunts, Jessie, an elderly and timid spinster, told me she was going to see the film. I tried to dissuade her. I thought she would be shocked by the violence. "I want to see it," she persisted, "James Morrison was a relative of ours." I did not take Jessie very seriously, and I took her even less seriously when, a few days later, she told me she had seen the film, "and the family resemblance was unmistakeable." Jessie was a real innocent, but, of the family, she was the one most interested in old lore, which she retailed at inappropriate moments, and often to the embarrassment of other members of the family. Fortunately I asked her where she got that particular item of information from. She replied, "Magaidh a' Chaiptein" - meaning, Maggie, the Captain's daughter. That meant nothing to me at the time, although I had heard the name frequently when my uncles and aunts were reminiscing. I asked Jessie's oldest brother, Rev Roderick Morison, then in his middle seventies, if he had ever heard the story about James Morrison. He said, "No," but added that he had never been interested in family gossip. When I told him Jessie got the information from Magaidh a' Chaiptein, his mood changed. "She was in a position to know," he said.

Around the same time I had a letter from another member of the family, Dr William Morison, whose adult life was spent in County Durham, where he had a medical practice at Annfield Plain. He said he heard the old sailors in his youth speaking of the family's relationship with James Morrison of the BOUNTY. More significantly he recalled them saying that Morrison had been "king of a South Sea Island." That phrase could not have been suggested by anything in the literature of the BOUNTY until the belated publication of Morrison's own Journal, in a limited edition, by the Golden Cockerel Press, in 1935. It rings true as the sort of phrase that might be used by sailors who heard James Morrison tell, *viva voce*, the story he unfolds in his description of his sojourn in Tahiti. A claim that a James Morrison from Stornoway was the James Morrison of the BOUNTY could be founded on nothing more substantial than the similarity of names. A claim, made before the publication of the Journal, that a James Morrison from Stornoway was on the BOUNTY and afterwards became "king of a South Sea Island" implies some contact with the man himself.

There the matter rested until, after my retiral in 1978, I was leafing through William Matheson's account of the life of the Blind Harper of Dunvegan, and discovered, in one of the genealogies at the end of the book, who Magaidh a' Chaiptein really was. She was a daughter of Neil Morison, who was a Captain in the Royal navy. More importantly, she was a granddaughter of Lillias Morison, whose brother was a Lieut in the navy. Lillias lived to be a centenarian. When Magaidh a' Chaiptein was in her late teens, Lillias was living alone in Stornoway, just a few doors away. There must have been considerable commerce between grandmother and granddaughter. Thus there is only one link (Magaidh a' Chaiptein) between my informant (Jessie) and a woman who was in her twenties when the mutiny took place, was herself related to the mutineer sufficiently closely to be called his cousin according to the usage of the time, and had a brother and son in the navy, when James Morrison was drowned in circumstances which must have been widely known throughout the fleet.

When I commented on the BOUNTY connection in the *STORNOWAY GAZETTE*, Mrs Rhoda Macleod, sister of Joan Mackenzie, a well-known Gaelic singer, told me there was a tradition in her family that a great uncle, "had made a name for himself in the mutiny on the BOUNTY." She was not familiar with the literature about the BOUNTY and assumed the mutineer's name must be Mackenzie, her own maiden name, until she read my note, when she realised that, if the connection was on the distaff side, the mutineer's name would have been Morison. She had been told by her grandfather's cousin, Christina Macmillan, 6 Swordale, who was accepted as a reliable bearer of local tradition, that, in addition to the mutineer, another relative had been a ship's captain who lost his life off the English coast, and the family had been related by marriage to a family of Morisons who had been tacksmen at Aignish. Mrs Macleod added that another of the family, known as Big Peggy, had been in the habit of visiting what she called "posh relatives" in Newton Street, along the seafront of Stornoway Harbour, where, at the turn of the century almost every house had at least one ship's captain. The link between the Mackenzies and the Morisons in Mrs Macleod's family tree is provided by Isabella Morison who married Murdo Mackenzie, the last tacksman of Aird. The family tradition does not identify Isabella Morison, and no marriage or baptismal records of the period exist, but, if Isabella was a daughter of James Morison, merchant and tacksman in Stornoway, who was the mutineer's father, everything falls into place. If Isabella was the mutineer's sister, the mutineer was clearly a great uncle of her descendants. The other pieces fit equally well. My great grandfather, the mutineer's nephew. Roderick Morison, was drowned off Penzance in November 1833, when the Stornoway owned vessel MARY ANN, of which he was mate, was driven ashore with a cargo of timber from Canada. None of the crew was saved and the local papers of the period give a vivid picture of the wreckage which strewed the beach, including personal letters addressed to their wives at home. In Stornoway the Local Lodge of Freemasons staged a concert to raise funds for the support of the widows and orphans. The Aignish link, in the Mackenzie family tradition, was through Lieut John Morison, Magaidh a' Chaiptein's grand uncle. The "posh relatives in Newton" visited by Big Peggy, in more recent times, were Roderick Morison Jnr, the mutineer's grand-nephew, who lived at number 29, and Mrs Pope, the mutineer's great grand-niece, who lived at number 1.

I have attempted to find confirmation for the local tradition in the surviving naval records, but so far without success. The material is voluminous, but incomplete, and often inaccurate. For instance, James Morrison's place of birth is given as London in the muster roll of the BOUNTY, but as Bandon, Cork in the muster roll of the VICTORY, which he joined after his trial and reprieve. Both cannot be right, but both can be wrong. The Bandon entry would appear to have arisen through the slippage of lines when copying from one list to another. The London entry is almost certainly wrong. James Morrison first joined the navy as a clerk in Leith. It is easy to see why a lad from the Western Isles should look for employment in Leith, but why would a well educated lad from London seek advancement in such an unlikely direction? As I show in the course of the book, Highlanders, even a generation after Culloden, had reason to conceal rather than advertise their provenance. The boatswain's mate of the BOUNTY spelt his surname in the English style with two "rs". The merchant in Stornoway, whom tradition says was his father, spelt his surname with one. This, however, raises no difficulty. Such is the pressure to conform with English usage, the great majority of Lewis Morisons, even Gaelic enthusiasts, use two "rs" although they are not sons of Morris but descendants of "Mores the sone of Kennanus, whom the Irish historiance call Makurich," according to John Morisone (c 1630-1708), who wrote the first account in English of the Island of Lewis and who was, according to tradition, the mutineer's great great grandfather. In this connection it is of interest that while the name of one of the BOUNTY'S carpenters was McIntosh, his wife in South Shields used the name Tosh, as if avoiding the telltale Highland prefix. Although it is not the sort of evidence one could adduce in a court of law, James Morrison's descent from the Morisons of Ness, who were the breves or hereditary judges in Lewis for several centuries, through John Morisone, who wrote the 'Prose Map' of Lewis referred to above, and his son, Roderick, who was the famous Blind Harper of Dunvegan, may help to explain how a boatswain's mate in the navy, at the end of the 18th century, was able to write a vivid and perceptive account of life in Tahiti, and conduct his own defence, when on trial for his life, in a manner which astonished those who heard him.

There is a letter in the Seaforth Muniments in the Scottish Record office which may have some bearing on the mutineer's identity. On 1st March 1817, the Factor in Lewis wrote the Proprietor, "Mr James Morison tells me that there has been ú300 remitted from the effects of his son to Mr William Mackenzie and that his two years rent would be paid from that firm." William Mackenzie was the Seaforth's legal agent in Edinburgh, who clearly must also have been acting in some transaction for James Morison as well. There is no will or deed in the Scottish legal records for the period, to which the letter could relate, and the inference must be that the payments arose from some transaction outwith the jurisdiction of the Scottish courts. The letter of 1817 was written ten years after James Morrison of the BOUNTY was drowned off Madagascar. He was then master gunner on HMS BLENHEIM which had just completed a very profitable tour of duty in the Far East in which rich prizes were taken. Unfortunately the naval records, which might provide the other end of the story, are missing but I am assured that ú300 was quite a credible sum for a master gunner to have at his disposal, and ten years quite a normal period for the winding up of such a transaction, where death had to be presumed. It is not possible to close the gap in the written records but the family tradition is so strong, and involves so few links, it must stand unless positive proof to the contrary can be produced.

I am indebted to a number of people and institutions for help in reconstructing James Morrison's naval career. In particular I am indebted to the State Library of New South Wales for photocopies of Morrison's papers and other information; the late Owen Rutter; the Public Record Office in Kew and Mrs M. Hawkins, who researched there on my behalf;

the Scottish Record Office; Mr Iain MacIver of the National Library of Scotland; the Inter Library Loan Department of the Highland Regional Council's Library Service; the Maritime Information Centre; the Mitchell Library in Glasgow; Mrs Rhoda Macleod; Dr Tony Paterson; Mr K. D. Smith; Mr D. J. Macleod, and Mr Geoff Taylor. Above all, I am indebted to the aunt who set me off on this expedition more than sixty years ago.

A SCOTSMAN: FAMOUS BUT UNKNOWN

In the autumn of 1779 James Morrison, aged 18, left his native Stornoway to seek his fortune in the Royal navy. In 27 years almost continuous service, he fought in three major wars. He played a significant part in several historic battles and was wounded and shipwrecked at least thrice. He was caught up in a famous mutiny, and was both marooned and imprisoned. He was tried for his life and condemned to death but reprieved. He was restored to his former rank and finally drowned at sea, in an accident due entirely to the stubborn pride of his commanding officer. He never rose above the rank of gunner but he won the respect of one of Britain's most famous admirals. His name appears in more than a hundred histories, and in thousands of magazine and newspaper articles. His career and character are still debated, nearly two hundred years after his death.

He is a central figure in an historical novel by Charles Nordhoff and James Norman Hall. Some of his ships sail fleetingly through the Hornblower stories, providing a factual backround for Forrester's vivid fiction. Naval events he was involved in are discussed in such unlikely places as Borrow's "Romany Rye."

Three major films have been made around the best known incident in his career. Among those who appeared in them were Charles Laughton, Clark Gable, Marlon Brando, Trevor Howard and Gordon Jackson. In one of them a young actor from Tasmania, named Errol Flynn, made his first screen appearance. Morrison himself was played by less well known actors, like Wallis Clark and Keith McConnell, but the best of the films was inspired by the publication of his *Journal*, in an elegant first edition, nearly a century and a half after it was written.

Byron wrote a long poem, "The Island," loosely based on events in which Morrison was involved. Mary Russell Mitford wrote a less well known poem on the same theme. It has even been suggested that Coleridge's "Ancient Mariner" was inspired by a voyage in which Morrison participated, but this is speculative and unlikely to be true.

Morrison's *Journal* and other writings are preserved in the Mitchell Library in Sydney, New South Wales, and are frequently studied by historians, some of whom travel considerable distances for the purpose.

One of the vessels on which he was shipwrecked has given its name to a coral reef in the Pacific. The wreck has recently been examined by underwater researchers, who have recovered, among other things, some of the vessel's guns, a telescope, and the surgeon's equipment, including a bottle still smelling of oil of cloves, after two hundred years at the bottom of the Pacific. It is one of the ironies with which the story abounds that, while Morrison escaped from the sinking ship, despite the fact that he was locked in a prison and shackled with irons, a young fellow-islander, Neil Carmichael, from Balallan, was drowned in a simple accident, when the training ship SIR WALTER RALEIGH was assisting in the exploration of the wreck.

It is surprising that a person of Morrison's modest rank in the navy is remembered at all but he has achieved a status which can be accurately described as fame. or, perhaps, notoriety, according to one's point of view. At the same time he is almost completely unknown. He is remembered only for one maverick incident in a long career of useful service to the state. His name is known because he was involved in the mutiny on the BOUNTY but his identity, and even his nationality, have been largely forgotten. He has ceased to exist as a real person. He has become merely a football, kicked this way and that, in a never ending debate about the characters and motives of two other men. Some writers praise him as a man educated far above his station. Others dismiss him as a sea lawyer and a whiner. He has been called a born journalist because of the quality and comprehensiveness of the record he has left us. On the other hand his *Journal* has been attacked as a concoction and a fraud. These contrasting points of view have little relevance to Morrison himself. They are predetermined by the attitude of the writers to Captain Bligh and Fletcher Christian, the main protagonists in the mutiny.

James Morrison's career has been misappropriated by writers and film makers to such an extent that one is tempted, as I have been, to measure his importance by the names of the actors who have appeared in fictional reconstructions of events in which he was an actual participant. To find the real man we must put him in his proper setting: in the context of the island he belonged to, and the circumstances of his day. Despite the fact that he was not one of those who make history - or seem to make it - his career serves to illuminate the social changes taking place in the Gaelic-speaking islands of Scotland after the Jacobite Rebellion of 1745, and the contribution islanders made to the creation of a great overseas empire from which they derived very little direct benefit.

So far as his native island is concerned, the true significance of James Morrison is that he was the first Lewisman, of whom we have any detailed information, who ever joined the navy voluntarily. He was a pioneer in a great tradition, which reached its highest point in the Second World War, when Stornoway men - as they were called, irrespective of their precise origin - were sought after throughout the British Fleet.

In addition to Morrison, large numbers of islanders served involuntarily, at the same time and in the same campaigns. They were the anonymous victims of the Press Gang. Men were snatched at random from merchant vessels or from fishing boats. Sometimes they were taken from their own homes; although that was illegal, even under the oppressive laws of the time.

The hundreds who were cajoled or coerced into joining the army at the same time can be fairly accurately enumerated because they were generally recruited in large groups by regiments territorially based. The campaigns they served in can be traced through the history of the regiments. It is sometimes possible to pick up information about identifiable individuals. Their battle honours are remembered, and their ties with the areas from which they came are known. During their years of service they were generally commanded by officers who shared their language and held their respect, perhaps even their affection, although in civil life, the classes from which they were drawn - landlords and crofters - were already on a divergent and, ultimately, a collision course.

With those pressed into the navy, it was different. They were picked up at random, often far from home. They were scattered throughout the fleet, passing from vessel to vessel, without regard to their origin or their affinities. They were insignificant individuals, lost among a multitude of other men, pressed from the Lowlands, England, Wales, and Ireland-sometimes even from foreign ships. Their commanding officers, for the most part, had no knowledge of their language, no sympathy with their culture, an ingrained suspicion of their loyalty, and, in the early years at least, a system of discipline based on coercion and punishment, which was wholly alien and repulsive to people who responded, traditionally, to personal leadership.

We have no idea how many from Lewis, and the other Hebridean islands, were forcibly "recruited" into the navy, near their homes or in remote seaports, but we do know that there are few families in any of the islands who do not have a tradition about relatives taken by the Press Gang during the period I am concerned with - roughly from the battle of Culloden to the battle of Waterloo.

These facts give Morrison's story an even wider significance. Because he made the navy his career, and sought promotion; because, too, of his involvement in the mutiny on the BOUNTY and his skill as a writer; it is possible to reconstruct the main lines of his career. In a sense he is the "ringed bird", whose movements have been recorded, giving us a general picture of the fate of hundreds of others who cannot be traced. The service rendered to the state, in a tumultuous period of British history, by James Morrison and the hundreds of forgotten men for whom he is our "marker", is an imporant element in any bill of reckoning between the Outer Hebrides and the Kingdom of which they form a part. It is time to begin to tot up the score.

2
THE LONG SHADOW OF CULLODEN

Although it is possible to reconstruct, at least in outline, the story of the first Lewisman who joined the navy voluntarily, it is not easy.

The greatest difficulty arises from the mass of material available in the Public Record Office at Kew and other naval archives. The Record Office has hundreds of thousands of documents covering the naval history of the period. One is not looking for a needle in a haystack, but a needle in a field of haystacks, with no guarantee that the needle is there. Even some of the smaller archives are daunting for the amateur researcher. I thought, for reasons which will emerge later, there might be some information relevant to James Morrison among the papers of Admiral Sir Thomas Troubridge. When I tracked down the Troubridge archive to the National Maritime Museum at Greenwich, I was dismayed to learn there were twenty-two boxes of letters, and they had never been catalogued. I was invited to get in touch with the archivist if I wanted to make a search. I decided not to, even though her name was Macleod.

In addition to the overwhelming mass of material there is the irritating fact that there are many gaps. Ships' logs for certain years are missing as well as muster rolls, lists of prize money and seamen's wills. There are documents of all sorts in great abundance, except the ones you particularly want. And then there are the ghosts. The navy in the later years of the 18th century seems to have been swarming with James Morrisons. James Morrisons from Scotland, England, Ireland and even from America. Many of them on the muster roll of ships on which I expected to find the Lewis James Morrison but at the wrong date. This was very confusing. My man seemed to be on two ships at the same time. Or, if he wasn't, which of the two was the man I really wanted? Then at last, a little clue. Perhaps a note of the age, or a cross reference to a previous ship, or the grim initials "DD", signifying "discharged dead." With that would come the realisation that the James Morrison I had stumbled on was a will o' the wisp leading me into a limitless bog.

Eventually I was forced to go back to Sir Thomas Troubridge. Not to the twenty-two boxes, fortunately. I found a short-cut through the maze. One thing most writers on the mutiny on the BOUNTY are agreed about is that James Morrison was posted as master gunner to HMS BLENHEIM in 1805 at the specific request of Sir Thomas Troubridge. I reasoned that a distinguished Admiral would not ask for a particular gunner on his flagship unless he had some personal knowledge of him, and a high regard for his skill. Troubridge, as a famous admiral, has his place in the Dictionary of National Biography, and numerous naval histories. It was relatively easy to make a list of his ships, and then look at the muster roll of each, for the relevant dates, to see if the ship's gunner was a James Morrison, of the right age.

I didn't do the work myself. I had an efficient "bloodhound". A professional researcher, the widow of a naval officer, who knows her way around the labyrinth of paper in the Record

Office and has a passion for the hunt. She quickly reported that Troubridge and Morrison had in fact served together, and fought together, in a famous naval victory, as captain and gunner respectively, on a 74-gun ship of the line! The name of the ship rather staggered me. They met on HMS CULLODEN!

The first CULLODEN was laid down a few months after the massacre on Drumossie Moor. It was a fifth rate man of war. Someone, possibly the Butcher himself, the Duke of Cumberland, decided it was too insignificant a vessel to commemorate so great a victory. The name was quickly changed to PRINCE HENRY and a new CULLODEN was laid down. This time a ship of the line carrying 74 guns. Altogether there were four successive warships named CULLODEN in the British navy and a store ship as well. The first CULLODEN, as I have explained, was quickly renamed. The second remained in service for nineteen years before being sold. In 1771 a third CULLODEN was built. Again, a ship of the line with 74 guns. It was wrecked on Long Island shortly after James Morrison joined the navy. A fourth CULLODEN was built almost immediately. This was the ship on which Sir Thomas Troubridge and James Morrison became acquainted. Like its two predecessors it was a ship of the line carrying 74 guns, and it remained in service until 1813. So far as I know the name CULLODEN was not used by the navy thereafter.

It seems incredibly insensitive to us, looking back, that the government of a kingdom which proclaimed itself "united", should name a vessel after a battle in a bitter civil war. Especially a battle with a bloody aftermath which anyone concerned with the honour of the British Army would wish to forget. It was in the same mood of triumphalism Handel dedicated "Judas Maccabeus" to the Duke of Cumberland. A dedication which gave so much offence to Highlanders that even down to the present day there are a few music lovers in the north who refuse to listen to "Judas Maccabeus" because of the apotheosis of the "Butcher" as "the conquering hero".

The relief and exultation in the south of England after the defeat of the Jacobite Rebellion is easier to understand when we put the events of the period in a European context. A few months before "Johnnie Cope" was routed by the Jacobites at Prestonpans, the Duke of Cumberland had been thrashed by the French at the battle of Fontenoy, in Belgium. The Jacobite Rebellion was part of an intermittent but protracted struggle between Britain and France, at a time when it was still possible that France might become the predominant power in Europe, seriously threatening Britain's security. It all seems remote and irrelevant today when the British Empire has disappeared, and Britain, France and Germany are partners in the European Union, but the threat of French power was very real in the middle years of the eighteenth century. It is sometimes suggested that the British National Anthem is anti-Jacobite because of the verse, now omitted, which calls on God to scatter the King's (or Queen's) enemies and "frustrate their knavish tricks". The anthem, however, was popular "in both Playhouses" in London, before the Jacobites crossed the Border into England, and relates to the threat from France rather than the threat from Bonnie Prince Charlie. Even so, it seems unfortunate we should be saddled with a National Anthem which is mediocre both poetically and musically, was inspired by national paranoia, and had its origins in the playhouse. Perhaps the most interesting point is that the name CULLODEN, having featured in the naval List for more than half a century, was quietly dropped in 1813. By that time the prowess of the Highland Regiments and Island seamen in the Napoleonic Wars had made the name completely untenable for one of His Majesty's Ships.

When James Morrison joined the navy in 1779 Highlanders were still hated, despised, and perhaps feared, as the 'rabble' which had almost succeeeded in toppling the Hanoverian dynasty. Part of the difficulty of sorting him out from others of the same name in the naval Records may have been his reluctance, in the prevailing mood of the time, to advertise his provenance, even although he and his family had not been Jacobites.

James Morrison was born just five years after the battle of Culloden. His father, also James, was in all probability one of the excited "council of war" held in May 1746, when the rumour spread that Prince Charles Edward was marching on Stornoway with a force of five hundred men, to burn the town. Charles, in fact, had only two companions. He was sheltering at Arnish, in the home of a Catholic family, drying out his shirt after walking twenty miles across the sodden Lewis moor, in the hope of chartering a vessel to take him to France. A few years ago I had the task of conveying to the National Museum of Antiquities in Edinburgh one of the sheets in which the Prince slept that night. I was acting as courier for a descendant of his hostess, Mrs Mackenzie of Kildun, in whose family it had been treasured for more than two hundred years.

Before the Prince reached Stornoway from Scalpay, his pilot, Donald Macleod of Gualtergill, in Skye, had succeeded in chartering a boat to take some cargo to Orkney. Unfortunately, he had a drink too many after the bargain was struck. It leaked out that the real destination was France, and the "cargo" the Prince, with a reward of thirty thousand pounds on his head. The canny SY merchants panicked. They backed out of the bargain to provide a ship but made no attempt to capture the Prince and claim the reward. They made a lot of noise, in the hope that he would go away and, much to their relief, he did.

There is no actual record that James Morrison Snr. took part in the affair. But he was a tacksman and merchant in Stornoway and two of his relatives, Rev Aulay Macaulay in Harris and his son, Rev John Macaulay in Uist, did their best to capture the Prince. The clergy seem to have been more ruthless than the laity. Whether they were also more avaricious is something about which we can only speculate. Clearly the people of Lewis, or at least the English-speaking business community in Stornoway, had accepted the Hanoverian succession and wanted to be left in peace. The vengeance of the Hanoverians, however, was both protracted and indiscriminate.

The penal Disarming Acts, imposed on the loyal as on the Jacobite clans, were still in force whan James Morrison enlisted in the navy a quarter of a century later. A few months after he joined his first ship, the town of Stornoway was pillaged by a privateer from Dunkirk, called the FEARNOUGHT, commanded by an Irishman, Luke Ryan. The people of Stornoway were no longer able to beat a drum and assemble a force for the defence of the town. As the "Glasgow Mercury" put it at the time, "If they should now arm to prevent privateers from pillaging them, they are liable to penalties inflicted by the Statute. If they remain unarmed, they are at the mercy of every boat's crew the enemy may choose to send on shore." It was in this ambiguous period when the Highlands had accepted the Hanoverians but the Hanoverians had not accepted the Highlands, the Lewis connection with the Royal navy began.

James Morrison entered the navy as a clerk. He was English-speaking, literate and numerate. He had at least a passing acquaintance with the classics. And he wrote with a firm and legible hand. Although he and his family, for at least four generations, had been able to read and write English, James Morrison came from the Gaelic heart of Lewis. He was descended from the Breves, the hereditary judges under the Lords of the Isles. He was a great-grandson of Roderick Morison, the Blind Harper of Dunvegan, and a great great-grandson of John Morison of Bragar who, almost exactly a century earlier, had written the first extant account in English of the Island of Lewis, aptly described in Togail Tir as "a prose map." The Gaelic/English divide in the period just after Culloden was not between incomers and locals. It was the indicator of a creaming off process, which separated the upwardly mobile from those who, from choice or lack of opportunity, remained crofters and fishermen. The difference between then and now is that, in the late 18th century, all the Lewis people who spoke English were bilingual, whereas now all those who speak Gaelic are bilingual.

The navy in the 1780's was desperate for seamen. Monoglot Gaelic-speakers were seized by the Press Gangs along with monoglot Welshmen and monoglot Irish. The language of discipline was the cat o' nine tails, and it needed no interpreter. It was different for a man making the navy his career. English was essential for the ambitious. There was a long history of good education in Stornoway by the time James Morrison was born. A hundred years earlier, John Morison of Bragar put it on record that there was, "a flourishing school planted and maintained by the Earls of Seaforth all the time in the town of Stornoway." As if to underline the point, he finishes his description of the island with a little flourish of Latin. Martin Martin confirms the existence of a school in Stornoway teaching English and Latin before 1700, and Agnes Mure Mackenzie claims, in a footnote to one of her histories, that Greek was taught in Stornoway before it was taught in the High School of Edinburgh. W. C. Mackenzie in his biography of Col. Colin Mackenzie, who became Surveyor General of India, postulates that there must have been a particularly able teacher of mathematics in Stornoway in Colin Mackenzie's youth. James Morrison and Colin Mackenzie were close contemporaries. What applied to the one would have applied to the other, so far as education is concerned. Promotion in the Georgian navy depended on influence, except when it was modified by bribery. Morrison had no influence, and no spare cash for bribery: his career, as we shall see, was shaped at critical moments, by the quality of the education he got in his native town.

When he joined the navy at Leith, he was posted to HMS SUFFOLK, a seventy four gun ship, as clerk. In the navy, at that time, only the captain of a man-of-war had a clerk, although the first lieutenant, on the larger ships, sometimes had a writer to assist with the paperwork - of which there was plenty! As captain's clerk, Morrison would have been regarded as an "idler" to distinguish him from the seamen. The term idler did not imply that the clerk had nothing to do: simply that, unlike the seamen, he did not stand watches, but normally worked by day and slept by night.

Although his tasks were clerical, the captain's clerk was not protected from the rigours of shipboard life. When a man-of-war was in action, the captain stood exposed on the quarter deck, to set an example to his crew. His clerk stood beside him, keeping a record of signals made and received. On one of his early voyages, possibly the very first, Morrison received a musket wound in the arm which marked him for life. When not in action, or standing by the captain in some other emergency, Morrison would have worked in a tiny office towards the stern of the ship, close to the sleeping quarters of both captain and master.

As his subsequent career testifies, he was a man of considerable intelligence, with an avidly enquiring mind. His early initiation, close to the working heart of a ship, must have given him an insight into many matters with which he had no personal concern, except as the channel through which others communicated; ranging from the grand strategy of the fleet to which SUFFOLK was attached, to the political controversies and personal jealousies, which threatened to tear apart the navy and the nation.

A few weeks after he joined the SUFFOLK, the fleet based at Leith was ordered to the Leeward Islands for a key role in a war in which, very shortly, Britain was ranged against America, France, Spain and Holland. From his "fly on the wall" position as Captain's clerk, the young Lewisman had a rare insight into the best and the worst in the Georgian navy. He took part in a long sea chase after a French fleet, superior in numbers to the British, and commanded by one of the greatest seamen of the age, Admiral Guichen. He was on the quarter deck beside his captain when Rodney, the commander in chief, used new and revolutionary tactics, invented by a Scot, which eventually changed the pattern of naval warfare, but initially produced nothing but chaos and controversy. As recently as 1988, one of the best known historians in the USA, Barbara Tuchman, writing about the American War of Independence, was still trying to unravel the sequence of events which young Morrison observed as they actually happened, standing by his captain's side, on one of the ships at the centre of the British line. It is a pity Morrison did not leave us a detailed record of his whole career, as he has of his voyage on the BOUNTY. It would have cast new light on a long-running naval controversy.

Although it is no longer possible to estsblish what precisely he did or thought on voyages other than the BOUNTY, it is possible to reconstruct the events in which he took part. An insignificant player perhaps, but a very sharp eyed observer, often looking on from a point of vantage.

3
COCKPIT OF THE CARIBBEAN

The SUFFOLK was based at St Lucia, one of the loveliest of the West Indian Islands. Roughly the size of Harris, St Lucia is dominated by mountains just slightly higher than the Clisham but so very different from the hills of Morrison's home. The slopes are covered almost to the summit with banana trees, giant ferns, bamboo and other rich tropical trees and plants. In the south of the Island there is a volcano, inactive but by no means extinct. The average temperature is higher than the highest maximum for a single day ever recorded in the Western Isles. In the forests are strange and colourful tropical birds, and in the undergrowth snakes, including in Morrison's day, the deadly *fer de lance*, later exterminated by the introduction of the mongoose. Among the local foods are plantain, mango, paw paw, dasheen, and cloves. Today the list also includes bread fruit, but that came later, and procuring it involved Morrison in the most difficulty days of his life.

Later, in his account of Tahiti, he showed that he had a keen eye for the detail of a strange countryside and its inhabitants but he would not have had much opportunity of seeing the flora and fauna of St Lucia at close quarters. In the Georgian navy crews were seldom free to go ashore. The risk was too high that they would not come back. Men disciplined by fear had no natural loyalty to their ship or their commander. Their one anxiety was to get away, even on a remote foreign shore. Morrison, however, must have known a good deal about the West Indies even before he got there. The Union of Scotland and England in 1707 opened up to Hebridean fishermen a lucrative market for salt fish in the West Indies. At first the trade was carried in hired vessels, but in Morrison's youth the merchants in Stornoway began to acquire boats themselves. These were stout handsome vessels from twenty to seventy tons burden, all their own property. As a lad he would almost certainly have heard tales of the West Indies from seamen who had been there, just as, little more than ten years after his voyage on the SUFFOLK, he himself brought back to Lewis even stranger tales from the South Pacific.

It was not trade or tourism, however, that took him to St Lucia. The little island was the cockpit of the Caribbean, just as Flanders has been the cockpit of Europe. Lying within sight of the larger islands of Martinique and St Vincent, St Lucia was of supreme strategic importance in the struggle between Britain and France for dominance of the area. At Gros Islet Bay there was an anchorage where a fleet could lie with comparative safety even in the hurricane season, and a beach where vessels could be careened for repair, or to have the dense tropical growth, which accumulated in a matter of weeks, scraped from their hulls. The practice of lining the hulls of sailing ships with copper to protect them from the wood boring teredo worm was just coming in when Morrison joined the navy and the SUFFOLK was one of the old type with the result that her sailing qualities were greatly diminished by the time she went into action against a French fleet fresh out from home.

As well as offering safe harbours, St Lucia was strategically placed in relation to the prevailing winds - a decisive consideration with sailing ships. As Rodney put it in a letter to the Admiralty, "Cruisers from St Lucia can always stretch to windward of all the other islands and intercept any succours intended for them." Its strategic importance was reflected in its troubled history. In the recurring struggles between Britain and France for possession, thirteen British Regiments earned the right to carry the name St Lucia among their battle honours. The island changed hands between Britain and France many times before James Morrison was stationed there, and it changed hands six times in the twenty years after he left.

France had been humiliated by Britain in the Seven Years' War. Under the Treaty of Paris, in 1763, she lost Florida, Louisiana and Canada to Britain, but was given back the islands of Martinique and Guadaloupe. As well as leaving France with a festering grievance, the Treaty of Paris had consequences for Britain which the victors had not foreseen. The expulsion of French forces from the mainland of North America east of the Mississippi made the revolt of Britain's American colonies possible, almost inevitable. So long as the French were pressing up the Mississippi from Louisiana, and down the Great Lakes from Canada, the American colonies were in danger of encirclement and dependent on British naval power for their survival. When the French threat was diminished, the colonies were free to cut the umbilical cord which bound them to the mother country.

Britain was deeply divided over the American War. Many of the ablest British politicians, like Burke and Fox, sided with the "rebels". After all, they were merely challenging an autocratic and repressive government in a colony, as many British politicians were doing less effectively at home. The intervention of France, on the side of the American colonists, however, simplified the issue. The war was no longer a domestic political issue: the future of Britain itself was at stake and Britain was ill prepared to meet the challenge.

After the Peace of Paris, which ended the Seven Years' War, the British navy sunk into a state of indolent corruption while the French were busy rebuilding their fleet, ready for the return match when it came. By the time young James Morrison joined the British navy, France had better ships than Britain and a more efficient system of signalling: a critical matter when trying to manoeuvre a fleet of unmanageable sailing ships to windward of an enemy.

Long before France entered the war, the British public were calling for the recall of a hero from the past: George Brydges Rodney who had won several notable victories in the Seven Years War. By the Peace of Paris he was Vice Admiral of the Blue, and had been formally thanked by both Houses of Parliament for his services to the nation. Unfortunately he was a gambler and a reckless spender. As France moved towards participation in the American War, Rodney was a refugee in Paris: unable to return to London for fear of being thrown in a debtors' prison. Living in Paris he could see the direction in which French policy was moving but there was nothing he could do except fume at the activities of the American Ambassador, Benjamin Franklin, whom he, a single-minded English Tory, regarded as an "old rascal". He was specially incensed to see a notorious rebel - as he regarded him - swaggering through the streets of Paris: John Paul Jones, an American Scot, who had just carried out a daring raid on Whitehaven, across the Solway from his native Kirkcudbright. Much to Rodney's chagrin, Paul Jones was presented with a gold hilted sword and made a Chevalier of France by Louis XVI in recognition of his achievement.

Then suddenly and unexpectedly, Rodney was enabled to return to Britain. A French nobleman paid his debts. It is difficult to understand the motive behind the Marechal de Biron's generosity. It may have been pure altruism. He may have been returning some obligation of which we do not know. He may even have been doing it to show up the meanness of the British Government. The one thing certain is: he was not serving the interests of France when he let Rodney loose to destroy its navy. So far as we are concerned, it was this quixotic gesture by a French nobleman which brought James Morrison, from Stornoway, under Rodney's influence, like a tiny satellite revolving unobserved around a mighty star.

Morrison was already in St Lucia when Rodney sailed. Under an inert command, HMS SUFFOLK and the other vessels in the Leeward Islands Fleet, did little except lie at anchor, achieving nothing, as weed accumulated on the timbers and the sailing qualities of the ships deteriorated by the day. With the slow communications of the time they had no idea Rodney was sailing towards them, to take over as Commander-in-Chief, or that an even larger French fleet was heading towards them with hostile intent. The change in their situation hit them with the sudden fury of a West Indian hurricane, and caused the same sort of havoc among the ossified shellbacks, unexpectedly stirred into action.

As soon as Rodney was appointed Commander-in-Chief of the Leeward Islands, the politicians began to hurry him into action, as politicians do, without much regard for the practicalities of the situation. "For God's sake go to a, without delay!" they urged him. Rodney, equally impatient but with some understanding of the facts was writing his wife, "I wish to Heaven the wind would come fair that I might get to sea... then I should only have to discipline the fleet and have done with writing, a thing I detest."

When the wind at last came fair, Rodney sailed to Gibraltar to relieve the beseiged garrison. On the way he fell in with a Spanish convoy which he captured and sent back to Britain. By the time he reached his station at St Lucia, Britain was ringing with his praises. His thirteen year old daughter wrote excitedly about the 'songs going about the streets.' She deplored the poetry 'such rhymes you never saw' but approved the sentiment "the chorus always 'Brave Rodney for ever'." She was specially thrilled to tell her father that the King had been heard to say at his drawing room that he knew, 'When Rodney was out, everything would go well.' It didn't, but it wasn't Rodney's fault. Or perhaps it was!

The change in the tempo of life in the fleet after Rodney's arrival comes over clearly in the SUFFOLK'S log. Some of the entries may actually have been written by young Morrison, as he copied out the notes of his superiors, or made records from their dictation. A handwriting expert might give a firm opinion. To an amateur there are certainly similarities with the only surviving document we know for sure is in his hand.

In February 1780 most of the entries are routine. The state of the weather: "squally with rain", "fresh breeze and fair". Where the ship is lying, the depth of the water and how she is moored - a kedge or a bower, for instance. How the crew is employed: "took on sundry stores", or "blacking yards and tarring rigging." The monotony is broken only by the occasional signal for a court martial on Admiral Parker's flagship, or a call for guards to attend a punishment. "Jno Pope 13 lashes and Willie Alexander 10 for desertion."

By April, just a few days after Rodney's arrival, the fleet was at sea, and signals were flying thick and fast as he tried to hurry up the laggards and keep them all in station. "No regard was paid to rank," he wrote his wife. "Admirals as well as captains, if out of their station, were instantly reprimanded by signals or messages sent by frigates; and, in spite of themselves I taught them to be what they had never been before - OFFICERS." The re-education of his captain and the other senior officers in the Fleet, must have been watched with interest by the young man from the Western Isles on his first venture into the wider world.

Rodney knew that a French Fleet, larger than his own and under the best French seaman of his generation - Comte de Guichen - had arrived in the West Indies. De Guichen's tactics, however, were the very antithesis of Rodney's. The British wished to destroy the French Fleet so that they get on with the war against the rebellious American colonists. The French believed wars were won ashore, by armies. The first aim of an admiral was to keep his fleet in being, to protect the land forces from blockade The result was a mammoth game of hide and seek. For weeks on end the two fleets were in and out of touch with each other, each commander determined to keep his fleet to windward. The British wished to bear down on the French and bring them to battle, the French were determined to keep open a line of retreat. We can almost feel Rodney's frustration in the signals decoded and noted down by Morrison or one of his shipmates.

"CENTURION, FORTUNE, CORNWALL, and MAGNIFICENT signalled to make
more sail."

"Admiral made signal for fleet to bear down in his wake."

"French fleet in sight to windward."

"Admiral made signal for line of battle ahead at two cables distance."

"Signal for rear to close the centre."

"Enemy bearing down in line of battle abreast."

"Admiral made signal to prepare for a battle."

Every time the "prepare for battle" signal was hoisted, de Guichen's magnificent seamanship took the French fleet out of reach. There were times when flags were not urgent enough for Rodney. Racked though he was with pain from gout, and in need of constant attention from his personal physician, he transferred his flag to a frigate and went racing round the fleet urging everyone to get the last knot out of their sluggish ships.

"YARMOUTH hailed us and said it was the Admiral's direction that the ships ahead
make more sail and preserve the line of battle at two cables distance."

"FORTUNE hailed us and said it was the Admiral's orders that the van shorten sail and not part from the centre on any account."

"At midnight tacked in each other's wake."

As the days wore on, the signals becme more frequent and more urgent.

"Make more sail!"

"Get in station!"

"Close the centre!"

At last Rodney caught up with the French. A fortunate change of wind direction brought him an advantage which, if pushed home, would have utterly destroyed a fleet larger and better equipped than his own. It was the supreme moment of his life but it all ended in frustration. Up until that time, British naval tactics had been rigidly governed by rules laid down by bureaucrats at the Admiralty. Each ship in a British line of battle was supposed to lay itself alongside the corresponding vessel in the enemy fleet and slug it out, broadside to broadside, until the enemy vessel was sunk, or it was possible to board her. In such an engagement, the French aimed high to "wound" the rigging, make the opposing ship unmanageable, and prevent it from coming alongside to board. The British aimed low, to sink the enemy or sweep the decks for boarding.

Rodney wanted to break away from the rigid idea of laying the two fleets side by side. He planned to enter the battle at an angle, as it were; break through the enemy line and encircle the tail, so that a vastly superior force was concentrated on the destruction of part of the enemy fleet. That left the enemy van free to make its escape, but only by sacrificing half the entire force as prizes or wrecks, completely altering the balance of power. The alternative was for the enemy van to turn back to help the rear. That was a cumbersome movement for vessels under sail. It was bound to disrupt the line and might leave the whole fleet in disarray, to be picked off one by one.

This novel tactic had been suggested to Rodney by a Scot, John Clerk, who learned his navigation watching the movement of ships off the Port of Leith. Some of Rodney's admirers have argued that he didn't know of Clerk's ideas until after the battle and worked out the tactics for himself. Barbara Tuchman, the modern American historian I have already quoted, has no doubt that Rodney's plan at the battle of Martinique was borrowed from "that alert Scottish intelligence that so often causes uneasiness below the Border." It certainly caused uneasiness among Rodney's shellback captains on the day.

Well before they caught up with the French fleet, Rodney explained to his captains what his strategy would be but they misunderstood him, or, in the heat of battle, they forgot. The multitude of signals issued during the chase, as recorded in the SUFFOLK'S log by young Morrison and his shipmates, no doubt added to the confusion. And the signalling system of the day was far from perfect even at its best. Some of the captains have been accused of disregarding Rodney's plan because they resented his promotion over them. Others ignored it because of a genuine fear that, if they did something so completely unorthodox, they might be shot, like Admiral Byng, for disobeying long established Admiralty rules. Whatever the cause or causes of their disobedience, the result was chaos.

Rodney, in his flagship SANDWICH, engaged the enemy closely. At one time he was under fire from three French warships all more heavily armed than his own. SANDWICH emerged from the fight a virtual wreck, holed in three places below the waterline; kept afloat by constant pumping. Altogether the hull sustained more than eighty direct hits. The main and mizzen masts were both broken. The sails were in ribbons. Of 120 men killed and 353 wounded in a fleet of twenty warships nearly one in seven was on the flagship. TERRIBLE had no casualties at all. VIGILANT and BOYNE only two each. At the height of the battle, when one member of a gun crew on the SANDWICH was killed, a woman he had smuggled on board took his place and served the gun. When Rodney heard of it, after the battle, he summoned her to his cabin, blasted her to hell for her breach of King's Regulations, and then gave her ten guineas for her courage. He must have wished that some of his captains had shown as much spirit.

Young Morrison was in the centre of the line with a grandstand view of what happened to the SANDWICH. And that's what it largely was - a grandstand view. He was a looker-on. His commanding officer, Captain Crispen, was one of the old school: muddled by unfamiliar orders. As a contemporary commentator put it, "YARMOUTH kept firing to windward [of the admiral] without judgment or effect. The SUFFOLK made a like useless noise under the Admiral's stern." Meanwhile, with nearly half the French fleet at his mercy, if he had followed Rodney's plan, the second in command, Admiral Parker stuck to the stereotyped Admiralty rules, and sailed away from the battle in a vain pursuit of the fleeing French van. One of the captains, when he realised what he had done, went mad with worry. Two were court martialed. Of the two, one, a Lieut, who had taken command when his captain was killed, was completely exonerated. It was proved the ship was so badly damaged as to be unmanageable. The other was sent home in disgrace. There might have been a wholesale purge, if Rodney had thought it practicable. He complained he hadn't enough reliable captains to make up courts martial to try the others. As he put it pungently in his private correspondence, "I refuse to employ delinquents to try delinquents."

To the end of his life, Rodney believed the battle off Martinique was his finest hour. He had caught the enemy at such a disadvantage that, if his captains had supported him, he would have achieved the most decisive victory in the history of the British navy, up to that time. Many naval authorities agree with him, but point out that part of the fault lay in his own character. He thought he had explained his plan to his subordinates but he lacked Nelson's gift of gaining people's confidence and getting them to understand what precisely was required of them.

It was James Morrison's baptism of fire, on his very first voyage, just a few months after he joined the navy. In his humble station as captain's clerk he was far removed from the questions of grand strategy which caused controversy within the fleet, but it would be surprising if he did not pick up a good deal from the signals and correspondence he handled in the course of his duties, and the tittle tattle he heard around him. His career had begun at a turning point in the development of British naval strategy.

Whatever he may have thought about these matters in retrospect, there was little opportunity for reflection at the time. Rodney moved his flag temporarily to another ship while SANDWICH was patched up at sea, and the hunt for de Guichen's fleet was resumed. For fourteen days and nights before the first engagement Rodney had not gone to bed. He slept in snatches on the deck. If he drove himself as hard as that, it is not likely a youngster at the bottom of the heap was on a bed of roses.

It was mid May before the two fleets were at grips again. The SUFFOLK log for 14th May notes, "Enemy to windward, stretching to the north, with all sail set." Again there were repeated signals from Rodney to "make more sail." Then a signal in the night to form a line of battle. Followed by a hail from one of the frigates with an urgent message from Rodney to "keep in line." At daylight the enemy could be seen to the north, "distance three leagues." So it continued for several days. Then Morrison, or one of his shipmates, noted in the log that the van of the fleet was in action and SUFFOLK was hailed again with a summons to "make more sail." Next day the skirmish was over and the enemy fleet were out of sight again. The signal for "line of battle" was taken down and four of the fastest frigates were sent scouring for the enemy into the north east.

The flash of guns at midnight seemed to indicate they had made contact. In the morning the enemy was in sight again but still three leagues away. The strain was telling on the SUFFOLK'S crew. Laconically, the captain's log records, "Punished John Taylor for striking centinal on duty and Henry Carter, seaman, for mutiny. Twelve lashes each." Morrison, as he made that entry, had no idea that one day he would face a much more serious charge of mutiny himself, which almost cost him his life.

The signals to "make more sail" continued thick and fast. Then at 2 p.m. "Admiral made signal to prepare for battle." At 3 pm the SUFFOLK log notes, "our van began to engage enemy centre." At half past 3, "we began to engage." Two hours later young Morrison's second battle was over. The enemy could be seen, with all sail set, some twelve miles distant, four of them "seeming much disabled." On this occasion the SUFFOLK redeemed her reputation. The casualties were among the highest in the fleet. Clearly she had been in the thick of the action.

We do not know for sure whether it was in this engagement Morrison was wounded but it seems almost certain it was while he was still on board the SUFFOLK he acquired the scar which was referred to as a mark of identification when he was being pursued as a mutineeer and a deserter after the affair on the BOUNTY.

The SUFFOLK suffered considerable damage in this second skirmish with the French. Some of the deck was ripped up. Shot lodged in the vessel's side. The bowsprit and jib boom were "wounded" and the main top gallant mast was cut off. With this damage, and the earlier neglect of weed growth on the hull, SUFFOLK was in no condition to remain on station. She was sent back to Britain for a major refit, acting as convoy on the way to a fleet of merchant ships carrying rum, sugar, tobacco, pig lead, cotton, claret and coffee.

As soon as SUFFOLK had been repaired she returned to the West Indies where she was involved in a dramatic series of events which must have taught young Morrison a lot about the vanity of human wishes.

4
BEYOND THE DREAMS OF AVARICE

In the two years he spent as captain's clerk on HMS SUFFOLK, young James Morrison visited many of the Caribbean Islands now best known as holiday resorts. The ship's log, for instance, shows her on several occasions anchored off Port Royal in Jamaica, once known as "the wickedest town in Christendom." Morrison saw it between two earthquakes, as it were. The old town, which had been the headquarters of Henry Morgan the pirate, from whom it derived its reputation for wickedness, had already been decanted into the sea when he dropped anchor there but the earthquake of 1907 was still more than a century away. Morgan's reputation is now a bait for the tourist. The few surviving remnants of the old town he ruled over are cherished by the Jamaica National Trust. His wickedness is sanitised in a museum. The pirate, however, would have been very much more alive for a young man in the 1780's, when privateers and piracy were still rife in the area, and the prosperity of navymen, from the admiral to the captain's clerk, depended largely on prize money.

However much Morrison may have been caught up in f'c'sle gossip about Henry Morgan when his ship was in Jamaica, the island which must have featured most vividly in his recollections of HMS SUFFOLK was St Eustatius, a tiny dot on the map of the Caribbean, no bigger than Bernera in his native Lewis.

St Eustatius belonged to the Dutch, and they had made this insignificant volcanic rock into the greatest emporium on earth. Geography, history, Dutch shrewdness and fiscal policy had combined to create what became known in young Morrison's day as "the Golden Rock". St Eustatius, not far from the larger and now better known St Kitts, had a safe and commodious anchorage. It was in the hands of a neutral trading nation, surrounded by warring rivals, Britain, France, Spain and now the "upstart" United States. It was, moreover, a free port. The wealth of all the nations of Europe and America could flow in and out of its harbour free of taxes. The Dutch grew fat and careless on the profits of the trade. At the height of its prosperity as many as two hundred trading vessels sometimes lay in the harbour overnight. Even when trade was slack there were normally more than seventy. The goods they traded in were lodged in a line of warehouses a mile long. Around the time of Morrison's visit the annual rental of the warehouses was over a million pounds per annum - an immense sum in the money values of the time. Another Scottish visitor, in time of peace, found everything on sale from sailors' clothes and iron pans to painted silks, French hats, and costly wines. British goods were obtainable cheaper than at home.

To many in Britain, St Eustatius was exactly what it seemed: a wholly beneficent peaceful trading post but Rodney and the British Admiralty saw it differently. St Eustatius was the main source of arms for the American "rebels". It also helped American traders circumvent the British blockade and obtain the wealth without which they could not continue the war. "Enemy" ships, as Rodney saw them, under flags of truce, sailed in and out with cargoes of contraband. French, Spanish and American privateers found in St Eustatius a safe haven from which to prey on British shipping. In the bills of lading, of the time, cannon balls were listed as fruit, and gunpowder as grain. In spite of their neutrality, the Dutch were far from even handed.

While the SUFFOLK was back in Britain being repaired, a hurricane devastated several of the Caribbean Islands. The havoc in Barbados was so terrible, Rodney was convinced there must have been an earthquake as well as a storm. He didn't believe wind alone could do such damage. Two British squadrons were almost completely destroyed. What happened to them gives us some idea of what life at sea was like when young Morrison joined the navy. Admiral Hotham's squadron was scattered by the storm. VENGEANCE was damaged in the harbour at St Lucia. AJAX and MONTAGU were driven out to sea, and limped home badly damaged. EGMONT and ENDYMION were dismasted and had to run for Jamaica. VENUS and ALCMENE were dismasted and finished up in Antigua. BLANCHE and CHAMELEON foundered with all hands. ANDROMEDA and LAUREL were wrecked on the coast of Martinique with heavy loss of life. DEAL CASTLE was wrecked at Porto Rico, and ST VINCENT drove ashore at St Lucia. Rear Admiral Rowley's squadron suffered even greater casualties. Four of his ships foundered in the storm with all hands. Two were wrecked with further heavy loss of life. Eight were dismasted. It was a major catastrophe. A French fleet was reported to be on its way from Brest. Repairs were urgent. St Eustatius was packed with goods to such an extent that holes had to be cut in the roofs of the warehouses to get at the contents, but oddly, the Dutch had no spars or cordage to spare[oo] at any price to repair the British fleet.

Not long before, despite their neutrality, they had been very ready to help the French make good the damage sustained in the various encounters with Rodney's guns. Five years earlier the Governor of St Eustatius had incurred the wrath of the British in a less material but, perhaps, more provocative way. He had returned the signal of the American vessel ANDREW DORIA as it entered the port. This was the first occasion on which a foreign power had urecognised the flag of the newly formed United States of America. It may have been a routine gesture without any intended significance but the British government treated it as a direct challenge: an act of hostility.

As James Morrison on the SUFFOLK was returning to the Caribbean, secret orders were on their way to Rodney, informing him that Britain intended to declare war on Holland so that the American "rebels'" trade through the harbour at St Eustatius could be stopped. Rodney was delighted to have the opportunity, as he saw it, of smoking out the nest of pirates. In January 1781 Morrison's ship was "moored in line of battle" in Gros Islet Bay in the north of St Lucia. The bay is still described on some maps as Rodney Bay, and the island which guards the entrance is still called Pigeon Island because the crusty old admiral kept pigeons as pets. In February the SUFFOLK, with the rest of the British Fleet, was off the entrance to the harbour of St Eustatius, and the Governor was given an hour in which to surrender if he wished to avert an attack. He had little option. In Rodney's opinion St Eustatius could have been made impregnable, if the Dutch had paid as much attention to defence as to their profits. As it was, the harbour was defended by four cannon, "manned", according to a contemporary Dutch writer by a constable, a boy and a maid. The contents of a mile of warehouses, and the numerous ships and their cargoes lying in the bay were captured without a shot. In addition a convoy of more than thirty merchant ships which had already sailed was pursued and overtaken. Rodney, or so it is alleged, despite his strictures on the misuse of flags of truce, left the Spanish flag flying for some weeks, after he captured St Eustatius, and vessel after vessel, laden with goods of every kind, sailed into the trap and was added to the booty. It was, in Rodney's own phrase, "a vast capture." He estimated the value as over two million pounds: perhaps two hundred million or more, today.

Rodney was strict with his men, boasting to his wife: "no man has been allowed to plunder even a sixpence." Diplomatically, he insisted the booty had been seized "for the King and the state" and would go "to the public revenue of my country." He disclaimed all desire for personal gain. "My happiness is having been the instrument of my country in bringing this nest of villains to condign punishment." No doubt, at the same time, he hoped the King would follow precedent and treat the booty as a naval prize. He was not disappointed. On March 31st, the King issued instructions that the Crown's claim to the "ships, vessels, merchandise, and military stores and other effects" should be relinquished for the sole benefit of Rodney as commander-in-chief and the forces under his command." One can imagine the excitement that news must have spread throughout the fleet. Prize money was very unevenly divided among the various ranks, but, out of such a huge sum, even the humblest seaman stood to gain a rich reward. The young captain's clerk from Stornoway, still finding his sea legs on his first ship, must have imagined he was already a "made man." That, however, was only the beginning of the story.

Just twenty years before James Morrison took part in the capture of St Eustatius, the Captain of HMS ACHILLES noted ruefully in his log, "The men in great confusion, the day before having received fourteen pounds prize money, and could not get their anchors up to save the tide." The celebrations were so great they were all too drunk to work the ship. Fourteen pounds in one day was quite a windfall for a seaman in an age when a ploughman earned only three or four pounds in a year. James Morrison and his shipmates could have expected much more from the treasure of St Eustatius. What they actually got is quite another matter.

HMS SUFFOLK was one of the warships detailed to escort the great convoy of prizes back to Britain. In Rodney's view the greatest convoy of prizes which had ever sailed from the West Indies. It was a thankless job. Rodney found it hard enough to keep his highly trained and disciplined naval vessels in their stations for a few hours in a battle with the French. Keeping an even larger fleet of merchant ships together for an Atlantic crossing was a problem of quite another dimension.

The vessels were of all sizes, types and speeds, with very different sailing qualities and under idiosyncratic captains used to going their own way. naval vessels, in time of war, were always on the alert. Each morning, before day break, all the guns were run out, loaded and ready, and every man was at his battle station, in case the rising sun revealed an enemy sail within sight. The merchant skippers, on the other hand, were reluctant to abandon the easy ways of peace. Many of the ships were undermanned, because of the owner's greed, or the activities of the press gang. They couldn't respond to orders quickly. It was a common practice to shorten sail at nightfall, so that there was no need to send men aloft in the dark if the wind freshened. When this happened a ship might be many miles adrift from her place in the convoy when daybreak came. She might even be out of sight and precious hours could be wasted hunting for her while the whole convoy waited. It is little wonder navymen referred to the merchant vessels in a convoy as "mules." The regulations prescribed quite heavy fines for captains in a convoy who got out of station, or refused to obey their orders promptly, but, as Shakespeare said, in another context, "Your dull ass will not mend his pace with beating."

When the great convoy first set out it must have been a magnificent sight. A vast fleet of vessels under full sail, spread over many square miles of open sea, formed into a vast square, or long narrow columns, whichever arrangement the commander-in-chief thought best for protecting his charges. There was always the risk of the stray privateer trying to snatch a prize from the edge of the flock, or the more formidable threat of a hostile fleet strong enough to take on the escort as well as the convoy. The orderly chessboard pattern of the assembled fleet would have been lost as soon as anchors were weighed and a busy time would have ensued for Morrison as captain's clerk: recording signals to errant vessels to get back in line or exchanging messages with the other naval vessels, scattered round the vast area occupied by the slow moving convoy. In charge of the complicated operation was Commodore Hotham, under whom Morrison was to serve later, in the Mediterranean, in a series of actions which have found their way into the history books.

Before the convoy sailed, Rodney sent a fast vessel home to say it was on its way. He asked that a powerful squadron should be sent out to meet it. To make a rendezvous possible, he informed the Admiralty the convoy would "make the latitude of the Lizard" while still at least 600 miles to the west. As everyone on board realised, safety and danger loomed together as the English Channel drew near. On one side were the British naval dockyards and safety. On the other, just a few miles off, were the French ports and the risk of interception. As the unwieldy convoy zigzagged along the parallel of latitude which ran through the Lizard, keeping as close to the appointed line as sailing ships could, anxious eyes must have scanned the horizon, hour after hour, for the first sight of the relieving squadron's sails. The British navy, however, was hard pressed. The Admiralty had other uses for its ships. When the expected sails at last appeared, they revealed a much superior French fleet which had slipped out of Brest to intercept the prizes.

Hotham ordered the convoy to scatter to reduce the inevitable damage to the navy's great haul of goods and ships. They were to make their way if possible to the shelter of Bantry Bay in the west of Ireland. There the British navy maintained a strongly fortified base in the shelter of Bere Island. In the naval records of the period, the base is generally referred to as Beerhaven: the transmutation of the name a symbol of the uneasy relationship between Ireland and England. A relationship not unlike that which existed between Morrison's native Lewis and the wider English-speaking world he chose to enter when he made the navy his career. The British naval base in Bantry Bay continued in use until 1936, providing a source of income for many Irish families roundabout, and attracting ambitious Irish youngsters into the naval service, voluntarily, like Morrison himself, quite apart from the many who were pressed. But still, despite the magnetic attraction of the wealthier and stronger British state, the Irish never forgot that overlooking the anchorage was Dunboy Castle, the ancient seat of O'Sullivan Bere, famous in Irish history for its stubborn resistance to an English force under Sir George Carew in 1602. When the Irish realised the castle was doomed, they attempted to blow it up. The attempt failed. Carew took it by storm and hanged the garrison on the spot. It is not likely that Morrison knew the story. Even if he did, he would probably have seen it from the English point of view, in spite of his Gaelic origins because that was the side on which his bread was buttered.

In any event, there was no time for ancient history. The terse entries in the SUFFOLK's log give a vivid, if laconic, account of a period of intense excitement in young Morrison's life. On May 3rd 1781, the SUFFOLK was in action off the Lizard. On May 4th the SUFFOLK took French prisoners on board in circumstances that are not fully explained. On the 8th the SUFFOLK'S log records that HMS ENDYMION'S cable had broken and she had lost the French prize she had in tow. Three days later, HMS SUFFOLK had retrieved the ENDYMION'S prize and took it in tow herself. By the time Commodore Hotham's scattered fleet was able to regroup, in the safety of Bantry Bay, twenty vessels from the convoy had been captured by the French. Further losses were sustained later in the law courts.

Rodney had been greedy and indiscreet. Some of the property seized belonged to British merchants with friends in high places. Costly litigation followed. In Parliament, the opposition condemned the whole operation at St Eustatius as a crime against humanity. In the rolling periods which made him one of the great orators of all time, Edmund Burke denounced the seizure of the treasure at St Eustatius as "A cruelty unheard of in Europe for many years". "The wealth of the opulent, the goods of the merchant, the utensils of the artisan, the necessaries of the poor, were seized upon, and a sentence of general beggary pronounced in one moment upon a whole people," he declared. He made no reference to the fact that the British merchants, who lost property at St Eustatius, had been trading with the enemy in time of war, providing arms and other essential supplies, which put the lives of their fellow countrymen at risk. Nor did he add that, with the deference to wealth and privilege which characterised the age, the wartime profiteers were allowed to leave St Eustatius in comfort with all their personal belongings, including the family plate, their domestic servants, and their slaves. In the battle with the French and the hubbub in Parliament, the dreams of Morrison and his shipmates that they were rich for life vanished like last night's dream. In two years, on his first ship, the young captain's clerk from Lewis had seen many aspects of life in the wider world and the voyage was not yet over.

When Morrison and his companions left the shelter of Bantry Bay, HMS SUFFOLK, with some of the merchant ships which had escaped from the French attack, headed up the west coast of Ireland, making for the warship's home port, Leith. The log at this stage is peppered with entries relating to the firing of guns to get errant merchant vessels back into line in the convoy. The brush with the French had clearly not improved the discipline. It was still quite an armada. The log notes that on a Sunday morning, when the ship's crew assembled for Divine Service there were 51 sails within sight.

The rigours of the long voyage were now beginning to tell. Deaths aboard were frequent and became more frequent with every passing day. SUFFOLK seemed to be in the grip of an epidemic, but still naval routine went on, with regular gunnery practice, and even more regular floggings for petty misdemeanours.

3rd June. "Departed this life Wm Dransfield... Fired three shots at a ship to windward for not obeying a signal."

4th June. "Fired five shots at a light transport for not obeying the signal... Sailmakers employed on repairs."

5th June. "Punished Richard Pike with 24 lashes for drunkenness and Isaac Cooper with 12 for neglect of duty..."

6th June. "Departed this life Henry Allen, invalid... Fired a shot at a ship for not obeying a signal... Departed this life David Yeoman, invalid..."

There was a flurry of excitement when a passing vessel refused to answer signals and the SUFFOLK gave chase. Eventually a boarding party was sent out. The uncommunicative stranger proved to be the POLLY SNOW of Cork bound for the West Indies. Whether on legitimate or illegitimate business is a matter for conjecture. As we have seen, many English merchants in the West Indies were providing arms for the enemy. One would expect the merchants of Cork to be even less inhibited.

From this point on the crew were kept busy heaving the lead. Sometimes as much as 170 fathoms of line was used without touching bottom. The convoy was taking no risks of running aground. The Admiralty hydrographic survey of the area was still three quarters of a century in the future. The convoy was in home waters in one sense, but still in an uncharted sea.

Under the date 7th June, 1781, there is an entry in the log which must have stirred young Morrison deeply, especially if he wrote it himself. SUFFOLK had left Ireland well behind. It was now "off the north point of Lewis." It was only a fleeting glimpse of home, and the grim work of burying the dead went steadily on. Sometimes there was a funeral service, sometimes not. Presumably the burial service was read when the deceased was a member of the crew, but SUFFOLK had many prisoners on board both French and American. On the day the Butt was first noted as the nearest point of land there were three deaths: a seaman, a marine and a French prisoner of war. On the 9th of June, with the Butt still their nearest landmark, the crew of the SUFFOLK exercised the "great" guns and small arms, and fired several broadsides. I wonder whether the rumble of gunfire was heard on shore, and, if so, what the Niseachs made of it.

On June 13th when the SUFFOLK was still quite close to Lewis - just nine miles from the Butt - the ships's water ration was reduced to three pints per man per day for all purposes. Deaths continued regularly as SUFFOLK sailed between Orkney and Shetland, in sight of Foula, which appears in the log as Foul Island. The sailmakers were still busy repairing the sails and rigging damaged in the encounter with the French. The gunners were still busy firing shots at errant ships of the convoy. Then a boat's crew was sent off to investigate another strange sail. A trader from Dantzig bound for Newry.

While still in the neighbourhood of Foula the SUFFOLK was joined by another British warship, HMS TERMAGANT. Morrison could not know it at the time, but the TERMAGANT was to play a crucial role in the later events of his life.

The voyage round the north of Scotland was slow. Three weeks elapsed between the first mention of the North Point of Lewis and the sighting of Edinburgh Castle "some ten miles off." On the 25th June 1781, the SUFFOLK finally anchored in Leith Roads, almost exactly a year and a half after she had sailed. The first task next morning was to bury two more "invalids" and send the rest of the sick ashore. On the 28th the prisoners were landed and marched to Edinburgh Castle.

The month of July was spent taking on stores and getting the ship prepared for another voyage. By the 6th of August the gun deck had been whitewashed, and sprinkled with vinegar and the SUFFOLK was ready for sea. Morrison, however, was no longer on board. He was ashore in Leith Hospital, but whether because of the musket wound in his arm, or because he had fallen ill with the rest, it is impossible to discover. Either way his initiation was at an end. The battle hardened seaman who was admitted to Leith hospital must have been very different from the callow youth who joined the SUFFOLK, less than two years before, as a clerk. We do not know, however, whether by that time he had acquired the tattoos which figure prominently in later naval records - the identification marks recorded against his name when he was entered on the "run" list of HMS BOUNTY as a deserter and a mutineer.

Under the left breast he had a star tattooed, and round his left leg a garter with the motto "Honi soit qui mal y pense." Why should a young seaman from the Western Isles tattoo himself with the insignia of an Order of Chivalry, established by an English King Edward III who tried to conquer both Scotland and France? Was it by any chance connected with the fact that, almost at the same time as Morrison, a young man from a very different background joined the navy, and was posted, with him, to the Leeward Islands: Prince William Henry, third son of George III, who later became Duke of Clarence and finally succeeded his older brother as William IV, "the Sailor King".

To begin with the young Prince was immensely popular in the fleet. He carried out the normal duties of a midshipman, and got involved with his companions in escapades ashore which must have been widely discussed. Everyone in the fleet would have heard the story of the occasion on which Don Juan de Langara, the Spanish commodore, was entertained on board the PRINCE GEORGE. The young Prince William was one of the guests, treated with all ceremony as the King's son but when the Spaniard left he was astonished to see that the Prince was now a plain midshipman, commanding the barge which took him ashore. "Well does Great Britain merit the empire of the sea," he said, "when the humblest stations in her navy are filled by princes of the blood."

Later, when he was given a command, Prince William showed traits of character which were not so endearing, and the Admiralty solved a considerable problem, with British pragmatism, by promoting him step by step until at last he °became a full admiral, but keeping him safely ashore. He had all the trappings of his naval rank but no opportunity of doing damage.

While he was still a midshipman, the Prince did a short stint in Scottish waters which took him for a time to James Morrison's home town. According to local tradition, Prince William had a lively time in Stornoway. He is said to have got up to sailorly pranks ashore with some of the local bloods, notably Lewis Maciver, Gress. I have also heard it suggested that he left a strain of Hanoverian genes among the local population. Whether that is fact or a later invention, based on his notoriety as a womaniser, I cannot say and whatever happened between him and some of the local ladies, it is on the record that he did not think much of us in the mass. "The inhabitants here are in a more miserable state than the slaves in the West Indies," he commented "They do not talk English; it is not even understood here: they will talk Erse and wear the Highland dress." A great many of them, as it happens, were wearing "the Highland dress" with great distinction, at that very moment, in his father's army.

5
PORTENTS OF THINGS TO COME

Morrison spent two months in Leith Hospital. By the time he was discharged his ship, the SUFFOLK, had sailed and he was posted to a much smaller vessel, the TERMAGANT. The SUFFOLK was a ship of the line with 74 guns. The TERMAGANT was a 6th rate ship with only 26 guns, and was reduced, shortly after Morrison joined the crew, to an 18 gun sloop. TERMAGANT was less than a quarter the size of SUFFOLK. In the odd reckoning of the time - a hangover from the English navy of the 15th century - TERMAGANT was reckoned at 374 tuns (not tons!) builders' measure, while SUFFOLK was reckoned at 1616 tuns. The measure did not relate to the ship's displacement but to the number of tuns, or casks, of wine the builder calculated the hull could contain.

The move to a smaller ship changed the course of Morrison's life in some ways that were obvious to him at the time, and in others which were hidden from him but are clear to us with the benefit of hindsight. The first and most obvious change was that Morrison passed into a sort of limbo for a time. In his day you didn't join the navy, you joined a particular ship, and you remained part of the crew even if you were no longer on board. Morrison appears on the muster roll of the TERMAGANT as a supernumerary "for victuals only." His pay still came from the SUFFOLK, and it was only due when the ship came to its home port and paid off. A young man in his position might go for years without receiving a penny. Nothing to show for his service but a chit entitling him to collect his pay in a remote port, at a distant date, when a ship with which he had lost all contact went into dock and the crew were paid off. He could borrow from the purser of the ship he was on for current needs, like the purchase of tobacco, or clothes, but he was often forced to "discount" his pay chit. In other words he would sell his pay chit to his purser, or more likely an agent ashore, for a good deal less than its face value, leaving the money-lender a handsome profit on the difference when the ship eventually settled its affairs.

It is a fair assumption that, while he was still in hospital, Morrison would have discussed the incidents of his time on the SUFFOLK with his fellow invalids. One incident which may have been mentioned, but which would not have carried then the sombre overtones it had at a later date, was the mutiny on board the SYLPH. Just about the time the SUFFOLK left Rodney's fleet at St Eustatius to return to Britain with the great convoy of captured ships, a marine on the cutter SYLPH reported to his captain that he had been asked to join a conspiracy to seize the officers and sail the cutter to America or France. Six of the SYLPH'S crew were tried for mutiny and condemned to death. "To deter others from so heinous a crime," as Rodney put it in a letter home. He refused all pleas for clemency. The comspirators - despite the fact that no mutiny had actually occurred - were hung from the yardarm, one on each of six different ships, lying in the roads at St Eustatius. Rodney was determined that as many men throughout the fleet as possible would know the penalty for mutiny through their own involvement in an execution. However the incident appeared to young Morrison as he reminisced with his friends in the hospital at Leith, the abortive mutiny on the SYLPH must have loomed like a great shadow in his mind when, some ten years later, he was homeward bound from the Pacific, a shackled prisoner, charged with participation in a real mutiny, which shook the navy as few mutinies before or since.

The move from the SUFFOLK to the TERMAGANT, however, brought him a piece of good fortune which helped him in his darkest hour. For part of his short stay on the 18-gun sloop, he came under the command of Charles Stirling, a Scot, from a well known naval family which claimed descent from a brother of William the Lion. When James Morrison was court martialled for his alleged part in the mutiny on the BOUNTY, Stirling stood by him and gave him a certificate of character which contributed towards his reprieve.

Stirling was promoted captain because of the gallantry he showed when attacked by a much more heavily armed American privateer. Later on, in the Napoleonic War he captured four French privateers, and played a notable part in the capture of Montevideo. He was thanked by both Houses of Parliament for his services, and eventually became Vice Admiral of the White. His career finished rather under a cloud. He was accused of accepting 700 dollars for taking a schooner under his protection in a convoy. It was an obscure transaction, but a Court Martial held it proved in part, and he was retired on half pay. Fortunately he was still riding high in the opinion of the Admiralty when Morrison needed the all-important testimonial to his character.

Almost all the captains Morrison served under eventually rose to be admirals. When he first joined the TERMAGANT, the captain was Arthur Kempe who became a full admiral. Early in his career he played a prominent role with the ships supporting General Wolfe at the capture of Quebec. He also took part in Captain Cook's great second voyage of exploration into the Pacific when the little fleet covered in all more than sixty thousand miles, and spent a thousand days at sea with the loss of only one man out of 118 in spite of the dreaded scurvy. The young Lewisman must have heard, at least at third or fourth hand, on board the TERMAGANT, of Kempe's adventures in Tahiti, Easter Island. Australia and South Georgia. It is not unreasonable to assume that the stories he heard whetted the curiosity which moved him a few years later to volunteer for the voyage of the BOUNTY, even although that meant accepting a lower rank than he had by that time achieved.

His spell on the TERMAGANT was uneventful in naval terms. Much of the time, the vessel seems to have been in and out of Sheerness. It was, however, during this period Morrison's naval career was given definite shape. As Captain's clerk on the SUFFOLK he might have had aspirations to become a purser. No one could become purser without serving for at least two years as a clerk. A strange hybrid in the navy of the time, the purser was in some respects a private contractor, buying and selling, with the opportunities for making money by commercial shrewdness which that process offered, and all the temptations to dishonesty to which a greedy monopolist is exposed. At the same time a purser was an official of the Victualling Office responsible for every ounce of perishable commodities like cheese, on board his ship, involved in endless paper work, and subject to incalculable risks.

If a ship went down, for instance, he might find himself held accountable for the stores lost in the wreck. In spite of that the pickings were so great it was still a coveted post.

Around the time Morrison joined the navy, Alex. Tweedie, a type founder and publisher in Edinburgh, made a strange proposition to the Admiralty. He offered to provide the navy with one recruit, free of cost to the public purse, for every gun on whatever ship the Admiralty was prepared to make him purser. The bigger the ship, the more recruits, and, presumably, the richer the pickings for Alex. Tweedie. When the offer was turned down he vented his disappointment in a savage poem attacking Charles James Fox who was at the Admiralty at the time. Fox is not mentioned in the poem by name but, in the published version, now one of the curios in the National Library, every time Fox is alluded to the name is replaced by a drawing of a small dog-like animal with a rabbit in its mouth. Tweedie included the poem in an odd medley of a book which is partly a paean of praise of Rodney, describing the events young Morrison played a very humble part in, partly a bitter complaint that the fleet had been withdrawn from Leith, leaving Scotland exposed to French and Dutch privateers, but also a vehicle for his personal grievance that Fox was reserving purser's posts for his friends "though contrary to the interests of the nation."

Despite the fact that he joined the navy as a captain's clerk, however, it seems unlikely that James Morrison shared Alex Tweedie's ambition. To become a purser, he would have to put up a guarantee of several hundred pounds, which does not seem the sort of money a young Lewisman would have at his disposal in the 1780's. The new line his naval career took, brings us back to his native Stornoway and the education he received there.

On 13th November, 1781, James Morrison appears on the muster list of HMS TERMAGANT as a midshipman. A midshipman in the Georgian navy was not an officer but all officers had to serve as midshipmen before becoming lieutenants so that it was an essential step on the ladder of promotion. It seems unlikely, however, that Morrison became a midshipman because of personal ambition. It looks rather as if he were asked to carry out a midshipman's duties because TERMAGANT was too small to have a captain's clerk and they had to find something for him to do.

He was already into his twenties when he became a midshipman whereas the normal age of entry for an aspiring officer was around 13. Some naval families bent the rules and had sons entered on a ship's muster roll at the age of five or six. Their obligatory years of sea service were accumulating on paper while they were still at school or even in the nursery. Morrison was already too old to be aiming at commissioned rank. Besides promotion depended almost entirely on influence, and he had none. Rodney, to take a well known example, made his son a captain at the age of 15 and gave him command of a ship. This accelerated promotion later backfired, when the young man was court-martialled for some breach of regulations and debarred from rising further in the service. As a result he became the longest serving captain in the history of the British navy. Apart from looking after his own family, Rodney was pestered by Lord Sandwich, at the Admiralty, to find billets for other ambitious sprigs of aristocratic families. As he sailed for the campaign which brought James Morrison under his command, Rodney was fuming over a letter from Lord Sandwich asking him to appoint a friend's son to "a sloop with six pound guns," or anything, "to take him off my hands," and to do a like service for another young man "concerning whom I am tormented to death."

A young man from Stornoway, son of a petty merchant and tacksman, did not have the sort of influence one needed to get a start in the Georgian navy. The fact that he ceased to be a midshipman when he left the TERMAGANT is not evidence of ambition abandoned. It signifies rather that he had found his feet in the navy and discovered his real metier. In January, 1783, at Sheerness, he was transferred to HMS HIND, "by order of Admiral Roddam," as acting gunner. By the end of the same year he was in Chatham sitting his examination for promotion as a master gunner.

I have before me as I write a photocopy of the report on his examination. It is signed by three master gunners and a teacher of mathematics. The examiners certified that Morrison was "skilled in Vulgar and Decimal Arithmetic, the extraction of the Square and Cube Roots, and in practical Problems of Geometry and Plain Trigonometry." His Lewis upbringing had not furnished Morrison with the influence to climb in a service where nepotism was rife, but it did give him the education to succeed in the branches of the service where only merit counted. He had entered the service as a clerk, and finally got his foot on the ladder of promotion because of his modest skill as a mathematician. Clearly he was both literate and numerate to an unusual degree for a seaman of his time.

James Morrison was a contemporary of Colin Mackenzie, the Stornoway man who became the first Surveyor General of India, and was a very distinguished mathematician indeed. In his biography of the Surveyor General, the historian, W. C. Mackenzie, postulates the existence in Stornoway, in the latter part of the eighteenth century, of a good school and a remarkable teacher of mathematics. The fact that James Morrison became a gunner and had no difficulty with the mathematical part of his examination would seem to bear that out. A third outstanding Stornowegian of that generation, Alexander Mackenzie, the great Canadian explorer, was not so well equipped academically. After his first attempt to reach the Pacific had brought him instead to the Arctic, he returned to Britain to study navigation. And he confessed to great difficulty in writing an account of his travels. Alexander Mackenzie, however, left Stornoway as a boy. Such education as he got was picked up in New York or in Canada. He is in fact the exception that proves the rule. An inspired teacher of mathematics there must have been, although who he was remains a mystery.

Apart from his mathematics, Morrison, of course, had to know a lot about gunnery. In the words of his examination report, he had to be able to tell when a cannon was truly bored and not honeycombed; how to "dispart a Cannon, so as to direct it justly to the place aimed at," and "how to adjust Shott to a Cannon, and a due Proportion of Powder." He had to be capable of judging heights and distances at sea. He had to know all the technical details of every type of cannon used in the navy. He had to know how many men were required to attend all the different types and sizes of gun in time of service. Finally he had to know "how to Charge and Discharge a piece of Ordnance readily and artist-like, and how to spunge the same, and to Muzzle, and secure it in bad weather." He had also to produce certificates from the commanders he had sailed under of his Care, Sobriety, and Obedience to command, and a certificate from the navy Office of his length of service.

Having satisfied themselves that Morrison was competent in all these matters, John Evans, gunner of the ROYAL GEORGE, Jos. Neate, gunner of the REVENGE, Jas. Watt gunner of the ALBION, and Josh. Hawkins, "Teacher of the Mathematics", "humbly certified" that he was "a person fitly qualified to be appointed a Master Gunner of any of His Majesty's Ships of War of the Third Rate." A third rate, was a 74 gun ship of the line, like the SUFFOLK, on which his career had begun. There were a few larger ships in the navy, but not many. The 74 gun third rate was the main fighting ship during the American War of Independence and the French Revolutionary and Napoleonic Wars. As Master gunner on a 74 gun ship, James Morrison had under his command the largest group of petty officer on board. He had two gunner's mates, and eighteen quarter gunners. He himself ranked as a warrant officer and his appointment was made by the Ordnance Board which was completely independent of the Admiralty. He had a small cabin in a corner of the gunroom, which was at the stern of the ship, on the lower deck, lighted only by gratings in the deck and by the gun ports. He was entitled to have his own servant to wait on him. In fact the master gunner sometimes had two servants. The gunroom also housed the lower status officers on the ship and the chaplain and junior marine officer had cabins in the corner, like the master gunner himself.

As the name implies, the gunner and his petty officers were responsible for maintaining the ship's armaments including small arms in readiness for immediate use. They were responsible for more than a hundred separate items of the ship's stores of which the most troublesome to handle, not surprisingly, was gunpowder. The gunpowder had to be protected from both fire and damp. It was stored in barrels with copper or wooden hoops to avoid the risk of sparks from iron hoops. The barrels were stored away from the hull of the ship, protected by charcoal from seepage. No lights could be taken into the powder room. It was illuminated through windows by lanterns in a neighbouring room sealed off from it. The guns for the most part were Scottish. At one time iron smelting was carried out in the South East of England using charcoal. By Morrison's day the industry had moved to the coalfields in the north, and the main supplier was the Carron Ironworks near Stirling. Carron Ironworks, in fact, gave its name to a new weapon coming into use just about the time Morrison joined the navy - the carronade: a short barrelled gun, deadly in the close ship to ship fighting favoured by the British navy.

In addition to the duties of looking after the guns, the gunner's crew were regarded as a group of elite seamen charged with special duties in working the ship and maintaining the rigging and other equipment. Youngsters sent to sea to train as midshipmen were generally put under the master gunner's care. The great drawback of being a gunner was that it was a dead end job. Once Morrison became Master Gunner on a 74 gun ship he had little opportunity of rising further in the service. He might get promotion to one of the few larger vessels but the benefit of that was marginal. There was no post of gunner of the fleet or even of a squadron. Thanks, in part at least, to the good education he got in his native town, James Morrison, just four years and two days after he joined the navy, had qualified for the highest rank open to him in the branch of the service he had chosen. The route to his goal, as we shall see, was a rough one and, even after he had attained it, he had hardships and adventures enough for any man.

Almost every vessel on which James Morrison served was involved in dramatic events which have found their way into the history books. The HIND, on which he was acting gunner, while preparing for his master gunner's examination, was an insignificant vessel. A sixth rate man of war, mounting only 24 guns, she was converted into a store ship not long after Morrison joined the crew. She was, however, despatched in May 1783 to take part in one of the most important events in modern history - the British evacuation of New York which signalled the end of the American Revolution and established the United States of America as an independent power. It also marked a triumph of freedom and democracy over the British Crown and aristocracy which stimulated the slow and hesitant progress, within Britain itself, towards Parliamentary reform in the following century. Effectively, Britain had lost the American colonies in 1781, when Lord Cornwallis surrendered to George Washington's forces at Yorktown, but it was another two years before the Treaty of Versailles formally ended the war, and Britain pulled out of New York.

The HIND sailed from Spithead on 24th May. In July it was lying off Staten Island taking on stores from the New York garrison. On the 10th September it was back in Spithead. As far as I have been able to discover, James Morrison, in his tour of duty in the HIND had to fire the ship's guns only twice, apart from any practice the vessel engaged in. On 19th January, 1783, just two days after he joined her, he fired a salute of 19 guns to mark the King's Birthday. On 23rd September he fired a salute of 21 guns to mark the anniversary of the King's Coronation. It was a simple piece of ceremonial but not without its drama. The ship's log records the incident laconically, "James Boyle in loading one of the guns had his right arm blown off. Sent him to shore to hospital." Even when using blank shot, in harbour, on a ceremonial occasion, the guns of the Georgian navy were chancy things to handle.

Apart from the voyage to New York, the HIND paid a brief visit to Europe following the signing of peace. In October 1883 she was off the island of Texel in North Holland, and next day she was moored in the estuary of the River Weser, off Bremerhaven. The purpose of the visit to Bremerhaven does not appear from the ship's log and, unlike the earlier visit to New York, to help bring the curtain down on Britain's American Empire, it had no particular significance. The end of the war did, however, affect James Morrison very directly. On 4th December 1783 the ship's company was sent up river to London to be paid off and the HIND was put out of commission. It was a fortnight later, on December 18th, that Morrison sat his examination as a gunner in Chatham. He gained his promotion, or at least his entitlement to it, but he had lost his job. He no longer had a ship.

At that point the scent runs cold. For the next four years I have been unable to trace him. He may have found other employment in the navy although this seems unlikely when so many ships were paying off. He may have found work ashore in the South of England. He may even have returned to Lewis where, at least, he would have had a roof over his head.

William Bligh, with whom he was soon to be inextricably linked, was ashore, on half pay, at the same time and for the same reason. But he had influence. He had married a Glasgow woman, Elizabeth Betham, whose father was a customs officer in the Isle of Man. More importantly her uncle, Duncan Campbell, was a merchant with wide interests in shipping, ranging from the West Indian trade to the contract for convict ships lying in the Thames. Duncan Campbell gave Bligh employment in the West Indian trade to tide him over the lean years until the fateful day when, as Captain of HMS BOUNTY he accepted a Lewisman as his boatswain's mate.

6

IT WAS ALL A QUESTION OF CLASS

We lost sight of James Morrison in December 1783, when his ship paid off at the end of the American War of Independence and he disappeared into the swirl of London, presumably looking for work ashore. He emerged from obscurity four years later and the next five years of his life are documented in great detail, both in his own writings and those of other people. His own record, now preserved in the Mitchell Library in Sydney, New South Wales, begins in a direct, sailorly fashion:

"On the 9th of September 1787 I entered on board His Majesty's Armed Vessel Bounty, Lieut Wm. Bligh Commander, then lying at Deptford. On the 18th October following she drop'd down to long reach and in a few days after saild for Spithead where she anchor'd on the 4th of November... She saild on the 23rd of December with a fresh Gale Easterly, which increased to a heavy Gale by the 27th in which the Ships Oars, a spare Topsail yard and Top Gallant Yard were wash'd from the Quarters, one of the Eye Bolts being drawn from the side. She also ship'd a sea, which broke the Boats Chock and tore all the planks from the large Cutters Stem, and wash'd some empty Casks overboard which were on the Deck. Another Sea stove in part of the stem between the deadlights, but did very little other Damage except breaking an Azimuth Compass & wetting a few bags of bread in the Cabbin; the breach in the stem was soon secured, and the Ship hove to, as it became dangerous to Scudd."

It was a stormy beginning to a stormy voyage, but, as he stood on the deck of the BOUNTY, watching the coast of Britain disappear to the northward, Morrison's heart, we can be pretty sure, was filled with anticipation and excitement. He had got a ship again, and that itself was an achievement in a time of peace. He was bound for the South Pacific, a fabled region among seamen of his day. We know he was familiar with Anson's account of his voyages of exploration, because he quotes from them in his Journal. It is fair to assume he was equally familiar with the accounts of Cook's famous voyages of exploration in the Pacific. Morrison had served for a period under a captain who had sailed with Cook. On the BOUNTY he was now serving with another: Lieut Bligh.

There was great competition among ambitious young men for berths on the BOUNTY. Influence was used to get the sons of gentlemen accepted as able seamen when the complement of midshipmen was complete: a fact which left the BOUNTY with two few real seamen to work the ship in bad weather. Morrison himself had to accept a lower rank than he was entitled to, in order to get a place. He was a certificated master gunner, entitled to be a warrant officer with a personal servant of his own, on a ship of the line, but on the BOUNTY, a tiny vessel, he was merely the boatswain's mate.

"The boatswain's mates were the most vocal and feared of the petty officers," writes Brian Lavery in his book NELSON'S NAVY. "They had to wake the crew in the morning 'with a voice designedly of most alarming loudness'... Their calls were an essential part of the signalling system of the ship." It was also the boatswain's mate who had to wield the "cat" at floggings, and on other occasions to keep men sharply at their duties with his "starter" - a rope's end, freely applied to laggards. The boatswain's mate was seldom popular on board a ship. It was the sort of job to appeal to a natural bully. It tells us a good deal about Morrison's character that he retained the respect, and indeed the esteem, of almost everyone on the BOUNTY, throughout the difficult voyage - except Bligh himself.

The film about the BOUNTY, in which Charles Laughton played the leading role, has created the impression that Bligh was a brutal captain who flogged his men until their bones came through their skin. That is quite untrue. On the long voyage from Deptford to Tahiti, Morrison was only once called on to use the "cat". Bligh had many failings but brutality was not one of them. Morrison's journal, as we shall see later on, helps us to understand what the real flaws were in his captain's complex character.

For his duties on a long and hazardous voyage Morrison's pay was around ú2 a lunar month, subject to deductions towards the cost of Greenwich Hospital, the Chatham Chest for the maintenance of distressed seaman, and the pay of the ship's surgeon: a useless wretch who drank himself to death before they reached Tahiti. People in all walks of life today look for annual increments but, when James Morrison joined the navy, seaman had not had an increase in pay for 124 years. A few years later, when the pay of soldiers was increased during the Napoleonic Wars, and seamen and soldiers frequently mixed together on shipboard where they could compare notes, seamen's pay became a source of discontent and a cause of mutiny. There is no evidence, however, that pay was an issue in the mutiny on the BOUNTY, although the small reward they received for a life of hardship at sea must certainly have contributed to their reluctance to leave Tahiti after tasting the delights of life on a tropical island where food was plentiful and "love" was free.

The BOUNTY was originally the BETHIA. She was renamed, when the navy bought her, to reflect the ostensibly philanthrophic purpose of the voyage: harnessing science in the service of commerce, to provide food for the poor. Sir John Barrow, who was probably the most famous civil servant who ever worked at the Admiralty, with the possible exception of Samuel Pepys, puts it rather grandiloquently, "In the year 1787, being seventeen years after Cook's return from his first voyage, the merchants and planters resident in London, and interested in the West India possessions, having represented to his Majesty, that the introduction of the bread fruit tree into the islands of those seas, to constitute an article of food, would be of very essential benefit to the inhabitants, the king was graciously pleased to comply with their request; and a vessel was accordingly purchased, and fitted at Deptford with the necessary fixtures and preparations, for carrying into effect the benevolent object of the voyage." The vessel was fitted out as a sort of floating greenhouse by Sir Joseph Banks, the great naturalist, and her crew of 46 included two gardeners, to attend the bread fruit plants which they were to gather in Tahiti, and transport to the West Indies, retaining a few specimens for the Royal Garden at Kew.

We can see with hindsight, and it may have been apparent to some even at the time, that the voyage was inspired by commercial greed rather than philanthrophy. The aim was not so

Transplanting of the Bread-Fruit-Trees from Otaheite. (T. Gosse 1796).

much to provide more food for the slaves as to reduce the cost of feeding them for the slave-owners. Even apart from that, the enterprise was misconceived and mismanaged. It stands as an early example, admittedly on a small scale, of the dangers of social engineering based on partial knowledge, represented in more recent years by the notorious Ground Nuts Scheme after the Second World War and the collectivisation of agriculture in Soviet Russia. To bring bread fruit from Tahiti to the West Indies to feed the slaves, cost the navy two ships out of the four that were used in the project. The BOUNTY was deliberately destroyed by the mutineers. The PANDORA was wrecked by careless navigation. Of something like 300 officers and men employed, at least sixty lost their lives. Eight of that total died of natural causes, in most cases brought on or exacerbated by the privations to which they were exposed. Thirty nine were drowned, the majority as a result of bad navigation, and four by the callousness of their commander. Ten were murdered in the lawlessness which resulted from the mutiny, and three were hanged.

It says a great deal for the character of the Lewisman, whose career I am concerned with, that he came through this bloody ordeal with his reputation undiminished, despite the attempts of Bligh, and some modern apologists for Bligh, to defame him.

The mutiny was punished by the Admiralty as a great crime, but the seeds of mutiny, as we shall see, were sown in the Admiralty itself by those who devised and planned the expedition. Moreover the whole project was a senseless waste of time, money and human lives. When Bligh eventually brought bread fruit to the Indies, on HMS PROVIDENCE, the slaves refused to eat it. It would have been better if he had never been sent to get it in the first place.

BOUNTY and PROVIDENCE - the "philanthropic" intention behind the scheme was well advertised in the names of the vessels employed, but no one had the sense to find out beforehand whether the trick would really work.

Morrison's first landfall on the voyage was Tenerife - or Tennariffe, as he spells it. Today visitors go to Tenerife for the sunshine and seabathing, but there were few luxuries for the crew of the BOUNTY.

"Four quarters of Miserable Beef a few pumpions [pumpkins] & a Goat and a Kid (which died soon after) were all the refreshments this Island afforded," Morrison complains. "The Beef was for the most part thrown overboard as soon as it was served out by the People who were not yet sufficiently come to their Stomacks to eat what they supposed to be either an Ass or Mule." Everything was both scarce and dear, he adds, except wine. Some wine was purchased for the ship, and "several Casks for Gentlemen in England and the West Indies." That must rank, I think, as the first mention in Lewis history of the legitimate purchase of Duty Free.

The BOUNTY left Tenerife a few days later "with a fine breeze and pleasant weather." The ship, in spite of the "Miserable Beef," was still apparently a happy one. Fletcher Christian, whose quarrel with the captain eventually precipitated the mutiny, was appointed to act as Lieut, and the crew accepted without demur Capt Bligh's decision to cut the ration of bread by a third, because it was probably too late in the season to round Cape Horn, and the voyage might last longer than the BOUNTY had been provisioned for. A few days later, however, the first storm signal appeared among the crew, when, as Morrison puts it, "the Cheese was got up to Air."

"On opening the Casks two Cheeses were Missed by Mr Bligh, who declared that they were stolen. The cooper declared that the Cask had been opened before, while the Ship was in the River, by Mr Samuel's order and the Cheeses sent to Mr Bligh's house. Mr Bligh, without making any further inquiry into the Matter, ordered the Allowance of Cheese to be stoppd from Officers and Men till the deficiency should be made good, and told the Cooper He would give him a damn'd good flogging If He said any More about it." Mr Samuel, who was both Clerk and Steward, put Mr Bligh's command into effect "on the next Banyan day."

Banyan days in the navy were days on which no meat was served. The name derives from Gujerati traders, known as Banians, whose religion forbade them to eat "anything which once had life." Vegetables, presumably, were not supposed to have life. On the Banyan days bread, butter and cheese were served instead of beef.

When Samuels, following his captain's order, dished out butter to the men without cheese they refused to accept it, "alledging that their acceptance of the Butter without Cheese would be tacitly acknowledging the supposed theft." The result was that they had neither butter nor cheese on their meatless days until the shortage in the cheese had been made good.

In recording this incident, Morrison appears to be accusing Captain Bligh of diverting some of the ship's stores for his own private use. Indeed he names the seaman - John Williams - who claimed to have taken the cheese, along with a cask of vinegar and some other stores, to Bligh's house, in a boat sent up the river, when the BOUNTY was lying at Long Reach. It is possible, of course, that the missing cheeses had been sent to Bligh's house on the steward's own initiative, in an attempt to curry favour with the captain. Both practices were rife in the Georgian navy.

Whatever the truth is about the cheese, Morrison put his finger on an important trait of human nature when he underlined for us the fact that the seamen on the BOUNTY resented the imputation of theft even more than they resented the withdrawal of their ration of cheese on the banyan days. They were prepared to go without butter as well as cheese, rather than lie down under their Captain's accusation. That was something a natural leader of men would have understood, although clearly Bligh did not. The real significance of the incident, however, is that it focusses attention, almost at the beginning of the voyage, on one of several blunders the Admiralty made, through false economy, in planning the expedition.

The purser on a naval vessel, as I mentioned in an earlier chapter, was in charge of all the stores on board his ship. He was responsible for the shortfall if food went bad. It was in his interests to be niggardly with everything he doled out to the men in order to leave himself a working margin. Friction was inevitable between the purser and a crew on short rations, but, normally, if it got out of hand, the captain was there, behind and above the purser, to assert his authority and smooth things over. Even when the captain sided with the purser, the crew had the satisfaction of taking their grievance to a "higher court" and the trouble generally subsided. On the BOUNTY, however, to save a few pounds, the Admiralty had appointed Bligh both captain and purser. There was no "court of appeal", no second opinion, to reinforce the man taking hard and provocative, if necessary, decisions.

Right from the start of the voyage, as a direct result of Admiralty policy, the Captain was involved in confrontation with the crew. His interests, as purser, were set in opposition to theirs, as consumers; diminishing simultaneously his popularity as a leader and his authority as the captain. On a long voyage, on an overcrowded ship, this undermining of the Captain was potentially disastrous and the consequences should have been foreseen. Instead of anticipating the danger, the Admiralty compounded it by a number of equally short-sighted decisions.

As a Lieut, Bligh had considerably less authority over the officers than if he had been Post Captain. As Lieut he couldn't discipline them directly, but had to nurse any grievances he had agaisnt them until the end of the voyage when he could have them court martialled. He should have been promoted before the voyage began, or someone senior to him should have been given the command.

Again although the crew were to be employed ashore for a considerable period, and desertion from the navy was rife in such circumstances, the BOUNTY had no file of marines to maintain discipline. It is significant that, when Bligh was sent back to Tahiti on the PROVIDENCE to complete the BOUNTY'S abortive mission, he demanded that these weaknesses should be remedied and most of them were. It is true he was not made Post Captain. He was still a Lieut when he sailed on the PROVIDENCE, but he had a much larger ship, with an escort to help him thread a passage through the dreaded Torres Straits; he had a purser and he had marines.

There were three elements in the explosive cocktail which produced the mutiny on board the BOUNTY. The Admiralty's cheeseparing approach to the expedition was the first, and in some ways the most important. The second was a flaw in Bligh's own character, although it was not the brutality generally attributed to him. The third was the strange contorted mind of Fletcher Christian, who was a friend and protégé of Bligh's, but at the critical moment turned against him.

In his account of the dispute about the missing cheeses, James Morrison illustrates the problems which arose because there was no purser interposed between the captain and his hungry seamen. Later in his Journal he provides important clues to the defects of character which brought Bligh and Christian into conflict. The Journal and the oral testimony at the Court Martial of this pioneering Lewisman are the most important guides we have in unravelling the mystery of what really happened on the BOUNTY, and why it happened at all.

Arguments about food continued to preoccupy the crew of the BOUNTY as they headed for Tierra del Fuego and Cape Horn. At the Equator the usual ceremonies were performed, but James Morrison's Journal dismisses them with a bare mention. Of much more importance was the fact that the pumpkins were beginning to spoil with the heat, and the crew had to eat them quickly. The rate of exchange decreed by the steward was one pound of pumpkin in lieu of two pounds of bread, which on the face of it seems unfair. When the men complained, however, they came up against the same difficulty as before. The Captain was not a court of appeal. In his capacity as purser, he was the source of the injustice. Instead of listening to the men and either reasoning with them, or upholding their complaint, Bligh lined up the crew and told Mr Samuel, the steward, to call the first man in each mess, "to let him see who would dare to refuse it, or any thing else that He should order to be Served, saying 'You dam'd Infernal scoundrels, I'll make you eat Grass or any thing you can catch before I have done with you.'"

The trouble was renewed when the men complained they were getting short weight in their rations of beef and pork. The casks were not weighed when they were opened, and the men asked the Master to look into the matter. The crew were once more assembled by the captain and told it was, "Needless to make any Complaint for they would get no redress as he was the fittest Judge of what was right or wrong. He further added that He would flog the first Man severely who should dare to attempt to make any Complaint in future and dismissed them with severe threats." After that the men accepted the inevitable. This was made easier for them by Bligh's impartiality - he treated the officers just as he treated them.

"The Officers were not so easy satisfied and made frequent Murmurings amongst themselves about the smallness of their Allowance and Could not reconcile themselves to such unfair Proceedings; but they made no Complaint seeing that the Men had drop'd it and did not appear either in publick or private to take any notice of it. When a Cask was broachd they saw with regret all the prime pieces taken out, for the Cabbin table, while they were forced to take their Chance in Common with the Men, of what remain'd without the satisfaction of knowing whether they had their Weight or Not; being forced to take it as Markd. This Circumstance, while it served to increase their distress and to draw forth heavy Curses on the Author of it in private, helpd to Make the Men reconciled to their part, seeing that it was not level'd at them alone but that all shared a like fate." Morrison suggests, indeed, that the officers suffered more than the men. They were less able to 'stand the Wrangle in the Gally,' when the hungry seamen elbowed and jostled each other for their share of the victuals - a process in which several were injured, as they got into stormier waters, and the ship began to roll.

Bligh's treatment of his Officers raises a number of questions. Was it an egalitarian sense of natural justice or did it spring from something much more complex? When I was considering this question, a friend drew my attention to a suggestion, in the appendix to George Borrow's "The Romany Rye", that the mutiny on the BOUNTY was due to the obsession of the lower classes in England with the notion of gentility. Bligh had worked his way up from the lower deck, which was unusual in the Georgian navy where so much depended on influence and privilege. It says a good deal for his ability as a seaman but as Borrow puts it, he "was certainly neither a lord's illegitimate, nor possessed of twenty thousand pounds." As a result the ordinary seamen thought he was "no better than themselves", and treated him accordingly. Fletcher Christian, on the other hand, had great influence with the crew because he was "genteely connected."

This curious theory about the origins of the mutiny was suggested to Borrow by one of the men cast adrift with Bligh, in an open boat, after the mutiny. Borrow does not name his informant but says he was familiar with him in his youth, and heard from him of an incident, during the open boat voyage, when one of the crew "with a mutinous look" told Bligh that they all considered themselves "as good men as he." "Bligh, seizing a cutlass, called upon him to take another and defend himself, whereupon the man said that Bligh was going to kill him and made all manner of concessions."

"Now why did this fellow consider himself as good a man as Bligh?" asks Borrow. "Was he as good a seaman? No, nor a tenth part as good. As brave a man? No, nor a tenth part as brave. Of these facts he was perfectly well aware, but bravery and seamanship stood for nothing with him, as they still stand with thousands of his class: Bligh was not genteel by birth or money, therefore Bligh was no better than himself. Had Bligh, before he sailed, got a twenty-thousand pound prize in the lottery, he would have experienced no insolence from this fellow, for there would have been no mutiny in the BOUNTY. 'He is our betters' the crew would have said, 'and it is our duty to obey him.'"

The suggestion that the mutiny was due in part to the English obsession with class, receives some support from Sir John Barrow, who was one of the first, and one of the most authoritative, writers about the mutiny. "It was Bligh's misfortune not to have been educated in the cockpit of a man-of-war, which is to the navy what a public school is to those who move in civil society," he comments.

The two writers, Borrow and Barrow, are looking at the same situation from somewhat different points of view. Borrow, the friend of gypsies, believed that Bligh had no control over the lower deck because he lacked the "gentility" before which the ordinary people of England were prepared to bow. Barrow, the civil servant, felt that Bligh was disadvantaged among the officers in not having mixed, at an early age, with the class from which they were at that time mainly recruited. He hadn't acquired the self-assurance or the mannerisms of the upper class, and remained an outsider among them, even when he was their captain. In this comment Barrow may have been reflecting something of his own experience. He rose to high rank in the civil service, and was respected by the admirals and cabinet ministers whom he served, but he must have been always conscious, in a class-ridden society, that he had been brought up in a humble cottage near Ulverston in Lancashire.

The Lewisman looks at the situation from a different point of view from either. Coming from a society in which men had traditionally given great loyalty to their chiefs, but still regarded themselves as kinsmen and equals, he makes no reference to gentility or class but reports the facts objectively as he saw them. He makes no comment on Bligh's origins, either favourable or unfavourable, but he describes a situation in which Bligh clearly had more difficulty controlling his officers than controlling his men. It was not strength but weakness which impelled Bligh to subject his officers to the same rigorous control as the men where rations were concerned, and to bawl them out in front of their subordinates, as if he had to demonstrate publicly that he was in command of the ship. This equality of treatment, as Morrison records, was appreciated by the seamen and helped to reconcile them to their lot but, simultaneously, it undermined the authority of the officers over the crew, and of the captain over the officers. In the end it was Bligh's second in command, and early favourite, who led the mutiny, and he had so lost the affection and respect of the other officers that none of them was prepared to lead an attempt to retake the ship. Morrison made much of this point when he was tried for mutiny, and the master of the BOUNTY testified that, if an attempt had been made to suppress the mutiny, he would have expected the Lewisman to be one of the first to rally to the captain's side.

One of the great insights Scotland, and especially the Highlands, have contributed to the United Kingdom - although it has been assimilated slowly and not yet fully and seldom recognised articulately - is that a strong sense of egalitarianism is not incompatible with acceptance of the need for a chain of command.

7

BARE POLES AND BATTENED HATCHES

Many Lewismen of later generations have been round Cape Horn, but James Morrison is the first of whom we have any record, and we still have his own account of how he fared:

"March 1788. We met with no accident or occurrence worth mentioning except speaking the BRITISH QUEEN of London since leaving Tennariff. She was bound for the Cape of Good Hope on the whale fishery. On board this ship we sent letters for England supposing she would in all probability be the last we should see this side of Cape Horn. We saw several ships on the coast of Patagonia, but spoke none of them; and carried a fair wind and fair weather (except at intervals) till we made Tierra del Fuego, which happened on the 23rd March. The weather being fine we were all in high spirits, and hoped soon to get round the Cape, but a few days convinced us that Commodore Anson had not said worse of this place than it deserved...

"Fair weather in this clime is always the forerunner of foul and this we found by experience as soon as we were clear of Staten Land, but before it set in we got the top gallant masts down and made everything ready for it. The appearance of the country is rugged and barren, and the snow on the hills gives it a very inhospitable look at a distance. What it may be on a nearer view I do not pretend to say. We saw here vast quantities of seals, penguins, shags and other seafowl. White and black albatrosses - some of which we caught which made an excellent meal. Some of them measured upwards of eight feet from tip to tip of their wings. The black ones we called padries [padres?], but never caught any of them.

"The weather becoming very sharp as we stood to the southward, the people requested that their rum might be served without water. This was readily agreed to, as water was saved by it, and the water allowance was reduced to three pints per day which, in such weather as we had, was more than sufficient, having no method of using it otherwise than as drink, and this indulgence was not lost on the seamen whose spirits seemed to have an additional flow from it. They thought nothing of hardship and notwithstanding fatigue and increasing bad weather they carried on their duty with alacrity and cheerfulness anticipating the pleasure and profit they hoped to reap by the success of the voyage... The weather continued to grow worse every day, hail, rain, sleet and snow - or rather large flakes of half formed ice - following each other in heavy squalls, which often reduced us under bare poles and battened hatches, as the sea made fair breaches over us, running in a manner unknown in northern climes."

Morrison says the seas were so high they frequently obscured the sun when it was 20 degrees above the horizon. The ship tossed so violently it was impossible to walk the deck without a rope to hang on to. As a result several of the crew sustained injuries. The ship's surgeon was thrown down a ladder into the cockpit. As he was a drunkard, the heavy seas might not have been the only cause of his fall, but others suffered the same fate, including Peter Linkletter, a quartermaster. Linkletter was a Shetlander. He injured his back in the fall "of which he always complained afterwards." This injury may have contributed to his death on the homeward voyage with Captain Bligh, after the mutiny.

"Notwithstanding the severity and inclemency of the season and the continued gales and repeated squalls, which seemed to break with redoubled violence and threaten us every moment with destruction, such was the alacrity and carefulness of officers and men, that we never lost a spar, or a yard of canvas..." writes Morrison. The manner in which the ship was handled says a good deal for Bligh's skill as a seaman, but by the time the Journal was written up, Morrison had no reason to thank Bligh for any favours, and he pointedly gives all the praise to the officers and men. It was not the hardships of the voyage, however, which precipitated the mutiny. It was the soft living in Tahiti. Bligh was at his best when the going was hard.

While the hatches were fast against the great seas breaking over the ship, the men's quarters were always filled with smoke and, although the ship was sound, the straining of the timbers made her leak with the result that the hammocks were always wet. Bligh tried to counter the conditions as well as he could. Sweet wort was made from malt and a pint a man served hot each day. The men found this very acceptable and nourishing, but, in spite of it, they began to fall ill. There was little chance of throwing off illness in a wet hammock, in a smoke filled fo'c'sle, and the more who went sick, the heavier became the burden on those who were fit. The work of the ship, however, was "still carried on with alacrity and spirit; and the behaviour of the seamen, in this trying situation, was such as merited the entire approbation of the officers, and Mr Bligh's thanks in a public speech.

"After a fatiguing and ineffectual trial it was found that the passage round Cape Horn was not practicable at this season of the year. Though we had reached the 62 deg of South Latitude, and 29th of West Longtitude, yet we found that we lost ground, and though the ship was an excellent seaboat, it was as much as she could do to live in this tremendous sea where the elements seem to wage continual war... On the 18th of April Mr Bligh ordered all hands aft and, after returning them thanks for their unremitted attention to their duty, informed them of his intention to bear away for the Cape of Good Hope... This was received with universal joy and returned according to custom with three cheers. The ship was instantly put before the wind, and the reefed foresail, and close reefed main topsail set, which with the main sail and mizzen staysail were the chief sails that had been in use for some time; but they were seldom in use all at the same time. A hog was now killed and served out in lieu of the day's allowance, which though scarce anything else but skin and bone was greedily devoured; everyone by this time having fairly come to their appetites."

There was a disappointment in store, however. By the evening the wind had turned to the northward, and, although they had travelled 120 miles towards the Cape of Good Hope, Bligh, mindful of the Admiralty's orders, put about and made a final desperate attempt to round Cape Horn.

"These flattering appearances soon vanished and are always the forerunners of something worse," Morrison records. The wind "shifted again to the west and blew with redoubled fury." Four days later, on the 22nd April, Bligh finally gave up the struggle and took the longer, but easier, route by the Cape of Good Hope.

While they were battling with the Horn there were continual showers of sleet, in addition to the seas breaking over the ship. "No man could keep dry for one minute after he came on deck." As they sailed for smoother seas and a more temperate climate, the sick began to recover, the hatches were opened to let in air and stoves were lit to dry out the ship. Exactly a month later, on the 23rd of May, the BOUNTY arrived in Simon's Bay near the Cape of Good Hope, which was then a Dutch colony. They got fresh food and water, including bread and wine, and succeeded in catching large quantities of fish - "called Romans and Hottentots". They also tried eating "a large bird of the size of a goose of a grey colour which seemed to us unable to fly." They knocked down several of them and "from their immediately darting at the eye of those who came in their reach we called them Eye-peckers. They were full as heavy as a goose but their flesh rank and coarse and indifferent food."

After the rigours of the previous months, their stay in Simon's Bay was almost a holiday although there was heavy work to do as the BOUNTY was badly strained by the prolonged attempt to round Cape Horn. We learn from Bligh's own account that on the voyage to the Cape of Good Hope it had been necessary to work the pumps every hour to keep the vessel afloat.

Bligh, quite naturally and properly as captain, is concerned in his record with the provisioning of the ship; his relations with the Dutch authorities; the growth of Cape Town since his last visit eight years before; the military preparedness of the Dutch; and the price of mutton for the ship. The boatswain's mate from Lewis however - described more than a century later as 'a born reporter' - puzzled over a human tragedy.

When Morrison and his friends were fishing for "Romans and Hottentots," they visited a place they called Seal Island, about nine miles east of Simon's Bay. "The island is an entire rock," he writes. "It affords shelter for no animals but the seals, and sea fowls, with which it abounds, and, on firing a muskete, they rise up in vast flocks, making a great noise, and in a manner forming a cloud over the whole island, which is not more than half a mile in circumference." On the island he found part of a boat, which had obviously been dashed to pieces on the rocks. There were several bundles of seal skins still in the wreckage. He looked around but could see no bodies or bones. Had the crew of the boat drowned before it reached the shore, or had they perished in an attempt to swim to the mainland? When he got back to Simon's Bay, he tried to find out what had happened and was appalled by the indifference of the Dutch authorities. The island was frequented by sealers to get oil for the settlement. The boat Morrison stumbled on disappeared in a gale but the Governor didn't bother to find out what happened to the seven men on board.

The story of the missing boat's crew is the sort of thing one might record long afterwards from memory but Morrison also gives us details of the provisioning of the ship. Nine cwt of extra bread, 3 barrels of brandy, 2 barrels of arrack, two barrels of fine Dutch gunpowder from the Fort, and so on. His previous experience as captain's clerk may be reflected in the precision of the list, but, did he hold the information in his memory, did he note the details at the time, or did he borrow the information afterwards from some other source? These are questions which must be examined later when I consider the exact status of his celebrated and controversial "Journal".

Small though the BOUNTY was, she carried live goats and poultry, with hay and barley to feed them. The stock was augmented at Simon's Bay with five sheep and some pigeons. Then on the 1st July 1788, with the crew rested and refreshed, the BOUNTY sailed for a country which was then only six months old. Morrison calls it New Holland. Bligh calls it Van Diemen's Land. We call it Australia.

It was in January 1788 that Britain established a penal settlement at Botany Bay, and the modern history of Australia began. The continent was still generally known as New Holland, because the Dutch had been the first of the European nations to discover it. This is the name the Lewisman uses in his journal. His captain was more precise. He wrote of Van Diemen's land, which we now call Tasmania, which is where the BOUNTY was heading. Bligh, however, like Morrison, thought Van Diemen's Land was part of the main continent. It was ten years after the BOUNTY'S visit that Bass Strait was first explored, and seamen realised that Tasmania was an island. It was fifteen years after the BOUNTY'S visit before Britain formally claimed possession of Tasmania by establishing a penal colony at Hobart. The Lewis link with Australia, in this way, goes back almost to the beginning.

The BOUNTY anchored in Adventure Bay, south of the modern city of Hobart. "The country is mountainous and clothed with wood from the beach to the top of the mountains," writes Morrison in his Journal. "The trees are of several kinds and run to a prodigious size. We measured one which had fallen, by being burnt at the root by the natives, which was 27 yards to the first branch and 9 in circumference... The soil near the beach is sandy but, on the hills, is a strong red loam which affords excellent grass which we cut and dried for the sheep and goats... On the east side of the bay [we] planted some vines, pear trees and bananas, which we brought from Tenerife and the Cape, with several kinds of seeds, marking the adjacent trees with the ship and commander's name and the date of the year. We saw no quadrupeds but a dead opossum, but various kinds of birds, among which were black swans, ducks, hawks, parakeets, sea pies, and several others which we could not name, with numbers of gannets and other sea fowls."

I dont know how it strikes readers, but I take great delight in the picture of a Lewisman, in the 18th century, when much of the island was still in runrig and the cas chrom was high technology, planting bananas on an island in the South Pacific which was just clambering over the horizon of history.

It was on the same occasion Morrison became the first Lewisman, so far as we know, who ever saw a boomerang, although on the first occasion he saw one it was not actually used. "A few days before we sailed," he writes, "some of the natives came down on the rocks on the west part of the bay, where Mr Bligh, accompanied by Mr Nelson [the gardener] went in the cutter to see them, and made them several presents, of which they seemed to take very little notice. As they approached the boat the women stayed at some distance, and the men, in number ten, threw away their short sticks, and came close down on the rocks. Their colour was nearly all black but they appeared to be smutted in several parts with charcoal.

Their heads were all close shorn so that we could not tell whether they were woolly or not but thought that the short remains looked more like wool than hair. Their countenances were by no means agreeable, and their teeth black and uneven. They were quite naked and appeared harmless miserable creatures... Though they did not appear in the least curious to examine anything given them, they talked a good deal, which none of us understood, and would frequently jump up and shout, seemingly pleased, when the boat rose higher than common on the surf and again when she fell."

Morrison had no opportunity to go ashore to find out more about the aborigines, interested in them though he was. From the number of shells he saw in different places, as they passed along the coast, he came to the conclusion that shell fish was their main source of food. Actually the Tasmanians were expert hunters and trackers of game. They had, at least, a primitive notion of art, making rough drawings on bark with charcoal. They had no writing but marked stones with red and black bands as tallies for absent friends. They decorated themselves with red ochre, wore shell necklaces, and festooned themselves with flowers or berries. Their language is said to have been musical and soft, but who can really tell? The white man obliterated them ruthlessly and efficiently soon after he arrived.

The last pure blooded Tasmanian died in 1876, less than a hundred years after the first permanent white settlement at Hobart. The last survivor was 76 when he died, so he must have been born just twelve years after Morrison's visit. A man of Morrison's generation could well have known the first white man and the last aborigine to live in Tasmania. There is no virus more deadly than "civilisation".

8
A PARABLE FOR OUR TIME

Life on board ship was hard in the 1780's. Morrison records in his journal, as if it were a great event, that, during their stay in Tasmania, "bread was served at full allowance" and "Water Gruel boild for breakfast." Even a plate of porridge was a luxury!

As soon as they left Tasmania, rations were reduced again to conserve stocks, and symptoms of the dreaded scurvy began to appear. Bligh, despite his reputation for harshness, was deeply concerned with the health of his crew. He immediately ordered essence of malt to be served to those who were ailing, "with portable soup and rice from the surgeon's chest." Blood-letting was still a common cure for many ailments but, when the drunken surgeon bled one of the crew, the wound festered and the patient died. Under the stress of the long voyage tempers were beginning to get frayed. The Captain quarrelled with his two messmates, John Fryer, the master, and Thomas Huggan, the surgeon. Fryer and Huggan retired to their own cabins, taking their share of the provisions with them, and, as Morrison notes, "after that they had several disputes and seldom spoke but on duty; and even then with much apparent reserve."

Even before they left Tasmania, Morrison shrewdly records, "were sown some seeds of eternal discord between Lieut Bligh and his officers." Here he puts his finger on the essential difference between the mutiny on the BOUNTY and the numerous other mutinies, small and large, successful and unsuccessful, which occurred on naval ships of the period. The trouble on the BOUNTY began among the officers, not in the f'c'sle. It was a good deal more complicated than a rebellion of downtrodden seamen against the harsh condition of their lives.

Bligh, according to Morrison, "confined the Carpenter [a warrant officer] and found fault with the inattention of the rest, to their duty, which produced continual disputes every one endeavouring to thwart the others in their duty, this made the men exert themselves to divert the storm from falling on them by a strict attention to their duty and in this they found their account and rejoiced in private at their Good success." Evidence from other sources suggests that Morrison was incorrect in saying the carpenter was confined. Bligh withdrew his rations and starved him into submission, which was equally effective and equally humiliating. In fact it was more humiliating because the carpenter's disgrace was made public at every meal time.

That quarrel was quickly followed by another, this time with Fryer, the Master, who no doubt had a smouldering resentment against Bligh because he promoted his own favourite, Fletcher Christian, as acting Lieut, over the Master's head. The trouble between Fryer and Bligh arose over the signing of some records in the ship's books, presumably accounts. Morrison gives no explanation of Fryer's objection to signing. He merely says he refused "for reasons best known to himself." "Upon which, all hands were called aft, and the Articles of War read, and some part of the Printed Instructions, after which the books and papers were produced, with a pen and ink, and Mr Bligh said, 'Now sir, sign them books.' The Master took the pen and said 'I sign in obedience to your orders, but this may be cancelled hereafter.'"

The strains on board the BOUNTY were transformed and compounded, when they reached Tahiti and the weary mariners found themselves for several months in what must have seemed an earthly paradise.

At ten o'clock in the morning of the 25th October, 1789, the BOUNTY anchored Ma'taavye Bay, as Morrison spells it, although later he uses the variants Mataavye and Matavai. "We were presently surrounded by the natives in their Canoes, who brought off Hogs, Bread fruit and Cocoa Nuts, in abundance, and a trade for Nails, hatchets &ca, soon commenced," he writes. "Of the Cocoa Nuts the sick were desired to drink plentifully and these contributed so much to their recovery, that in a few days there was no appearance of sickness or disorder in the ship, and the Great plenty of Provisions with [which] the Natives supply'd us soon renewed their Strength." Food was so plentiful Bligh was able to stop "every species of Ship's Provisions except grog."

"Imediatly on anchoring, an order signd by Mr Bligh was stuck up on the Mizen Mast Prohibiting the Purchase of Curiosities of any sort except Provisions. There were few or no instances of the order being disobeyed, as no curiosity struck the seamen so forcibly as roasted pig & some bread fruit and these Came in abundance." Later, when he wrote his long description of life in Tahiti, as he lay a prisoner on HMS HECTOR awaiting trial for his life, Morrison concluded that the inhabitants were, "without doubt the Happiest on the Face of the Globe."

There is, however, a downside to the story. In a way the mutiny on the BOUNTY is almost a parable for our time.

In the fifty years from 1939 to 1989 the people of Britain experienced the harsh constraints of war, the austerity which followed the devastation, the sexual permissiveness which began in the early sixties, and the boom years of almost unlimited credit when money was splashed around in a manner which would have astounded the Prodigal Son. Then came the slump and the bitter realities of the nineties. The weary seamen on the BOUNTY went, in a single day, from deprivation to plenty, from the monastic abstinence of life on a long ocean voyage, to an island where the price of a woman was an iron nail. Within a few months they completed the cycle with a chastening return to the privations of shipboard life and the prospect of a long harsh voyage to a cold climate and an oppressive system of government.

In addition to the licence which demoralised many of the crew, lasting attachments were made between men from the BOUNTY and some of the women of Tahiti. When the time came to leave, the genuine heartbreak of parting with loved ones was added to the shock of returning to the harsh discipline and bare rations of the Georgian navy, and that at a time when the people of America had successfully thrown off the British yoke, when the writings of Tom Paine were acting like a yeast on British political life, and France was teetering on the brink of a bloody revolution. It would have required a much wiser and more charismatic leader than William Bligh to hold a crew together in such a demoralising situation, even if his position had not been made untenable from the start by the circumstances in which the Board of Admiralty had placed him. Following the mutiny Bligh made one of the most remarkable open boat journeys in history. He was still the same acerbic unlovable man he had been on the BOUNTY. In fact there are documented quarrels between him and at least seven of the eighteen men who accompanied him, but still he held them together. It was not hard tack and strict discipline which destroyed the BOUNTY, but easy living in Tahiti, and the irksome withdrawal symptoms when the good times came to an end.

On New Year's Day 1789 a double ration of grog was served to all the members of the BOUNTY'S crew who had crossed the Equator on a previous voyage. The greenhorns, who had crossed the line for the first time on the outward voyage to Tahiti, had to make do with the ordinary ration topped up with coconut milk. Morrison gives us no indication of his status. He had travelled widely in the West Indies on HMS SUFFOLK but there is no indication that she ever crossed the Equator. Unless he made a long foreign voyage during the four missing years which followed the end of the American War, he would have ranked as a greenhorn. As he sipped his exotic cocktail of rum and coconut milk I wonder whether he cast his mind back to Hogmanay in his native Lewis, in the midwinter darkness, with snell gales sweeping in from the Atlantic, or the Arctic? If he did he gives no hint of it. He had too much to write about in the drama unfolding around him. Like a juggler with half a dozen balls in the air, he had many themes to pursue at the same time.

First there was the mundane progress of the task which brought them to Tahiti: the gathering of the bread fruit plants. That required the continual presence of part of the crew ashore, giving them a taste of the easy life and the opportunity to talk, and perhaps conspire, in a way they could not do in the cramped quarters of a ship. While those ashore built a hut, in which the bread fruit plants were potted for transhipment to the Indies, those still on board were busy converting the cabin into a sort of greenhouse where the potted plants could be tended on the long voyage.

Then there was the growing tension between the Captain and his warrant officers, mainly about food. To begin with pork was abundant but, as the crew busily salted down carcase after carcase for the voyage home, the supply began to decline. As a prudent captain, Bligh was more concerned with basic rations for the ship at sea, than the natural gluttony of half-starved men ashore in a land of plenty. He claimed all the pigs that came aboard for the ship's stores, irrespective of who had bought them or to whom they were being given by native friends ashore. When Fryer, the Master, protested that pigs belonging to him had been seized, Bligh retorted that everything was the captain's as soon as it came on board. For good measure he added that he would take nine tenths of any man's property for the ship, and let him see who would say anything to the contrary.

"Those of the seamen were seized without ceremony," writes Morrison. "It became a favour for a man to get a pound extra of his own hog." If there had been a purser on board, the distinction between the ship's stores and the captain's stores would have been clear. Bligh could have stood aside from the chaffering, except when called in as the final court of appeal. The Admiralty's penny-pinching left him exposed, and his authority was eroded by constant bickering.

When the natives saw that the pigs they brought aboard as gifts, or bargains, were seized for the ship, they watched for a moment when the Captain was ashore. Bligh tried to close this loophole by ordering the Mate of the watch to keep a book beside the binnacle and note the weight of every carcase brought aboard the ship. The natives responded by cutting up the carcases and smuggling them on board, joint by joint, hidden in baskets of bread fruit. Bligh's maladroitness had made the acceptance of gifts a crime.

Morrison's third theme was the social relationship between the natives and the BOUNTY'S crew. He noted particularly the part played by the native women in establishing a line of communication across the language barrier. Several members of the crew had been to Tahiti with Capt Cook, including Bligh himself, Nelson the gardener, and Coleman the armourer. The women with whom they had been friendly on their previous visit quickly sought out their "quondum husbands", as Morrison describes them, and "by signs, at which these people are adepts," established "a method of discourse by which everything was transacted."

In addition to individual friendships struck up between the crew and the natives, both men and women, there was a good deal of more formal socialising. Matte, "the Chief whom we supposed to be King, & Eddea his Queen often slept on board the ship and frequently entertained Mr Bligh and the officers on shore with Hiwas (or Dances, plays &c) and such diversions as they thought most pleasing and from which he generally returned with presents of Cloth &ca. When any strange visitors came [on board the BOUNTY] they were entertaind by Mr Bligh who gratified their curiosity by firing a Gun, at which they appeard much amazed & always stopd their ears & fell down as soon as they saw the Flash, and a Pistol was to all appearance as much dreaded as a four pounder. Mr Bligh took the opportunity at such times, to show them the effects of round and Grape Shot, which to them appeard Wonderful, and they always exclaim'd in amaze when they saw the shot fall, scarcely giving credit to what they saw."

One incident in the social intercourse between ship and shore became an established ceremony in Tahiti. The Tahitians venerated Capt Cook almost as if he had been a god. His reputation among them was so important to the success of the expedition, Bligh concealed from the natives that Cook had been murdered in Hawaii, pretending that the great explorer was still alive. It was a stupid and dangerous deception, trading a short term advantage for a long-term loss of faith when the truth eventually became known, but it helped Bligh in his negotiations for the bread fruit plants. On Cook's last visit to Tahiti his portrait was painted by Mr Webber, one of his associates. On leaving, Cook presented the portrait to Poeno, the local Chief in Mataavye who later became a particular friend of Morrison. The Tahitians cherished the portrait as an ikon or totem and it became the custom for them to take it out to visiting ships and get the Captain to write on the back the date of his arrival and departure. When the BOUNTY arrived, Poeno took the picture on board to get it repaired and it remained on the Bounty until she sailed.

Although communication of a sort had been established through the native women and their eloquent sign language, Morrison regretted that his "Imperfect knowledge of the Language" prevented him from enquiring into the "misterious Customs" of the Island. One thing he did note, whether he interpreted it correctly or not, was the strange relationship between the king and his son. According to Morrison, as soon as a son was born to the king, the honours and titles passed to the child. The Father, as he puts it, "commences Guardian to his child and honours it as his superior." The child king never came on board the BOUNTY but frequently paddled round it in his canoe and Bligh went to pay his respects to him formally on shore. As the young king circled the ship, the enquiring Lewisman noted two points in particular. Everyone who saw the canoe did homage to the child. And the child, as king, sat in the bow, rather than the stern. "It is the custom of this country to prefer the Bow to the Stern," he noted.

Morrison makes no comment on the purpose or effect of the king's abdication in favour of an infant son but, if the custom is correctly described, it seems to formalise, in an exaggerated sort of way, the natural determination of parents to exalt their children and give them the best possible start in life. I wonder what a Tahitian would have made of the treatment of women and children in Georgian Britain? Perhaps it was with the hope of finding out that Morrison, as soon as he got to Tahiti, began to enquire what had happened to O'mai.

Omai, despite Morrison's spelling of the name, was not an Irishman. He was a native Tahitian taken to Britain by Captain Tobias Furneaux in 1773. Furneaux had gone to the Pacific with Capt Cook on his third voyage. The vessels lost touch with each other and came home separately. The arrival of Furneaux with Omai of Ulaietea created as great a sensation in Britain as the arrival of Cook did in Tahiti, with one significant difference. The Tahitians regarded the stranger as a god. The British regarded the stranger as a curiosity. Capt Cook took Omai back to Tahiti in 1776, but when Morrison arrived, thirteen years later, he learned that Omai was dead and the questions he wanted to ask, whatever they were, remained unanswered.

While friction between Bligh and his officers gradually eroded discipline on the BOUNTY, the other element in the mutiny also made its appearance soon after the arrival at Tahiti. What one might call the Lotus, or the Lotos, effect. The Oxford English Dictionary puts it succinctly. It defines the Lotus as a plant yielding the fruit ,"represented by Homer as producing a state of dreamy forgetfulness and loss of all desire to return home." Tennyson, using a variant spelling, celebrates the plant in his poem "The Lotos Eaters":

"Most weary seem'd the sea, weary the oar
Weary the wandering fields of barren foam.
Then some one said, 'We will return no more':
And all at once they sang, 'Our island home
Is far beyond the wave; we will no longer roam.'"

The crew of the BOUNTY were not intoxicated by the fruit of a particular plant. They were beguiled by the easy life of the people of Tahiti, and the contrast with the harsh discipline, and short rations on a British naval vessel at sea. On the 14th of January, at four in the morning, the small cutter was missed from its usual station alongside the BOUNTY. "Capt Bligh was acquainted with it, and the hands being called, it was found that Chas. Churchill, Jno Millward and Willm Musprat were missing," writes Morrison. "As Mr Hayward, the midshipman, had been asleep on his watch and a small bag with trade being found on deck, it was readily supposed that they had taken the boat especially as it was known that Millward was sentry from 12 till 2." An examination of the Armoury showed that the deserters had taken eight stand of arms and eight cartouche boxes of ammunition.

Hayward was clapped in irons, and Fryer, the BOUNTY'S master, was sent off in the large cutter to search for the deserters. At eight o'clock, Fryer returned with the small cutter but without the missing men. He had with him five natives who reported that the deserters had taken the cutter to Mataavye, and abandoned it there, transferring the arms chest to a canoe. They were believed to have sailed for a small group of islands enclosed by a reef, some twenty miles to the north. By this time the sea chests of the missing men had been searched. In Churchill's was a slip of paper with the names of three of the shore party. The inference was that they too were involved. Capt Bligh immediately went ashore and interrogated the men named in the paper. He accused them of conspiring with Churchill. "They persisted in their innocence," Morrison records. "And denied it so firmly, that he was inclined from the circumstances to believe them and said no more to them about it."

Bligh then turned to Matte, the King, or perhaps one should say the King's father, having regard to the curious custom of the Tahitians in exalting the son as a child king. Matte sent off a number of canoes to make a search but it was three weeks before Bligh got any news of his missing men. On 15th February Hetee-hetee came on board with news of their whereabouts. Morrison does not explain who Hetee-hetee was but his name was well known in Britain. He had spent seven months on board HMS RESOLUTION with Captain Cook, visiting the Friendly Islands, New Zealand, Easter Island and the Marquesas.

Capt Bligh immediately manned the launch and went in pursuit. The fugitives offered no resistance and had no means of escape. Their canoe had overturned and they had almost drowned. They were brought back to the BOUNTY and clapped in irons along with the midshipman who slept on duty. After a months detention the three deserters were paraded for punishment. Churchill was given two dozen lashes, and the other two four dozen each. Morrison gives no indication why Churchill was let off more lightly than his companions, despite the fact that he seemed to have been the ring-leader. Nor does he mention the fact that, as bosun's mate, the unpleasant task of administering the lashes would have fallen to him. I wonder in what frame of mind he discharged his duty?

He had an even more disagreeable task a few weeks later when one of the natives was given a hundred lashes, which must have torn his back to shreds. The trouble arose when the ship was being watered. It was a dark rainy night. The shore party were huddled in a tent. In the morning they discovered that one of the puncheons was missing together with some of the gunner's bedding and bits of an azimuth compass. Bligh upbraided the officers in the party for neglect of duty. They replied the night had been so dark and the rain so heavy they could not see or hear each other, let alone know what was happening outside their tent. They pointed out that the thief had also been confused by the dark. He had struggled off with a full puncheon, although there were empty puncheons near by which would have been easier to carry. There was no point in one of the natives stealing a puncheon of water. Water was plentiful. The prize was the container, not its contents. That explanation, of course, assumes that the thief knew the puncheon contained water. His attitude might have been different if he thought it was grog. Be that as it may, when Bligh reported the incident to Matte, the thief and the cask were soon produced. Matte suggested that the culprit should be shot as a warning to others. Bligh contented himself with a hundred lashes.

After the punishment the offender was put in irons. We do not know whether Bligh intended to punish him still further, or to keep him prisoner until the BOUNTY sailed. In the event he did neither. Despite his lacerations and the irons, the culprit was able to get hold of a marlin spike in the dark, break the lock of his chains, creep up to the fore scuttle unseen, and jump overboard. No one knew what was going on until the sentry heard the splash. Morrison passes no comment, but from the tone in which he records the incident I think we can assume he was glad the poor man escaped.

Around the same time there was a mysterious incident. The ship's cable was deliberately severed by some one, almost completely through, and just below the water line where the damage went unnoticed. It was only discovered when a squall from the westward brought the cable taut, and the part which had been cut came above the surface. Some of the officers thought the natives were responsible. They had been well paid for diving down to clear a cable when it fouled the rocks as the BOUNTY came in to anchor. Some one, they guessed, was trying to make himself another well paid job. Morrison disagreed. "Though they are not very guilty of keeping secrets this remained a profound one," he comments, implying that the garrulous natives could not have been involved. As it happens they were. One of them anyway. Morrison was astonished when, some months later, the culprit confessed to him and told him what else he had planned to do. By that time Morrison was no longer a member of the BOUNTY'S crew and his relations with the natives had assumed an entirely new character. I will pick up the end of the story later, in its proper context.

9

THE NOT SO FRIENDLY ISLANDS

By the end of March 1789 the BOUNTY had loaded more than a thousand bread fruit plants, and many other exotic specimens which Nelson, the gardener, wished to bring back to Britain. "We got ready for sea, getting them aboard by 1st April," Morrison records in his Journal. "The natives, to show the last token of their friendship, loaded us with presents and the ship became lumbered with hogs, cocoa nuts and green plantains for sea store." By the 4th all the water casks were filled, there was a good store of firewood on board, and buoys had been placed in the channel, to mark a safe course through the coral reefs to the open sea.

Some of the Tahitian chiefs remained on board until the last moment as if reluctant to let the BOUNTY go. "There was a tender scene," he notes, when they said their farewells before being sent ashore in the BOUNTY'S cutter. Bligh, in his most expansive mood, gave Matte a musket, two pistols, with balls and flint, and a chest full of other gifts. One of the carpenters, a Scot named Macintosh, with whom Morrison was to be later linked in a remarkable enterprise which neither of them could then foresee, gave Matte "an American Musquet" with which he seemed highly pleased. "As the labour of the day had been very great, double allowance of grog was given to all hands... Everybody seemed in high spirits and began already to talk of home."

The crew tried to predict how long the voyage would take, and to tot up the wages they would receive at the end of it. "One would readily have imagined that we had just left Jamaica instead of Tahiti, so far onward did flattering fancies lead them," comments Morrison. I suspect that, at the time, he was buoyed up by some flattering fancies of his own. His comment has the ring of hindsight: a knowledge of all the bitter experiences which lay between that double allowance of grog and his next return to Lewis, with a tale of desperate adventure which must have held his hearers spellbound.

In case the crew had gone soft during their sojourn in Tahiti, Bligh mustered them on deck next day, and stopped the grog allowance of those who weren't clean and tidy. He then kept them busy making and shortening sail to limber them up. It was a wise precaution. Before long a wind, blowing hard from the westward, had them shortening sail in earnest.

Nine days out from Tahiti they discovered an inhabited but still uncharted island. Morrison, as usual, was curious to note everything about the natives: their dress, their customs, their language, the design of their canoes. His thirst for information was insatiable. "Three of the natives came off in a canoe," he notes. "They seemed much surprised at everything they saw. As soon as they came on board they fell down and kissed Mr Bligh's feet, giving him the pearl shells they wore on their breasts suspended by collars of braided hair." Bligh in return gave each of them a knife and some beads, which they were pleased to get although they did not understand their use. He also presented the group with a young boar and a sow as they had none on the island.

The boar and sow had come from Tahiti. Although the islands were only a few days sail apart in a British man of war they clearly had little, if any, contact with each other. Not only was the fauna different, Morrison noted that "their language seemed to differ from that of the Society Isles though they knew the bread fruit by the same name." More particularly Morrison noted that their canoes were different from the Tahitian canoes, "being alike at each end and but indifferently built." Everywhere he went he took particular note of the design and quality of the canoes, indicating an avid, practical interest in boat building and design.

At Annamooka, in the Friendly Islands, which the Dutch navigator Tasman had named Rotterdam, Morrison noted, "their canoes will carry from 2 to 40 men. They have both double and single canoes equipped for sailing with well made rope, and large sails which they work in different methods." He describes the different methods in some detail, explaining how they made rope from coconut husk "well twisted in three strands." The canoes he concludes were "neatly built and well finished, and sail at an amazing rate in smooth water but in a rough sea they can never answer." Of particular interest is his comment that the Annamooka canoes "work to windward in the same manner as the Flying Proa of the Ladrones." Morrison had never been to the Ladrones so the comment must be based on his reading. It is one of several indications in the Journal of the extent to which he was steeped in the literature of exploration. The Ladrones, or Marianas, were named by Magellan on his famous circumnavigation of the globe in 1521. He must have found the inhabitants troublesome: the name Islas de los Ladrones means the Islands of Thieves. The largest island in the group, Guam, was the scene of a decisive battle in the Second World War. It lies well to the north of the BOUNTY'S course. Most of Morrison's comments, however, are based on direct personal observation.

He describes for us the fish hooks used in the Friendly Islands, "made of pearl, bone and tortoise shell"; the clubs, "about three feet long, of hard wood, neatly carved, and inlaid with bone and pearl"; the long spears "with barbs of three inches, fixed at equal distances for three feet in length"; the bows, "of about 6 or 7 feet long of very elastic wood"; the arrows, "pointed with the stings of the sting ray" and the slings, "made of the husk of the coconuts." Everything is noted precisely and when possible measured or quantified in some way. He was just as interested in the way things were made as in their appearance.

Turning from weapons of war to more domestic matters he writes, "their clothing is in both sexes alike, and is mostly one piece of cloth or matting tied round the waist and depending below the knees. The matting is chiefly worn at sea or in wet weather and is of several sorts, neatly made. Their cloth is made of the bark of the cloth tree and they have a method of glazing it to make it keep out wet, and stain it with brown or black which gives it a very handsome appearance. Both sexes dress their hair with lime or burnt shells which, though originally black, soon turns to red, purple and white. They are of copper colour and are well made. The women are handsome but know how to set a price on their favours. The men are tattooed from the knee to the waist which something resembles a pair of breeches. The women are not tattooed, but have on their shoulders several circles indented with burning hot bamboos of different sizes, and many of both sexes want a part, if not the whole of their little fingers, which we understood was cut off as a tribute to the memory of their deceased friends."

From dress he turned his attention to their well made earthen vessels and "many curious pieces of workmanship and ingenuity." "Their canoes appear to be the best made and the neatest work of any we have seen, though not so large as some." One thing disappointed him. "Tho the countenances of the men are open yet they have something in it that gives an unfavourable idea to strangers; perhaps this might have been heightened in our eyes by their actions which did not correspond with their name." The islands, or rather the islanders, were far from Friendly.

"They were very rude and attempted to take the casks from the waterers and the wood from the wooding party and if a musket was pointed at any of them [it] produced no other effect than a return of the compliment, by poising their club or spear with a menacing look." "As it was Lieut B's orders that no person should affront them on any occasion, they were emboldened by meeting no return to their insolence, and became so troublesome that Mr Christian, who had command of the watering party, found it difficult to carry on his duty. Of this he informed Lieut Bligh, who dam'd him for a cowardly rascal, asking him if he was afraid of a set of naked savages while he had arms; to which Mr Christian answered 'the arms are no use while your orders prevent them from being used.'"

And so, in the Friendly Islands, the long and close relationship between Fletcher Christian and his patron, Bligh, began to crumble in slights and recriminations publicly exchanged in the presence of the crew. Worse was to follow.

The Friendly Islanders were not overawed by the white man, as other islanders were. "The natives flocked to the ship in great numbers to traffic for hogs, fowls, yams, coconuts etc. all of which they seemed to know the value of and would not part with a single plantain without something in return," writes Morrison. Fryer, the master, was sent ashore with the cutter. A swarm of natives followed. When a grapnel was dropped to anchor the vessel, "the natives found means of unbending it from the rope by stirring up the mud and thickening the water and then diving down as they flocked about the boat." Seeing the danger, Fryer ordered one of his crew to haul the rope taut to make sure the grapnel was there but, before the guard realised that the rope had gone limp in his hand, the grapnel was on its way to another island. Bligh ordered the Chiefs to secure its return, "but to no purpose tho' they made fair promises."

When the BOUNTY was ready to sail, there was a frantic burst of trading which had consequences of its own. "Two hours liberty was given to the people [meaning the crew] to expend their trade." As this was likely to be the last island where Iron Currency was the most valuable, everyone got rid of their "trade" as fast as they could, purchasing mats, spears, amd many curiosities and a quantity of yams for private store with coconuts etc and everything the natives had or would dispose of. "What with yams and clubs in all quarters, the ship was fairly lumbered that there was scarcely room to stir in any part."

About noon the BOUNTY weighed and stowed the anchor, "and the fore topsail being loose we stood to westward with a light air." The ship was still surrounded by canoes. The

Chiefs were still on board. And Bligh was still waiting for the missing grapnel. The Chiefs assured Bligh they had sent a canoe to the island it had been taken to. It would be returned if he delayed his departure until the canoe got back. At that point Bligh boiled over. "The ship's company was armed and drawn up and the Chiefs made prisoners. The canoes were ordered to cast off and keep astern." It is difficult to imagine what Bligh hoped to achieve at that point by the arrest of the Chiefs. It was obvious it would not secure the return of the grapnel.

Then Bligh went even further. He humiliated his proud prisoners by sending them down to the messroom to peel coconuts for the dinner: a gesture as offensive as it was ineffective. He stormed back on deck and denounced his own men as "lubberly rascals", as if they were responsible for the loss of the grapnel. He declared, irrelevantly, that, with five men and a few sticks, he could disarm the lot of them - meaning his own crew! - in spite of their muskets. In a final flourish he aimed, "a pistol at Wm McCoy [and] threatened to shoot him for not paying attention."

While this was going on the wives of the arrested Chiefs were following the BOUNTY in a catamaran. "They wept bitterly and cut their faces and shoulders in a terrible manner as did the oldest of the Chiefs who struck himself several violent blows on the face and cut himself on his cheek bones with his fists." When he realised he could achieve nothing by this show of spite, Bligh suddenly changed his tactics. He ordered the catamaran alongside and dismissed his prisoners, heaping them with presents, as if they were old friends. Only one of the prisoners responded. The youngest among them stripped off his matted skirt and offered it as a return gift. The offer was spurned. The others, Morrison shrewdly observes, "seemed as if they only smothered their resentment, seeing that they could not revenge the insult. It was the opinion of most on board that, if a weak manned ship came in their way, they would remember this day's transaction and make them suffer for it."

The young Lewisman's comment might well be the epitaph of the British Empire. All the good that was done, often with high intentions, in the spread of parliamentary democracy and the rule of law, and by selfless missionary activities in the fields of education and medical care, was offset by stupid acts of arrogance and failures to understand the feelings of other people which rankle down to the present day. Shakespeare puts it in eight memorable words: "The evil that men do lives after them." James Morrison, brought up at the Gaelic-English interface, in the first generation after Culloden, clearly felt it in his bones. He was quite sure that someone else would someday pay for Bligh's humiliation of the Friendly Islands Chiefs.

A few days later, as if to justify the comment, Bligh treated his own closest friend with the same contempt, and Morrison, an innocent bystander, was caught up in the consequences. Here is the story as he told it himself:

"When the Chiefs were gone we made sail but the wind being light and frequently flattening to a calm we made little way during the night. As we neared Toofoa we observed vast columns of smoke and flame issuing from the volcano which appeared to be a very large one. The weather continuing the same all day we altered our position very little, being within 7 or 8 leagues of the island all the day and no appearance of a breeze. In the afternoon of the 27th Mr Bligh came up, and [was] taking a turn about the quarter deck when he missed some of the coconuts which were piled up between the guns... He said they were stolen and could not go without the knowledge of the officers, who were all called and declared that they had not seen a man touch them, to which Mr Bligh replied 'then you must have taken them yourselves.'

"[He] ordered Mr Elphinstone to go and fetch every cocnut in the ship aft, which he obeyed. [Bligh] then questioned every officer in turn concerning the number they had bought, & coming to Mr Christian asked him. Mr Christian answered 'I do not know, Sir, but I hope you don't think me so mean as to be guilty of stealing yours. Mr Bligh replied, 'Yes, you damned hound, I do. You must have stolen them from me or you could give a better account of them. God damn you, you scoundrels, you are all thieves alike and combine with the men to rob me. I suppose you'll steal my yams next, but I'll sweat you for it you rascals. I'll make half of you jump overboard before you get through Endeavour Straits. He then called Mr Samuel and said, 'Stop these villains' grog, and give them but half a pound of yams tomorrow, and if they steal then, I'll reduce them to a quarter. The cocnuts were carried aft, and he went below. The officers got together and were heard to murmur much at such treatment, and it was talked among the men that the yams would be next seized, as Lieut Bligh knew they had purchased large quantities of them [they] set about secreting as many as they could.

"The night being calm we made no way, and in the morning of the 28th the boatswain came to my hammock and waked me, telling me to my great surprise that the ship was taken by Mr Christian. I hurried on deck and found it true - seeing Mr Bligh in his shirt with his hands tied behind him and Mr Christian standing by him with a drawn bayonet in his hand and his eyes flaming with revenge. Several of the men were under arms, and the small cutter hoisted out and the large one getting ready. I applied to the boatswain to know how I should proceed but he was as much at a loss as I."

The mutiny on board the BOUNTY had taken place and, three years later, Morrison was condemned to death for his part in it, although it happened while he was asleep.

1783

...are to certify the Right Hon.ble The Lords Commissioners for executing the Office of Lord High Admiral of Great Britain, and Ireland &c. That in pursuance of directions from Charles Proby Esq.r Commissioner of his Majesty's Navy at Chatham We have examined Mr. Jam.s Morrison in the Articles ordered by their Lordships, for the Examination of persons previous to their being appointed to serve as Master Gunners in his Majesty's Sea-service & humbly Report as follows.

He is skilled in Vulgar, and Decimal Arithmetic, the Extractions of the Square, and Cube Roots, and in practical Problems of Geometry, and Plain Trigonometry.

He is capable of knowing, when a Cannon is truely Bored, and not Honey Combed.

He knows how to dispart a Cannon, so as to direct it justly to the place aimed at

He knows how to Scriate, or Round the thickness of the Metal of a Cannon at the Touch-Hole, Trunnions and Muzzle.

He knows how to adjust a shott to a Cannon, and a due proportion of Powder

He is capable of Taking, or Judging of Heights, and Distances, especially at Sea.

He is able to find the Weight of a Cannon, and knows the Names and Denominations thereof, and the Names of the particular parts of them, the Dimensions of their Bore, shott for them, and the Weight of the shott.

He knows the Length and Fortification of a Cannon of each sort and size, and how many persons will be necessary to attend each piece in time of service

The report of Morrison's examination in gunnery.

9. He knows when the Trunnions of a Gun are placed justly in the carriage, whether the Carriage itself is fit, and of a due length for the Gun, and whether the Trucks are equally high, and the recoil or return equally quick.

10. He knows how to Charge, and Discharge a Piece of Ordnance, readily and assist like, and how to spunge the same, and to Muzzle, and secure it in bad weather.

He has produced to us Certificates from the several Commanders he has sailed under, of his Care, Sobriety and Obedience to command. He has also produced a Certificate from the Navy Office of his having served Four Years, and two Days _____ in his Majesty's Navy.

We therefore humbly certify our opinion, that he is a person fitly qualified to be appointed a Master Gunner of any of his Majesty's Ships of War of the Third Rate. Given under our hands this 19 day of December 17__

John Evans

Jo:ᵗ Neate   } Gunner of the {   Royal George

I.ᵒ Watts   }   {   Revenge

Jos:ᵗᵒ Dawkins   Teacher of the Mathematics.   Albion

The report of Morrison's examination in gunnery.

10
IN SEARCH OF PARADISE

Brian Lavery, in his book "Nelson's navy", says there must have been more than a thousand mutinies, large and small, in the British navy between 1793 and 1815. Considerably more than one a week! These were eruptions from the lower deck by men oppressed from above. The mutiny on the BOUNTY was unusual, if not unique. It was led by an officer - the second in command on the ship - and his fellow officers did nothing to stop it. "The behaviour of the officers on this occasion was dastardly beyond description," comments Morrison. "None of them making the least attempt to rescue the ship, which would have been effected had any attempt been made by one of them." Some of the ordinary seamen who were under arms when he got on deck "did not know what they were about". They had been ordered to stand sentry, and they did, although their subsequent behaviour showed that they were loyal to their captain.

The young Lewisman's outspoken criticism of the officers is justified by his account of what led up to the mutiny, as he heard it from Fletcher Christian and others, after the event.

Christian's original intention had been to desert the ship rather than lead a mutiny. At least three of the midshipmen were privy to his plan but none of them alerted the Captain. One of the three, George Stewart from Orkney, sparked off the mutiny by a whispered word to Christian at a critical moment. Another of the three, Thomas Hayward, made the mutiny possible by falling asleep on his watch. just as he had fallen asleep on duty in Tahiti, enabling some of the crew to desert.

Stewart no doubt had sympathy with Fletcher Christian. He was desperate to get back to Tahiti. He had fallen deeply in love with the daughter of one of the chiefs. Hayward's motives for keeping silence are more difficult to fathom. He may have been showing his resentment against Bligh for putting him in irons after his first lapse. Whatever his resentment against Bligh, he went with him in the open boat after the mutiny and returned to Tahiti as a Lieut on the PANDORA when she came in search of the mutineers. On the voyage home he was distinguished by his brutality to his prisoners. On these later occasions one can only assume that he was trying to expiate his own two serious lapses of silence and sleep by punishing others for crimes they didn't commit. A very common pattern of human behaviour in the navy as in the church.

Morrison's account of what led up to the mutiny is based on hearsay but he gives the best insight we have into the mind of Fletcher Christian. It was directly from Christian he learned "the cause of this sad affair." "Finding himself much hurt by the treatment he had received from Mr Bligh he had determined to quit the ship the preceding evening, improvising a raft from a stout plank and some staves which he found lying at the larboard gangway." He informed the boatswain, the carpenter, and two of the midshipmen - Stewart and Hayward - of his intention. Instead of preventing him, or reporting him, they provided him with some roasted pig for food, and nails and beads to trade with the natives, in the unlikely event of his ever getting ashore. The various items were put in a bag provided by the righteous Mr Hayward. Morrison has no doubt of the significance of the point he is making. "The bag was produced," he adds, "and I knew it to be the same which I had made for Mr Hayward some time before."

Christian hid the bag "in the clue of Robert Tinkler's hammock" until the time came to use it. But Tinkler stumbled on it, becoming the fifth member of the crew and the third midshipman to have prior knowledge of the First Lieut's intention to desert. Tinkler's discovery, in Morrison's phrase, was "smothered and passed off." It seems unlikely that, in the close confines of a ship, a discovery of that sort could have been made and smothered without others knowing about it as well as those immediately concerned. Yet no one thought it his duty to raise the alarm.

Christian's plan was a madcap venture: more like attempted suicide than desertion. Tahiti, where he would have been welcome, was far beyond the range of a ramshackle raft. The nearest islands were the unfriendly Friendlies and everyone on board the BOUNTY expected the next white men who landed there to feel the fury of the chiefs whom Bligh had humiliated. As it happened there were too many people stirring during the first and middle watches for Christian to slip away. By half past three he decided to try to get a little sleep, until the ship quietened down. Christian was wakened by Stewart, when the young Orcadian came on watch. He had not had much sleep and, in Morrison's phrase, was "still much out of order." Stewart tried to dissuade him from "swimming away" and then murmured the fatal words, "the people are ripe for anything."

Hayward, who was in command of the ship, was asleep on the arms chest which stood between the guns. Hallet, the young midshipman, not yet seventeen, who shared the watch with Hayward was nowhere to be seen. In what Morrison represents as a sudden decision, without premeditation, let alone conspiracy, Christian opened his mind to Quintrell and Martin, two of the seamen on deck. They immediately wakened Churchill, the Master at Arms: the man whose primary duty it was to maintain discipline on board. He had already shown his disaffection by attempting to desert, for which he had received two dozen lashes. Four ABs, Thomson, Smith, Williams and McCoy joined them. At that point Christian went to the armourer, Coleman, and asked for a musket to shoot a shark which had come alongside. Without question Coleman opened the arms chest; the mutineers had guns, and the ship was secured. Capt Bligh was tied up, and sentries were posted to keep the gunner and the botanist in the cockpit. The ship's small cutter was launched in which Bligh and his supporters could be set adrift.

It was at that point Morrison was wakened by his immediate superior, the boatswain, and came on deck. He asked what he should do. The boatswain told him "in a confused manner" to assist in getting the cutter out. Christian ordered Hayward and Hallet to get into it. Then Fryer, the master, and Samuel, the clerk. Hayward and Hallet, "with tears in their eyes" begged to be allowed to remain on board. They did not fancy being adrift in the open Pacific in an overloaded cutter. Christian told them to be quiet. Bligh began to reason with

Christian. Christian replied, "Mamoo, Sir, not a word or death's your portion." The boatswain and carpenter came aft to Christian and begged him to give them the launch instead of the cutter. He hesitated but finally agreed.

Morrison seems to have taken a leading part in replacing the cutter with the larger and more seaworthy launch. "While I was clearing her," he records, "the Master came up and spoke to Mr Bligh." Afterwards he "came to me asking if I had any hand in the mutiny. I told him I had not, and he then desired me to try what I could do to raise a party and rescue the ship, which I promised to do." Before they could agree on anything further, Quintrell intervened and ordered the Master below where he was confined in his cabin. Morrison, however did his best. "Jno Millward, who was by me at the time, swore he would stand by me and went to Musprat, Burket and the Boatswain on that score," he records. "Churchill, seeing the Master speaking to me, came and demanded what he had said. I told him he was asking about the launch, but Alexander Smith, who stood on the other side of the boat told Churchill to look sharp after me saying, ''tis a damned lie, Charles, for I saw him and Millward shake hands when the Master spoke to them,' and called the others to stand to arms which put them on their guard. As I saw none near me that seemed inclined to make a push, and the officers busy getting the boat in order, I was fain to do so too... The boat was got out, when everyone ran to get what he could into her and get in themselves as fast as possible."

In spite of the scramble, not everyone who wanted to go was able to get into the launch, and not everyone who got in really wanted to go.

Altogether there were 19 men in the launch when it was cast off from the BOUNTY at the beginning of what is acknowledged to be one of the greatest open boat voyages ever undertaken. In getting back to Britain, to unleash the vengeance of the navy on the mutineers, Capt Bligh showed that he was a navigator of unusual skill, and a man of outstanding courage. By the time the launch was cast off it was so overloaded it was in danger of sinking. Morrison reckons there was less than seven inches of freeboard: a slender margin with which to undertake a four thousand mile voyage across the Pacific. When he saw the launch was in imminent danger of sinking, Bligh told some of those who were scrambling on board to remain on the BOUNTY. "Never fear, my lads, you cant all go with me... but I'll do you justice if ever I reach England," he shouted. Reaching England must have seemed a pretty remote prospect at that time.

One of those Bligh ordered to stay on the BOUNTY was Fryer the master, but Christian would not have him. Presumably he did not want anyone on board who could challenge his own authority. But why did Bligh want the Master to stay? Was it to have a competent navigator on board to protect the ship, even in his own absence? Or did he have a glimmer of hope that, with Fryer on board, there might be an opportunity to retake the ship? Or had his quarrel with Fryer reached such a pitch that he couldn't abide his company? We cannot tell.

According to Morrison, Bligh made one last attempt to end the mutiny before he was bundled into the launch. "I'll pawn my honour! I'll give my bond, Mr Christian, never to think of this if you'll desist!" he shouted. He pled with Christian to think of his wife and family. "If you had honour things would not have come to this," retorted Christian. "If you had any regard for your wife and family you should have thought of them before and not behaved so much like a villain." When Bligh attempted to speak again, he was ordered to be silent. William Cole, the boatswain, intervened to try to pacify Christian. He was brushed aside. "'Tis too late. I have been in hell for this fortnight past and am determined to bear it no longer... You know Mr Cole I have been used like a dog all the voyage."

Cole was Morrison's immediate superior, and, as he went to join Bligh in the launch, Morrison told him he was going to take his chance in the ship, in view of the Captain's promise to do them justice. "God bless you, my boy," replied the boatswain. "If it were not for my wife and family I would stay myself." It was an odd comment. The risk of going in the launch was probably greater than the risk of staying on the BOUNTY. Was he hinting that, if he were not a family man, he might have been tempted to return to the Tahitian paradise himself?

Morrison gives a list of some of the provisions put into the launch including two gang casks of water, three bags of bread and some bottles of wine. He claims to have handed in, himself, 25 or 26 four pound pieces of pork and two gourds of water. About eight o'clock in the morning the launch rowed away in the direction of the nearest land between twenty and thirty miles distant. Christian was now in command of the BOUNTY, and he appointed George Stewart, the Orcadian, as his second in command.

Stewart's position in regard to the mutiny is rather equivocal. It was his whispered word which sparked it off. But, when it did occur, he was confined to his cabin along with another midshipman, Heywood, whose fortunes became closely entwined with Morrison's during and after the court martial, and not always, I think, to Morrison's advantage. The Orcadian's promotion probably reflects the lack of seagoing experience in Christian's party. The captain, the master, the master's mate, the boatswain, the carpenter, the gunner, the quartermaster and his mate, and the best of the midshipmen had all gone with Bligh. Stewart, a midshipman in his early twenties, was the most senior officer, commissioned or warrant, on whom Christian could call. Morrison was promoted boatswain and told to take charge of the stores, a fact which did him no good when it came to his trial.

At nine o'clock, an hour after the launch had rowed away, a breeze sprang up, sails were trimmed and the BOUNTY was on its way back to Tahiti by way of Toubai. One of Christian's first orders was that the thousand bread fruit plants for which they had come to Tahiti should be thrown overboard: a task which occupied several days. He installed himself in Bligh's cabin.

At this point the young Lewisman made a second attempt to retake the ship: "As I had reason to believe from the countenance of affairs that the ship might yet be recovered if a party could be formed, and as I knew that several on board were not at all pleased with the situation, I fixed on a plan for that purpose and soon got several to back my opinion," he recorded in his Journal. His plan was to wait until they got back to Tahiti. On the night of their arrival there, he reckoned, men would be anxious to get ashore, and the judicious use of grog would ensure that the right people went, leaving the loyalists in command. "These matters being settled, I had no doubt but that everyone would stand to the test and, to prevent the others from knowing our design, [we] affected a shyness towards each other. I soon found to my unspeakable surprise that Mr Christian was acquainted with our intentions, some of his party overhearing some part of the business."

Although he knew there was something afoot, Christian did not know how many were involved, nor whether he was strong enough to take drastic action. He contented himself with taking the keys of the arms chest from Coleman, the armourer, who had always kept them. The keys were given to Churchill, the corporal at arms, who must be regarded as more deeply implicated in the mutiny than anyone apart from Fletcher Christian himself. The arms chest was moved into Christian's cabin and Churchill slept on top of it. Each of "Mr Christian's party" was given a pistol, and "a sharp lookout was kept by his party one of which took care to make a third when they saw any two in conversation."

The mutiny divided the crew of the BOUNTY into two groups: those who went with Bligh and those who remained with Christian. Almost from the first moment, however, it was clear there were three parties: those who had gone with Bligh in the launch; a small group of hardliners who stood by Christian and went with him eventually to Pitcairn Island; and a group of loyalists who would have prevented the mutiny from taking place if any of the officers had given them the leadership their duty demanded of them.

Perhaps we should say there were four groups. The loyalists who refused to go with Christian to an unknown destination, which turned out to be Pitcairn Island, were themselves divided between those who returned to Tahiti because they were desperate to get back and those who remained on Tahiti only because they had no other option. We have only Morrison's own word for the story of his two abortive attempts to organise a party and retake the ship, but his truthfulness is established by the fact that on Tahiti he organised an elaborate attempt to get back to Britain, which was thwarted in a most dramatic fashion at the last moment, but of which there was tangible and indisputable evidence.

Alexander Smith, who frustrated Morrison's first plan to retake the ship, was one of the hard liners who went to Pitcairn Island. After a period of bloody feuds in which Christian's supporters murdered each other, Smith, now calling himself Adams, was the sole survivor of the hard line mutineers. Twenty years later, when the colony on Pitcairn was discovered, Sir Thomas Staines described Adams as, "a venerable old man... whose exemplary conduct and fatherly care of the whole of the little colony could not but command admiration." Morrison, who tried twice to save the ship, was condemned to death by a naval Court Martial, and narrowly escaped hanging. Adams who thwarted him, was never brought to trial. In fact when the navy found him, they gave him a halo.

One of Fletcher Christian's first acts, on taking command of the BOUNTY, was to order new uniforms for the crew. Nothing, he said, had more effect on the minds of the Pacific Islanders than uniformity of dress. James Morrison seems to have agreed. The wearing of uniforms, he comments, "always betokens discipline, especially on board British men of war." The uniforms were made from discarded sails. Christian's old uniform was used for edging. The crew were thus in white canvas suits with blue piping.

Christian's next aim was to find an island, unfrequented by shipping, where he might live in peace now that the mutiny, in Morrison's phrase, "had for ever debarred him from returning to England or any civilised place."

His first choice was Toobouai. It had been charted by Capt Cook, but had such a bad anchorage Christian reckoned no vessel would call there if it could reach Tahiti. He found the opening through the reefs described by Captain Cook and got the BOUNTY safely into a sandy bay, but the reception from the natives was not encouraging.

When George Stewart, in the cutter, was marking a channel through the reef for the BOUNTY to follow, his party was attacked by natives in a canoe. They clambered aboard uninvited, stealing a jacket and other articles. He had to fire a pistol to scare them off. Next morning native canoes circled round the BOUNTY as if on reconnaissance, then paddled back to the beach where a large crowd had gathered with clubs and spears of shining black wood. They made a din by blowing conches and "their dress, being red and white, gave them a formidable appearance." By next day the number of canoes had increased greatly and at last an old man came on board the BOUNTY. Morrison assumed he was the local chief.

He "appeared to view everything he saw with astonishment and appeared frightened at the hogs, goats, dog etc, starting back as any of them turned towards him." There was some difficulty in communicating with him as he did not speak the Tahitian language. "Mr Christian made him several presents and he went on shore seemingly satisfied, promising to return again, but we supposed that his visit was not for the purpose of friendship as he had been particular in counting our numbers." As a precaution arms were handed out, "that we might be in readiness to receive the promised visit... Their ferocious aspect gave us plainly to understand in what manner to expect it."

The return visit, however, came in a manner that was unforeseen. About noon there was a stir at the beach, and "a double canoe, full of women neatly dressed and their heads and necks decorated with flowers and pearl shells," sailed out to the BOUNTY. "As they approached the ship they stood up and beat time to a song which was given by one of them, which appeared to be a person of some consequence and who we afterwards found was the daughter of a chief. They were all young and handsome having fine long hair which reached their waists in waving ringlets. They came on board without ceremony, being in number 18, and the men who paddled the canoe were six, five of whom followed."

It was a tense moment for the young Lewisman and his companions because, in the "meantime, about fifty canoes, manned with 15 or 20 men each, paddled round on the other side, closing in and blowing their conches... We supposed that the women had been sent as a snare to catch us with, as they came so readily on board, but being on our guard which they observed, and having changed our dress, they were disappointed and made no attempt."

It is tantalising to speculate what precisely Morrison means by the phrase "having changed our dress." Had they put on the new uniforms Christian had ordered them to make, impressing the natives as he intended, or had they stripped for action? Whatever he means, the sequel was disconcerting. While the women were being treated with civility and given presents, the men began to steal everything they could lay their hands on. One even stole the card out of the compass. The man who took it was "a stout fellow" and there was a scuffle before he was subdued in which the card was torn. He was, "given two or three smart stripes with a rope's end" before he was set free.

As the natives moved away in their canoes they produced weapons, which earlier had been hidden, and brandished them "with threatening gestures." One of them cut loose the anchor buoy and was making off with it when a musket was fired at him. The four pounder was then loaded with grape shot and the canoes fled towards the shore. Christian ordered the BOUNTY'S crew to man the boats and follow but "the landing was vigorously disputed by them plying the boats smartly with stones." They paid no attention to the muskets, "till they found some fall when they took to the wood and in a few moments were all out of sight."

The mutineers search for an earthly paradise where they could live in peace had begun in bloodshed as it was to end, a little later, in mutual destruction on Pitcairn Island. At the same time, Christian was probably right to distrust the natives of Toobuoai. In the canoes they left on the beach, when they fled, were lengths of rope, quite clearly prepared to bind up the BOUNTY'S crew if the women succeeded in distracting their attention. The Bay where this skirmish took place is "abreast of the opening (the only one in the reef) described by Captain Cook, and we called it from this time Bloody Bay."

Christian was still determined to make Toobouai his home. When the natives failed to appear on the morning after the skirmish at Bloody Bay, he tried to coax them back with gifts. The BOUNTY'S boats sailed round the island carrying a white flag in the bow of one and a union jack in the bow of the other, as if the natives would understand these sophisticated European emblems. At several points Christian went ashore and walked up to the houses. No one appeared, but he left presents of hatchets and other iron goods.

Toobouai had plenty of bread fruit, coconuts and plantains, but neither hogs nor goats, which explains why the chief was so nervous of the livestock on the BOUNTY. Christian decided to go to Tahiti to get hogs and goats with which to stock Toobouai, hoping gradually to bring the natives into friendship "either by persuasion or force."

Although Morrison had been appointed by Christian to a post of responsibility among the mutineers the gap between them was widening all the time. He disagreed completely with Christian's plan to return to Toobouai. He didn't believe it was possible to win the friendship of that particular group of islanders "whose savage aspect and behaviour could not gain favour in the eyes of any man."

On the passage back to Tahiti, Christian warned that anyone who named Toobouai to the Tahitians would be punished severely, and anyone who attempted to desert would be shot. He was trying to make sure that when they returned to Toobouai their tracks would be completely covered. The crew of the BOUNTY were now involved in a web of deceit. Bligh began the process when he concealed from the Tahitians that Capt Cook was dead. Christian compounded the deception. He thought it necessary to conceal from the Tahitians what had happened on the BOUNTY. If the Tahitians knew, the navy, sooner or later, would find out even if Bligh and his companions, as they all anticipated, perished in the open boat. So he told them the BOUNTY had met up with Captain Cook, who took the bread fruit plants into his own ship and sent them back to Tahiti for hogs and goats to provision a new colony he was setting up in Australia, then still known as New Holland.

All the time tension was growing between Christian's party and those, like Morrison, who were against him. The clothes and other effects left behind by the men who had gone in the launch with Bligh were distributed among the crew to win them over. "They were made up in lots by Churchill and drawn for by tickets but," says Morrison, "it always happened that Mr Christian's party were better served than those who were thought to be disaffected." Whether the imputation was true or false, there was no love lost between the groups and an open rift could not be long delayed.

As the BOUNTY sailed back to Tahiti the armourer was kept busy, making iron goods to trade with the natives. "The grand object of these people is iron and like us with gold it matters not by what means they get it or where it comes from if they can but get it," comments Morrison. His own particular task was to go ashore with Churchill and buy the hogs and goats Christian intended to take back to Toobouai. Christian himself, in the meantime, entertained the chiefs on board the ship "plying them with wine and arrack" of which, Morrison notes ominously, "they became very fond."

Morrison had no difficulty in buying hogs and goats. The BOUNTY had bought so much on the first visit he thought they had "impoverished the island" but now the place seemed full of animals. They could have supplied a fleet, let alone a single ship. The task of provisioning the BOUNTY was made easier because Christian was much more popular with the Tahitians than Bligh had been. "Mr Christian was beloved by the whole of them but on the contrary none liked Mr Bligh though they flattered him for his riches, which is the case among polished nations, those in power being always courted," was the Lewisman's double edged comment on Tahiti and Georgian Britain.

By the 16th of June the BOUNTY was ready to return to Toobouai. On board they had about 460 hogs, mostly breeders, 50 goats, a quantity of fowls, a bull and cow, and a few dogs and cats. They also had on board men, boys, women and a female child some of whom seem to have been stowaways. Christian told them they would never see Tahiti again, "at which they seemed perfectly easy and satisfied, never betraying the least sign of sorrow for leaving their friends, nor did I observe that they ever repined afterwards," comments Morrison.

It was a stormy passage back to Bloody Bay and some of the animals died. When the survivors were let loose ashore the natives were more terrified than they had been of the mutineers' muskets during the battle. Despite the relative proximity of the two islands the people of Toobouai seem to have been much more primitive than the Tahitians. They weren't interested in iron goods, preferring their stone adzes to the axes made by the armourer for trade. A few red feathers seemed to be the best currency and cocks with red hackles were much esteemed.

Christian had no difficulty in negotiating for a plot of land on which to establish his colony. When the first turf was cut at the site of their fort, the men were given a double ration of grog to celebrate. He ordered the union jack to be flown, and named the place Fort

George, as if he were still a loyal subject of the king. Work was interrupted when they discovered the site was over-run by rats but a few cats brought ashore from the ship soon dealt with the problem. Then there was a scare when they heard hideous noises and shrieks which they took to be a war cry, and saw a large crowd approaching. It turned out to be a funeral procession.

As Morrison puts it, with a little unconscious humour, "It [is] the custom in their island when a man of any rank dies for all his friends and relations and all who wish him well to attend his funeral. When the body is put into the grave, a priest makes a long prayer, and the bystanders rend the air with horrid cries, cutting their heads and breasts with shells, and smearing their body with the blood, after which the grave is filled up and they depart leaving the near relations of the deceased to enjoy their mourning in private."

None of the mutineers had any building experience but the fort they planned was formidable. They cleared a square a hundred yards long on each side, and dug a ditch 18 feet wide all round it. The soil from the ditch was heaped up to make a wall giving a height of 20 feet from the top of the wall to the bottom of the ditch. Guns were taken ashore from the BOUNTY and so placed that two four pounders and four swivel guns could be brought to bear in any direction.

While Christian pressed ahead with the fort and Morrison did his share of the work with the others, the young Lewisman was developing a plan of his own. He had no intention of remaining on Toobouai. His first aim was to return to Tahiti from whence there was at least a chance of getting back one day to Britain. As the fort progressed, Christian began to strip the BOUNTY to get material for the houses he hoped to build. When Christian talked of taking the masts out of the ship, Morrison saw his chance. He thought he could reach Tahiti in five or six days in the BOUNTY'S cutter. It was in bad condition and Christian, who may have suspected the use that might be made of it, prohibited repairs until the whole party was established ashore. Even with a leaky boat, however, Morrison thought the risk worth taking. Once the masts were out of the BOUNTY he reckoned he could prevent them ever being put back again by destroying the "purchace blocks and fall." It would be impossible for Christian and the hard line mutineers to pursue him.

He broached his plan to George Stewart, the young Orcadian midshipman. Stewart said he and Peter Heywood, another young midshipman, had been thinking along the same lines. They decided to keep quiet until the opportunity arose to make a dash for it. Then they began to suspect that other members of the crew were also planning to return to Tahiti. They had to take the first opportunity before a rival group made off with the cutter. "Had we the chance to meet with bad weather our crazy boat would certainly have made us a coffin," comments Morrison, "but Providence ordered things better and we had no need to make this rash attempt."

The intervention of Providence, as Morrison saw it, is a tangled story. Among the BOUNTY'S crew discipline was getting lax. Some of the men were trigger happy, shooting off at the natives on the slightest provocation. Fortunately the aim seems generally to have been bad. Then two of the men spent a night ashore without leave. When Christian asked for an explanation they replied, "the ship is moored and we are now our own masters." Christian whipped out a pistol and clapped it to one of their heads. "I'll let you know who is master!" He ordered them to be put in irons. By morning they were repentant and the incident passed off, but the sign of disintegration was there.

Then Christian lost his grip on the native population. To begin with there had been elaborate friendship ceremonies, which Morrison describes in detail. The exchange of gifts. The exchange of names: Chief Tummotoa greeting Christian as "Tummotoa", and Christian responding by calling the Pacific Island native "Christian". One special gift was a young plantain tree: the symbol of peace. Tummotoa plied Christian with pieces of cloth, baskets of provisions, fish raw and dressed, bread fruit, taro, plantains and coconuts. Christian responded with gifts of Tahiti cloth, which, unlike the Tahitians themselves, the Toobouai natives preferred to British; hatchets, of which they hardly understood the use, matting and red feathers. The Chief, according to Morrison, was "highly pleased but seemed to value the red feathers more than all the rest."

We can only guess at some native bonding ceremony behind Morrison's comment that, "Tummotoa spent the night in prayer at Christian's bedside." Whatever the ceremony, it was in vain. Having established friendly relations with the Chief at Bloody Bay, and his immediate neighbour, Christian decided to build his fort on the land of a third chief, some distance away, sowing jealousy and discontent between the three. As a result, when some of the BOUNTY'S Tahitian stowaways went ashore, they were attacked with stones and when Alexander Smith, who became the saintly patriarch of Pitcairn Island, went philandering, he was robbed and imprisoned by the local chief. Christian retaliated by burning the Chief's house.

Before starting the fire, he seized some clubs and spears, and "two curious carved images of their household gods, which were decorated with pearl shells, human hair, teeth and nails cut in a very curious manner... Round them was placed a kind of grove of red feathers from the tail of the tropic birds." Christian hoped to negotiate a peace treaty by returning the goods he had confiscated but events were now beyond his control.

As the conflict between the men of the BOUNTY and the people of Toobouai became sharper so did the rift within the BOUNTY between Christian's party - the hard-line mutineers - and those, like James Morrison, who had been caught up in the mutiny without active participation.

Tinnarow, the chief whose home was burned, came "loaded with baskets of provisions which he presented to Mr Christian as a peace offering, begging at the same time that his household gods might be restored." Christian was agreeable; provided Tinnarow returned some goods which his followers had stolen from the BOUNTY. The negotiations were progressing favourably when one of the Tahitian boys who had gone to Toobouai on the BOUNTY reported that Tinnarow's men had come to the meeting armed. There spears were hidden in the bushes close at hand. Fearing treachery, whether it was intended or not, Christian refused to eat some Yava with Tinnarow, to seal their compact. The chief rose in anger and stalked away followed by his men. Christian ordered the BOUNTY's crew to action stations, and a warning shot was fired from one of the BOUNTY'S guns.

"The shot," according to Morrison, "did no other damage than passing through a house where it cut away a rafter to which a man was hanging a gourd of water. He was so terrified that he left the house, as did all who saw it, being alike surprised, the shot being lost and, the house not in sight of the ship, they could not be persuaded that it came from her. [They] readily believed it to be something supernatural and could not be persuaded to return to the house to live."

Hard on the heels of this affray came a dispute about women among the BOUNTY'S crew. "Mr Christian's party, finding that the natives still kept their women from amongst us though they had no objection to their sleeping with them at their own houses, began to murmur, and insisted that Mr Christian would head them, and bring the women in to live with them by force," writes Morrison. "[They] refused to do any more work until every man had a wife. Mr Christian's desire was to persuade rather than force them. He positively refused to have anything to do with such an absurd demand. Three days were spent in debate and, having nothing to employ themselves in, they demanded more grog. This he also refused, when they broke the lock of the spirit room and took it by force. Mr Christian, to keep them in temper, ordered double allowance to be served every day, but all to no purpose. Finding all his endeavours in vain he called all hands aft to ask what was their opinion of what was the best plan to proceed on. It was soon moved that we should go to Tahiti and there separate, where they might get women without force. This proposal [was] at first overruled but was carried the next day. On a call for a show of hands sixteen appeared for Tahiti. It was agreed that those [who] went on shore [at Tahiti] should have arms, ammunition and part of everything on the ship, the ship to be left in charge of Mr Christian, in a proper condition to go to sea, with her sails, tackle and furniture."

Once that was settled, they sent a search party out to round up the cow they had brought from Tahiti and gather other stock and provisions. They hadn't gone far however, before "they were set upon by the natives, who beat and plundered them." Christian immediately armed a party of twenty men to do the job. They hadn't gone far before they too were ambushed: by 700 natives, armed with spears and clubs. The natives, according to Morrison, fought with more fury than judgment, or the whole party would have fallen into their hands. As it was the natives were driven back with heavy losses, and the stock collected without further trouble.

Shortly afterwards the friendly chiefs informed him that Tinnarow was preparing to recover the stock with an even larger force. Christian formed up the BOUNTY'S crew, and their Tahitian allies, and marched towards Tinnarow's district. Once again they walked into an ambush. "They started up in a swarm all round us, rushing on us with great fury and horrid yells," says Morrison. "We instantly halted and, facing different ways, gave a smart fire, which we repeated several times with good effect, notwithstanding which they kept pouring in from all quarters seeming not to regard death or danger."

The Tahitians had armed themselves with spears captured from the enemy, and fought bravely, side by side with the sailors, but the BOUNTY'S men were so outnumbered they were forced to retreat, first to a hillock, and then to a piece of open cultivated ground, where they could see the enemy at a distance and use their muskets to better effect. When the Toobouains realised that anyone who came out from the cover of the bushes was immediately picked off they became discouraged. The BOUNTY men gave three hearty cheers "on which," says Morrison, "they fled and left us masters of the field."

At this point Christian was faced with an unexpected problem. "Before we left the field," writes Morrison, "one of the Tahiti boys desired leave to cut out the jawbones of the killed to hang round the quarters of the ship as trophies, which he said would strike others with terror. [He] was much displeased when his request was denied... It was only the fear of being put to death that prevented him from setting about it, begging at least that he might be suffered to take one for himself. None of the others were inclined that way as they were perhaps better pleased with the plunder and saw that it was contrary to our inclination."

The encounter had been a serious one. Morrison says they learned afterwards that sixty men had been killed, and six women, who had been helping their menfolk by supplying them with spears and stones. In addition there were many wounded. Among those who were killed were, in Morrison's phrase, "several of note" including Tinnarow's brother, who was shot by Christian himself. The conflict caused consternation among the friendly chiefs. They feared they would be subject to reprisals once the BOUNTY sailed. Three of them asked if they could go to Tahiti with the vessel for their own safety.

Events in Toobouai seem to suggest that the mutiny on the BOUNTY was due as much to the lust of the crew as to the harshness of Captain Bligh. Many of the crew formed genuine attachments during their stay in Tahiti, but some of them assumed that native women were there to be used at will. It was a demonstration of white male "superiority" at its very worst. The streak of violence and evil, which led to the self-destruction of the hard-liners, when they got to Pitcairn Island, was beginning to show itself in Toobouai and it was fortunate for Morrison, and those who thought like him, that they had reached an agreement to split up when they got back to Tahiti.

"Having filled sufficient fresh water we weighed our anchors on the 17th [September, 1789] and dropped down to the opening without much trouble being much lighter than before" he records, almost, one feels, with a sense of relief. Having got clear of the reef we lay by and filled salt water to keep her on her legs, and at noon made sail, leaving Toobouai well stocked with hogs, goats, fowls, dogs and cats, the former of which were increased to four times the number we landed."

"Before I take my leave of the island it may be proper to give some account of it and its inhabitants," he concludes. In every situation, even when he was a prisoner in chains, Morrison was an observer and reporter, noting every detail with a sharp eye and a retentive mind.

11
EXTRACTS FROM A MINOR CLASSIC

When James Morrison wrote a description of life in Toobouai, more than two hundred years ago, it was the only extensive account in English of an island which had been charted for the first time a few years earlier, on a brief visit by Capt Cook. If Morrison's Journal had been published then it might have earned a reputation as one of the minor classics of 18th century travel. It was not published, however, until the 1930's, by which time it had been overtaken by many later and more detailed accounts, by better qualified observers, and Morrison himself is remembered as a mutineer rather than a travel writer.

This is what he had to say about Toobouai, just as he wrote it, apart from the modernisation of the spelling and punctuation:

"Toobouai lies between 20 degrees and 23 degrees south and about 209 east longtitude. [It] is about six miles in length from east to west, and about twelve miles in circumference. [It is] surrounded by a reef a full mile from the shore and, on the east part, near three miles, having but one break or entrance, on the NW, where the passage is but indifferent though in some places there is 4 or 5 fathoms. Within the reef are six small keys [islets] covered with wood, chiefly the toa, a hard wood of which the natives make their clubs and spears...

"The island is mountainous with a border of flat land running almost quite round of a mile or a mile and a half wide. [A] great part [of this] is covered with trees and underwood which makes it difficult to pass by any other road than the beach. To the eastward the land is fertile and the low land broader than on the other side, but the west end is rocky and barren. Off this part the water is in general very shoal and the reef nearest the shore. The lowland is, in general, coral sand, or rock covered with a fine black mould, which in many places is not more than a foot thick though in some it runs to a good depth. Near the foot of the hills are numbers of large flat stones and the earth is of a reddish colour, covered with ferns, reeds and bamboo... On top, the ridges are naked rock of hard brown stone. Though the water is shoal in some parts, yet in others there is no bottom with 40 fathoms of line.

"[Toobouai] produces bread fruit, coconuts, yams, torro, plantains and almost everything common to the Society Isles and the reef affords plenty of fish and large turtle. The cloth tree grows here to a larger size than in the Society Isles, though they do not cultivate it. They have most of the trees in common with the other islands. They have also a species of the primrose. The island is watered with innumerable rivulets from the hills which, being banked up for the cultivation of tarro, affords shelter to the wild ducks which are here in plenty. [The rivulets] afford also plenty of fine eels, shrimps, prawns and a fish like the miller's thumb.

"The island is full of inhabitants for its size and may contain three thousand souls. Their colour is nearly the same as that of the Society Islanders, but they are more robust and have a more savage appearance. This is heightened by the turmeric and the oil that they use to colour their cloth, which gives them a yellow, disagreeable look. The men wear their hair and beards in different forms as they please, and the young women wear their hair long, flowing in ringlets to their waist, and dress it with the white leaves of the fwharra or palm like ribbands, and odoriferous flowers. They also make necklaces of the seeds of the ripe palm apple, and flowers elegantly disposed, which not only sets their persons off to advantage but afford a continual nosegay to themselves and to all who sit near them... They are in general handsomer women than any we saw in those seas, nor do they make use of the lewd motions or gestures in their dances so much in use in the Society Isles, though they are equally good at that diversion and move with a becoming grace... Their dances seem [nearer] those of the Friendly than the Society Isles.

"Children of both sexes go naked until they are five or six years old. The boys have their heads mostly shorn, but the girls' hair is suffered to grow long... As it is not of a strong wiry nature [it] flows in ringlets [and], when they arrive at fourteen or fifteen, sets them off to much advantage. The old women cut off their hair when they mourn the loss of their relations but we observed no marks of this kind on any that appeared capable of child bearing. They never kill their children here as at the Society Islands... They are careful of them and use them very tenderly. They have no marriage ceremony but join and live as man and wife while they agree, nor is virtue deemed of any consequence among them. While they agree, they live on the estate of either, and, if they part after having children, the man takes the boys and the woman the girls, and each retire to their own estate. The children [are] no obstacle being no hindrance to their getting other partners.

"They have no tattooing, nor do they cut the foreskin, but keep away all surplus hairs from the body. As they seldom bathe in the sea they are but indifferent swimmers or divers, the rivers being too shallow for that exercise... Few or none of the women know how to swim at all. Their dress is similar to that of the Society Isles and both sexes wear pearl shells in the form of a gorget with collars of hair neatly plaited. These shells are common, but, as we saw no pearls, it is possible, as they always find them on the reef frequently dry, the oysters may lose their pearls while they lie open and half dead with the heat of the sun, after the surf has thrown them up.

"Their temper appears in many respects similar to the Indians of North America [rather] than any of their neighbours. They seem rather serious than lively and appear to be always ruminating on some important business. When they go abroad they have each a large piece of glazed cloth, of a purple colour, which they carry folded up, except [if] it happens to rain when they wear it by way of a cloak. If the rain continues, they strip and tie a girdle of grass and leaves about their middle... and, wrapping their clothes up in their cloak, proceed home or to the next house when they have dry clothes to put on.

"Their cloth and matting is made from the same materials and after the same manner but is much coarser [than in the Society Islands]... They have a method of dyeing and glazing it so as to make it turn the rain and scenting it with sweet flowers and perfumes. They prefer the cloth plant or Chinese paper mulberry to any other though they have several trees and shrubs fit for the purpose... This is the most durable [but] they do not bleach it so well as the

Society Islanders, and their principal colours are purple, red and yellow. The latter they extract from the turmeric which grows in abundance here, but the others we could not learn how they are prepared.

"Their houses are built of an oval form, and, at a distance, resemble a long haystack. They are from forty to eighty feet long and from fifteen to thirty feet broad, and about as much in height. The ridge is a strong beam, supported by two or more pillars, chiefly toa, and the sides and top are a frame of strong timbers squared to five or six inches and firmly lashed together. The thatch is neatly made and well put on of the fwharra or palm leaves and will last for several years. The thatch reaches the ground on the back and ends and on the front within about six feet. The front is closed with timbers neatly carved, and painted with a reddish colour. [It] has several openings about four feet high and two and a half feet wide, which have shutters, answering the double purpose of doors and windows. These shutters are carved with rude figures of men and women and the inside is neatly lined with reeds about four or five feet up. The floor is covered with grass to a good thickness and [there is] a division in the middle with a tier of stones to part the men and women.

"At the end belonging to the men is a place separated from the rest for the purpose of burying the males of the family. This place is fenced by a tier of flat stones set up [on] end and four or five feet high and here the women must not come. In this place they keep the images of their forefathers or titular deities, as they believe that their souls are fond of seeing respect paid to their remains, and that they always hover about the place of these representatives. They are curiously carved and decorated with human hair, and the teeth and nails of their departed friends [with] red feathers and pearl shells neatly disposed."

Funeral practices in Toobouai two hundred years ago were very different from those prevailing in Lewis today but they have this in common: the exclusion of women from certain parts of the ceremony. The male bias in human society runs deep and long.

From burial customs Morrison turns his attention to domestic furniture: "The chief of their furniture is mats for sleeping on, baskets of several sorts, neat platters of different sizes for holding their provisions [and] stools for beating pudding on, [with] a stone or pestle for that purpose. The stools and platters are made of the tummannoo, or callophylum mophylum, with the nut of which they scent their cloth. When they go to sleep they beat the mosquitoes out and make a fire at each door to keep them out, as they are very troublesome and, together with fleas and lice, keep them employed till sleep gets the better of them. The rats run over them all night in droves but, as we left several cats, it is possible that, in time, they may reduce their numbers. They have no snakes or anything more venomous than a centipede or scorpion, and their birds and insects are common to all the Society Isles.

"Their food is chiefly bread fruit (which they preserve, as the Society Islanders do, making it into a sour paste called mahee), yams, tarro, plantains, coconuts, wild roots and fish, which they bake in the same manner as at the Society Isles. They always cook out of doors and the women and their servants are under the same restrictions: a woman [cannot] touch what her child has touched while the child remains sacred. The women are [also] prohibited from eating the turtle, cavally, dolphin and albicore but may eat all the rest. They have abundance of the white salmon and plenty of delicious rock fish, with shell fish of several kinds, among which is a sort of cockles which are excellent when stewed. The turtle is also sacred to the men and is only used as sacrifices or eaten by the chiefs and priests.

"Their canoes are differently built from any of the other islands which we have seen. [They] are from 30 to 40 feet long and carry 12 or 24 men. They are narrow at the bottom, spreading out to 16 or 18 inches at the gunwale and carry their bearings to the top. They are about 2 feet deep, and sharp towards the head and stern, the head resembling the head of some animal with a large mouth and the stern rises into a scroll, neatly finished and carved. The canoes are built of several pieces well trimmed and joined together by seizings of the fibres of the coconut, the whole painted with reddish paint. On the sides are stuck, with bread fruit pitch, the scales of the parrot fish and small shells in a number of arches, which have a handsome appearance. They are built of tummannoo and bread fruit and are well finished, considering their tools which are no other than stone or shell adze, bones and sharks' teeth with coral and sand to rub them smooth, after which the skin of the stingray, nourse and shark serve to polish the work. Their paddles are three to four feet long and the blade is circular, having a ridge on one side like our oars but the other is hollowed out instead of being flat. Their fishing gear are hooks and lines, large seines, [and] spears of different kinds, pointed with toa, which every fisherman makes for himself. Their hooks are of pearl shell which they grind into shape with a stone and sand, and drill a hole with a piece of shell or a shark's tooth fixed in a long stick which they work between their hands after the manner of a chocolate mill... Different sizes of the branchy coral serve for files to cut the hollow of the hooks to their fancy. They have no 'beards' to their hooks but turn them with the bow more rounding and the point close to the back. They are of different forms as the fisherman fancies...

"They have no sailing vessels and never leave the land except they are blown off as all the islands of which they have any account are at too great a distance for them to hold any intercourse. When they fish within the reef, they seldom use their paddles but get along with long poles or staves to prevent frightening the fish they may be in chase of. The white salmon and the turtle they catch with their nets some of which are very large. They have several fine white beaches to haul their seines on.

"They have abundance of yava or intoxicating pepper, which grows without cultivation, and they use it in the same manner as the Society Islanders, preferring the method of chewing it to any other. They cultivate nothing but the tarro, a root of the nature of the yam, which grows in watery ground. The tops of [it] makes excellent greens. In the cultivation of this root both men and women labour, taking great pains to level the ground and bank it up so that the water may cover the whole of it. Their only method of digging is with a pointed stick, and hauling the brush up by the roots. When they find it necessary to level a piece of ground they carry the earth about in baskets, saving the stones for embankments. [They] find whether it is properly levelled by turning a stream of water into it. As some of them are always employed weeding or planting they always carry with them a long staff or wand with which they knock down the ducks they come within reach of. At this they are expert and frequently come on them unperceived, the leaves of the tarro keeping them from the sight of the ducks till they are within reach.

"Their war weapons are made of toa. They are spears or lances 18 or 20 feet long and regularly tapered from within 12 or 14 inches of the heel to the point. [They have] clubs which answer the double purpose of club and spear. These are from 9 to 12 feet long, two thirds of which is a round staff... The remaining part is a flat blade about 4 inches wide in the middle and tapering from the middle each way. The point [is] sharp enough to pierce a man's body. On the head of the staff, where the blade commences, is...a double diamond all wrought from the solid and the whole polished and finished in a style that some good artists would be surprised at. The old men have walking staves and handles of fly flaps made of the same wood, highly finished. On the top of their staves they generally have carved a double figure of a man representing a figure with one body and two heads, and some of two [bodies] standing back to back. Their fly flaps are made of the fibres of the coconut twisted and platted very curiously. When they are accoutred for war, they bind a piece of red cloth or matting, or both, round their waist with a sash, made of the fibres of the coconut platted into sennit, at each end of which hangs a tassel of the same. Round their waists they fill all the folds [with] a number of flinty stones. The shoulder mostly is bare. On their breast a pearl shell hangs in a collar of braided hair and their head [is] defended by a cap made of the fibres of the coconut after the manner and something in the form of a beehive. They are covered with white cloth and, on the top, a bunch of black feathers from the man-of-war bird. With a spear or club [they] are completely equipped. Some of these caps have a pearl shell on the front with a semi circle of feathers from the wild ducks wings round it... These are more for show than use, but the others will resist a severe blow and a cutlass will make no impression on them. They use neither slings nor bows in war, and, though their weapons bespeak them to be warriors yet it does not appear that they destroy the habitations of each other, as in other islands. Many houses appear to have stood for several years. Perhaps they satiate themselves with blood for they appear to fight furiously."

As one marvels at the range of Morrison's interests, and the precise detail of his observation, it is difficult to resist a sense of regret that no one has left us a comparable account of life in the rural villages of the Western Isles in Morrison's own lifetime. Such accounts as have come down to us - even Johnson's and Boswell's - are more discursive than precise and too remote from the ordinary people to give us the sort of information about the Hebrides which this remarkable Hebridean has given us about the South Sea Islands.

The nearest parallel was provided by Martin Martin nearly a century earlier, and much of his information about Lewis came from the mutineer's great great-grandfather, John Morison of Bragar. Martin Martin has quite a lot to say about the fiddlers of Lewis who flourished three hundred years ago. This is what James Morrison has to say about the music and religion of Toobouai in the late 18th century:

"The music[al instruments] are drums... conch shells with long tubes, flutes of a larger size than those of Tahiti but used in the same manner... The sound of the whole of them is more harsh and disagreeable than those of the Society Isles, though the workmanship is superior. Their Morais, or places of worship, differ from those of the Society Islands, being all flat pavements, and having a number of large flagstones placed on end in tiers or rows in the centre. They are planted with the tee, or sweet root, having a stalk about 6 feet long and as thick as a man's finger. These places have each a little house on one side and bear some resemblance [to] a burying ground. Here they offer sacrifices of men and turtle.

"When a sacrifice is to be made, all the males in the ditrict gather at the Morai and the old men and the priests (who are numerous) always bring their walking staves in one hand and a plantain in the other. [The plantains] are thrown in a heap with long prayers when, if the sacrifice is to be a human one, the victim is pointed out and knocked down... They soon despatch him with their staves, which are pointed at one end for this purpose. The body is instantly dissected with bamboo knives, and each takes a part, which he wraps in the leaves of the tee and each carries it to his own Morai... The head, bones and bowels are interred in the Morai and a stone put up, not to perpetuate the memory of the man but as a mark for the number that have been offered there.

"A feast is then made and eaten in the Morai, by the priests, of fish, bread, tarro etc, part of which is also offered with long prayers. The friends of the victim, if he happens to have any, put up with it quietly for fear they should follow him on the next like occasion. We knew of no more than two being offered during our stay, both of which were young men. Beside the general Morai, each father of a family has one, where they make frequent, though not regular, prayers and offerings.

"If they are taken sick they believe it to proceed from the anger of the Eakooa or Deity, or from some of their relations... Should they go to war in a wrong cause, they think that any sickness which befalls them at the time is sent as a punishment on them for their fault. On our first anchoring in Bloody Bay most of the inhabitants of the island flocked to that place, the land about which is an uncultivated swamp... In the course of the few days that they remained there, for want of their usual bedding, they caught colds, agues, sore eyes and running at the nose etc... All these they said fell on them through our means and on this account it was that we found such an alteration in their behaviour when we anchored for the second time."

The people of Toobouai may well have been right in blaming the white man for their flu, and Morrison mistaken in ascribing it to the swamp in which they slept. If he had known St Kilda as well as he knew the islands of the South Pacific, he would have heard of the "strangers cold" which afflicted the St Kildans every time a vessel called, exposing the small enclosed community to germs and viruses to which they had not acquired a natural resistance.

"The priests," Morrison continues, "who seem to have all the authority and be nearly on a footing with the chiefs, seeing that we were no other than common men and liable to accident like themselves, could not bear to see such superiority as the Europeans in general usurp over those who differ from themselves, and became jealous of us with respect to their religious authority... which they saw we not only refused to take notice of but even ridiculed. For this reason they used all the means in their power to keep the chiefs from making friends, thinking, perhaps, that if we stayed on the island, their consequence would have been lessened, which in all probability would have been the case.

"The island is governed by three chiefs - Tinnarow, Tahoohooatumma and Heeterirre... each of whom is absolute in his own district. Two are related by marriage, Tinnnatow having the sister of Toohoohooatumma to wife, yet they do not agree. Notwithstanding the smallness of their territories, they are continually at war. There are other chiefs who reside as private gentlemen. Of those we found Tummatoa to be one. On our first coming [he] acted for Heeterirre and Taroatchoa acted for his father. One of these [is] always, as it were, in commission and the other on half pay...

"Their language is a dialect between the Society and the Friendly Islands but not so much different from either as to prevent its being understood by both... It is more than probable that they are all descended originally from the same stock though so much different in their manners, customs and appearance. In other countries it is observed that the inhabitants of the northern and southern climes are more robust in general than those within the tropics... It is to be observed in those seas, in islands at an inconsiderable distance from each other in a north south direction... [that] the inhabitants of those isles where every necessity is supplied by nature [so that they] have no occasion to cultivate the earth... are less robust and vigorous than those who have exercise and labour procuring their food.

"The inhabitants of those islands drive about in their canoes to an amazing distance and I am therefore led to think that the whole of the islands in those seas might have been peopled from South America, notwithstanding the difference of their language, manners and customs, all of which are liable to change in length of time. The present language of all the islands in these seas differ no more than English does in different counties."

Apart from his own direct observations Morrison seems to have been able to communicate freely with the islanders, and to have spent a good deal of time with them 'round the cèilidh fire', so to speak. In Tahiti he learned that, some years before the BOUNTY'S arrival, there had been a civil war, in the course of which eight or nine canoes were driven out to sea and never heard of again. In Toobouai he found part of a canoe preserved on one of the Morais. He could tell from the design that it came from Tahiti, or at least from one of the Society Islands. It was washed ashore around the time of the war in the Society Islands, and, when it was found, there was the body of a man in it, with the flesh badly decayed and eaten off the bones by birds. It was clearly one of the canoes blown away from Tahiti during the battle.

Morrison was also told in Toobouai that the chief Tummotoa was the great great-grandson of a chief of Ryeatea, an island 120 miles north west of Tahiti. The chief of Ryeatea had been on a fishing expedition when his canoe was driven out to sea and wrecked on Toobouai. There was no way of getting back. He didn't even know in which direction Ryeatea lay. Toobouai was then sparsely populated, most of the other inhabitants being fishermen who had been similarly carried away by the wind and shipwrecked, some from an island a great distance to the westward, called Paroodtoo, others from an island to the eastward, called O'Gweeva. Tummotoa's great great-grandfather was acknowledged as chief by the other shipwrecked fishermen. He divided his "kingdom" into three districts, one of which he called Ryeatea after his home. When the BOUNTY mutineers left Toobouai and returned to Tahiti, Tummatoa went with them. He told the tale about his great-great-grandfather to the Queen Dowager in Tahiti, the mother of Matte, who immediately greeted him as a relation.

Her great great-grandfather had been chief in Ryeatea. His name was Tummatoa and he was blown out to sea in a fishing canoe and never heard of again.

Tummatoa, however, did not remain long with his relatives in Tahiti. He had become friendly with Fletcher Christian and elected to go with the BOUNTY on the voyage which eventually took them to the blood bath on Pitcairn Island.

12
A PLOT TO MURDER BLIGH

On the passage back from Toobouai to Tahiti the ship's armourer was kept busy making iron goods to be traded with the natives. The rest of the crew were equally busy, sharing out the ship's stores between those who intended to stay in Tahiti and those who were going in search of an uninhabited island, where Fletcher Christian hoped to spend the remainder of his days "without seeing the face of a European but those who were already with him." Sixteen of the BOUNTY'S crew elected to stay in Tahiti, and, as soon as the ship dropped anchor, they began to off-load their stores.

"Having only one boat that would swim, and a tolerable high surf going, we made it night before we got all on shore, being afraid to venture much in the canoes of the natives at one time, though they made a better hand of landing them in the surf than we could have done with the boat," writes Morrison. The arms and ammunition presented a special problem. On no account would they venture those in the native canoes. Every man in the shore party, except one, was provided with a musket, pistol, cutlass, bayonet, cartridge box, 17 lbs of powder and some lead with which to make ball. The odd man out was Michael Byrn, an Irish fiddler, enlisted by Bligh to entertain the BOUNTY'S crew and play for their shipboard dances. Whatever his faults, Bligh had always been careful of his crew's health. He knew that exercise was essential to keep men fit when they were cooped up for months on shipboard, despite the strenuous work of setting and trimming sail. But "Byrn being blind and of a very troublesome disposition it was thought that arms put into his hands would be only helping him to do some mischief."

Others, as we shall see, did the mischief instead.

The shore party got some of the carpenter's and armourer's tools, including a pig of iron for an anvil, a grindstone, and some bars of iron, but Morrison was disappointed in one important particular: "We wanted the saws, of which there was a whip and a cross cut in the ship, but Mr Christian told us he wanted them himself." He gave them two spy glasses and an old azimuth compass. The compass was defective but Morrison had taken the precaution to "provide cards and glasses privately." His concern about the saw, and his action in regard to the azimuth compass, in the very moment of landing, seem to suggest that he had already formed the audacious plan of building a ship and making his way back to Britain, which is perhaps the most remarkable feature of the Lewisman's remarkable story.

Christian's original intention was to spend some time in Tahiti and he asked the shore party to help in watering and provisioning the ship, but, much to Morrison's surprise the BOUNTY slipped her anchor during the night, and when daylight came they saw her standing away to the northward "on a wind." Morrison assumed the sudden departure indicated either that Christian was afraid the shore party might take the vessel by surprise, or that those who remained aboard with him might change their minds and stay in Tahiti.

Those who remained in Tahiti divided into little groups and went to live with the friends they had made during the months they were on shore gathering the bread fruit plants. The domestic arrangements were unusual to say the least. "I, having formerly made Poeno (Chief of Maatavye) my friend, and Millward, having made friends with Poeno's wife, we were now invited to live with them... and were treated like the rest of the family but with more attention and respect." Morrison gives no indication here, or elsewhere, that he had any particular female friend on Tahiti, but it would be surprising if he had not. Apart from the fact that they both lived with Poeno, one as Poeno's friend and the other as the friend of his wife, there is no indication of any special companionship between Millward, who was an AB, and Morrison. Eventually, they were both condemned to death for their part in the mutiny, but Morrison was reprieved while Millward was hanged.

Stewart and Heywood, the two young midshipmen, kept together, no doubt distancing themselves from the "other ranks". They made their home "on the land of Stewart's wife whose father was also Mr Heywood's friend." An Orcadian, Stewart was more anxious even than the others to get back to Tahiti. He had entered into a real marriage. His wife, Peggy, as he called her, was heartbroken when the navy eventually caught up with the mutineers and Stewart was carried off in chains. She died of grief not long afterwards, and their torrid love affair is celebrated by Byron in a long poem, "The Island". Byron takes great liberties with the facts in his romanticised version of the tale. He also take liberties with the geography of Scotland, confusing Orkney with the Hebrides and the Pentland Firth with the Minch.

Stewart was not the only one of the BOUNTY'S crew to enter into a permanent relationship with a Tahitian woman. While Morrison lists most of them as living with friends, he describes Richard Skinner, one of the ordinary seamen, as living "at his wife's fathers." There is no indication whether Stewart and Skinner went through any form of marriage ceremony, and, if so, whether it was Christian or native or a mixture, but Morrison draws a very clear distinction between the relationship entered into by these two and the others although they also were cohabiting with native women.

While most of the party remained at Maatavye, where they had landed, five went to live with friends at Oparee, some distance away where "the Young King" had his home. A few days after their return the whole BOUNTY party went together to Oparee to pay their respects to the Young King taking him gifts of cloth, matting, war weapons from Toobouai, ironwork from the ship and the inevitable red feathers. As a special gift, they presented him with the idols taken from Toobouai.

Before they were permitted to approach the king they were welcomed by a priest with a long oration, and each of them was given a plantain tree and a sucking pig or a fowl. A delicate question of etiquette then arose. The priest explained that they must strip off their clothing from head and shoulders before approaching the Young King because "he was yet sacred." Some, at least of the party, refused to strip, arguing that it was not customary in Britain "to remove any part of our dress, except our hats, and, if we were under arms, it was not our country manner to remove our hat, even to the King." The matter was amicable resolved, however, when someone suggested that, if each of the BOUNTY party was given a piece of Tahitian cloth, they would wear it over their own clothes as they approached, and ceremonially remove it in the Young King's presence. Morrison does not say who suggested the compromise, but it is interesting that a few leaderless seamen were able to resolve a problem which might have left professional diplomats in an icy deadlock.

The Young King then approached them, "sitting on the shoulders of a man." He saluted them with the word "manoa" (welcome), and addressed each of them by the name of his Tahitian friend, much as the House of Commons designates a member by his constituency rather than his personal name. The various gifts were welcomed by the King, especially the idols from Toobouai, not, however, because they were sacred, or spoils of war, but because of the number of red feathers with which they were decorated. The idols were held aloft to the multitude, gathered on the opposite bank of a river, and "produced a general exclamation of wonder." The boy King was even more delighted when the sailors formed three divisions and discharged their arms. As Morrison puts it "the Young Chief was so much pleased that he told us to follow our own country fashion in everything and take no heed of their ceremonies." They were then conducted to the Old Chief's house for a feast of baked hog, fish, bread, tarro, coconuts, plantains etc after which a portion of land was pointed out for the use of those who had settled at Oparee.

Next day a messenger from Matte, the chief mentioned by Capt Cook, brought a hog and a piece of cloth for each of those who had settled at Mataavye, and pointed out two pieces of land for their use. One area was well stocked with coconuts and the other with bread fruit. In return the sailors sent Matte many gifts including a bottle of wine which he gave to a sick neighbour as he had been told wine was good for sick people.

Morrison, with his ear to the ground as usual, learned, during the festivities, of a mysterious British sailor who had arrived in Tahiti in their absence. He also learned of an abortive attempt to murder Capt Bligh which, if it had succeeded, would have pre-empted the most famous mutiny in British naval history and left Fletcher Christian in the clear.

The chief, whom Morrison called Matte, had many names. He was also called Tinah, Too, or O Too. Eventually he became Pomare I, King of Tahiti, and established a royal dynasty. The last of the line was Pomare V who ceded his kingdom to France in 1880. Matte exchanged gifts with George III through the naval commanders who visited Tahiti on official business, and was very anxious to visit Britain but was dissuaded by the lesser chiefs from leaving the island at a time when they were likely to be at war. Geoffrey Rawson in his book "Pandora's Last Voyage" comments that Matte, or Tu, "was the friend and Tayo of Captain Cook, Captain Bligh, Captain Edwards and of the bosun's mate, James Morrison."

Cook, Bligh and Edwards all visited Tahiti as representatives of the British Government, with a ship's company and a ship's guns to back their authority. The Lewisman, however, was a nobody in the hierarchy of power and any influence he had with the paramount chief must have rested on his personal qualities. It was from Matte's brother, Wyetooa, Morrison learned of the plan to murder Capt Bligh.

Wyetooa was the "tayo", or particular friend, of Hayward, the young midshipman who fell asleep on watch, enabling three of the crew to abscond, when the BOUNTY was loading the bread fruit plants. Bligh had Hayward clapped in irons and, when the three absconders - Churchill, Musprat and Millward - were recaptured, they were twice flogged. It seems a barbarous punishment to us, but in fact Bligh was lenient. If he had not dealt with the matter summarily himself, but left the Admiralty to deal with it, when the BOUNTY returned to Britain, the three offenders would have been hung.

After the first flogging, the three wrote a letter to Bligh thanking him for dealing with them in that way but pleading to have the second flogging remitted. Bligh refused and, by his lack of compassion, made the subsequent mutiny inevitable. Churchill, Musprat and Millward were all in Christian's watch. If they had been under an obligation to Bligh they could have prevented the mutiny. As it was, they had a special grudge against him and Churchill, the ship's armourer, became one of the most active mutineers.

Wyetooa was not concerned with the three absconders but he was angry at Bligh's treatment of his "tayo", Hayward. He told Morrison it was he who cut the BOUNTY'S cable, as she lay at anchor. He hoped she would drift on to the reef and be so badly damaged the crew would have to come ashore. He would then have a chance to release Hayward from the chains with which Bligh had bound him. On the day of the flogging, Wyetooa was afraid Hayward might suffer with the others. He stood behind Bligh with a club in his hand. If Hayward had been touched, he would have felled Bligh at the first stroke of the cat, and jumped overboard before anyone knew what happened. He assured Morrison he could have reached the shore, underwater, with one dive.

When he heard the story, Morrison recalled that he had seen Wyetooa on board that day, standing close to Bligh, although he had no idea then what was passing in his mind. Morrison had good reason to remember the scene. As bosun's mate, it fell to him to administer the floggings. That gives us an insight into the complex relationships which existed on board. Twice Morrison was called on to adminster 24 lashes to Millward, as one of the three absconders, but, a few months later, Morrison and Millward were living together, amicably, in the same hut, as guests of Poeno and his wife. Whatever animosity Millward felt towards the Captain who ordered the flogging, he seems to have borne no grudge against the bosun's mate who administered it.

Morrison and his friends heard Wyetooa's tale when they were trying to unravel another mystery. As soon as they returned to Tahiti from Toobouai, they heard there was a white man, named Brown, on the island. Who was he? Where had he come from? Had his arrival any significance for those who had taken part in the mutiny or for those sucked into it involuntarily? A deputation was sent to Matte to find out who the white man was.

That raises the question, who sent the deputation? Morrison is tantalisingly silent on the point. He says simply, "We wished to know... and therefore appointed Churchill and Millward to go." Who are the "we"? There is no indication that any hierarchy of authority had been established among them after the departure of Fletcher Christian, and the assumption must be that they reached decisions by democratic consensus, like the old St Kilda Parliament. Not surprisingly rifts developed later and different groups pursued different plans. On this occasion, however, the delegates took their instructions and made their enquiries.

They discovered that while they had been at Toobouai a vessel had called at Tahiti and left the mysterious stranger behind. But what vessel? Poeno, the local chief at Mataavye, showed them a letter signed by the captain, T. H. Cox, in which the vessel was described as "His Swedish Majesty's Armed Brig Gustavus IIIrd" and the mysterious stranger as an Englishman called Brown, "an ingenious handy man when sober but when drunk a dangerous fellow." In a fight aboard ship, Brown had slashed one of his shipmates across the face with a knife. After that the ship became too hot to hold him and he expressed a wish to stay ashore. Capt Cox was only too glad to be rid of him. Because of the nature of his voyage, however, Cox was anxious to cover his tracks. He invented a false identity for his ship. It was not an armed brig, it was not Swedish and it was not called the Gustavus IIIrd It was a privately owned vessel of only 150 tons, on a voyage round the world in search of opportunities for trade, calling at lonely islands in the Indian Ocean and the South Pacific, before ranging as far north as Alaska.

The ship's real name was the MERCURY. It passed Toubaai at night while the BOUNTY was there. Capt Cox was surprised to see fires burning on Toobuai but he did not spot the BOUNTY in the dark and decided the fires must be connected with some native celebration. The MERCURY left Tahiti just ten days or so before the BOUNTY returned. It was a short visit but it had quite important consequences for Morrison and his companions. Capt Bligh had concealed from the Tahitians that Capt Cook was dead. He was afraid it might diminish his own authority among the islanders, if it was known that the man they thought all powerful had been killed in a dispute with people like themselves. Some of the Tahitians actually thought Bligh was Cook's son. They were astounded and angry when Capt Cox told them Cook was dead and showed them a painting depicting the scene. They resented having been lied to.

The man Cox left behind was also a bit of a handful. Morrison tells us that, as soon as Brown heard about the Captain's letter he got it from Poeno and destroyed it, "to prevent it from being of any further use in pointing out his character, which, according to his own account, was black enough." He had, according to his story, been a sergeant in Portsmouth Division of Marines, but being broke [meaning discharged for misconduct] had gone to India in the EURYDICE frigate. In India he deserted and "was cook to Col Baillie when he was taken by Hyder Ali, into whose service he entered and, turning Musselman, was made an officer." He soon got tired of military service with Hyder Ali, made his way to Fort St George, where he and some companions seized a small ship loaded with East India Company goods. He was arrested and tried but acquitted for want of evidence. He was, however, sent home to Britain, where, after another short spell in the navy, he deserted again, got a berth on the MERCURY and turned up in Tahiti to plague James Morrison.

At their very first meeting Morrison decided Brown was "a dangerous kind of man" and so he proved to be. One has the feeling that he was a romancer and a braggart but the tale of his adventure in India is not impossible and it has a symbolism of its own which is highly relevant to the theme I am pursuing.

The Colonel Baillie, whose cook Brown claims to have been, was in command of a small British Force in India, which marched into an ambush, laid by Hyder Ali, with an army of more than a hundred thousand men. The British troops fought bravely, and might even have cut their way out of the trap, if the ammunition waggons had not exploded, in the middle of the line, doing far more damage than the enemy fire. In an effort to save the few remaining British troops, Col Baillie tied his handkerchief to his sword in token of surrender. In spite of the flag of truce, most of the wounded were massacred where they lay, and the British officers were subjected to a long and harsh imprisonment in Seringapatam.

Accounts of the disaster, some true some false, filtered back to Britain and passed into common currency. From the casual manner in which Morrison mentions Col Baillie and Hyder Ali, it is clear that the BOUNTY'S crew were familiar with them. There was the story of Col Baillie's retort, when taunted by Hyder Ali, "You owe the victory to our disaster, not to our defeat." An even more widely known story concerned the stoic mother of another officer, Capt David Baird. When she was told that the officers had been chained together by the leg in pairs, her only comment was, "God pity the poor lad that's chained to oor Davie." Whether she made the comment or not, the story of Baird's captivity was untrue. He suffered greatly, because he was very badly wounded, but he was not chained to anyone else. In fact he wasn't chained at all. When one of their captors attempted to put irons on Baird's wounded leg, a friend, Capt Lucas, pled for him. The Indian gaoler was adamant. He had been given a set of irons for each prisoner. It was as much as his life was worth if they were not all used. "Then put a double set on me," said Lucas. That was done, and Baird remained unchained. Despite his wounds, Baird survived and went on to a distinguished career. His self-sacrificing friend, Capt Lucas, died in captivity.

Most of the British troops involved in that disaster were Scots. Well over half of them were from the estates of the Earl of Cromarty. They were serving in Lord Macleod's Highlanders, which later became the Highland Light Infantry, or popularly the H.L.I. Here we have a Lewis seaman, stranded on a Pacific Island, as the result of a mutiny in which he was inadvertently caught up. He meets a complete stranger, cast adrift in a casual way from a passing trader, and the subject of their conversation is a battle in India, in which a large proportion of those involved were Morrison's nearest neighbours from just across the Minch. Wherever one probes in the history of that era, the ubiquitous Highlander is to be found in the shadows, concealed behind the commanders who feature in the chronicles but would never have been heard of, but for the quality of the men they led.

It was to another Highlander Morrison turned when he first unfolded his daring plan to build a ship and make his way back to Britain. As he records it himself: "November, 1789. Finding ourselves settled, I began to think it would be possible to build a small vessel in which I had hopes of reaching Batavia and from thence to England. I communicated this to McIntosh and Millward and the matter was agreed on, but we resolved to keep the real motive a secret and to say that she was only for pleasuring about the island."

There were strong arguments for secrecy both from his Tahitian hosts and, more particularily, from some of his shipmates. There were one or two in the BOUNTY party who had no wish to return to Britain, because of the attachments they formed in Tahiti.

There were others who were even more reluctant to return, because of the active part they played in the mutiny. On the other hand it was more likely the Tahitians would cooperate in a project from which they would derive some benefit themselves than an attempt by their white friends to get away.

McIntosh, whom Morrison relied on most heavily, was one of the carpenter's mates on the BOUNTY. He was 25 years old and had a blameless record. He was one of those acquitted at the trial when Morrison was convicted and condemned to death. His home was in North Shields where his wife, according to some correspondence which survives, was known as Mrs Tosh. Whether the omission of the Mac was a result of carelessness, or whether it indicates that Highlanders were reluctant to advertise their origin in English seaport towns at that period, is not clear, but the difficulty in tracing Morrison's own origin from the naval records suggest a chameleon effect: a desire among Highlanders to assume the colour of their surroundings for reasons of self-protection or personal ambition.

Morrison's idea was that, if McIntosh designed a ship and provided the skilled craftsmanship, he would organise the venture and help with the heavy work. The difficulties were formidable. They had to fell the trees; transport them to the coast; and dress them into planks with quite inadequate tools. Morrison, as we already know, had failed in his attempt to get the BOUNTY'S heavy saws from Fletcher Christian. They had to design the vessel without plan or model. They had to improvise sails and tackle from unsuitable material. They had to find, by trial and error, which trees produced suitable timber for their various requirements. They had to do the ironwork without forge, bellows or anvil. In the end they had to transport the finished ship a considerable distance to the water without slipway or heavy blocks and tackle.

From the start Morrison seems to have had no doubt they would succeed. When he opened his mind to McIntosh the problem which worried him was not building the ship but sailing it home. "I observed that Matthew Thompson [one of the seamen] had got a quadrant and some of Mr Hayward's books, although he could neither read nor write," comments Morrison. Hayward was a midshipman. He had gone with Bligh in the open boat, leaving his navigational instruments and books behind him in the flurry. "I was determined, if possible, to get possession of them and with a little persuasion I got the quadrant for six small trade adzes and a gallon of wine," writes Morrison. "When I wanted the books, he began to have some suspicion, and was sorry that he had let me have the quadrant. I told him it was only for amusement. He said he had no cartridge paper and the books would answer that purpose. I told him I would give him paper in lieu which would serve that purpose better. This only served to confirm his opinion."

There is a hint of the inveterate envy, which has held men back across the ages, in the picture of the seaman, who could neither read nor write, but would sooner destroy the vital books of navigational tables than sell them to someone to whom they would have been invaluable. The Lewisman, however, accepted the situation with a shrug. "As I had a Seaman's Daily Assistant I took no further notice and affected to be easy about them though I was sorry that I could not get them."

Artist Robert Dodd's impression (1790) of the mutineers casting Bligh and others adrift.

It tells us a lot about Morrison that this audacious plan was conceived and developed by a humble bosun's mate, who had no authority over most of those around him. The officers had all gone, either with Bligh or Christian, but there were still two midshipmen on Tahiti who should have been the natural leaders in the project, and the navigators on the voyage. One of them, Stewart, was so infatuated with his Tahitian wife he had no wish to leave. The other, Heywood, was just a lad. Heywood became very close to Morrison in their captivity. It was he who preserved Morrison's Journal and, to that extent we are indebted to him, but there is reason to believe he was more concerned with protecting his own career than establishing Morrison's reputation: a point which will have to be examined further in the proper time and place.

13
MORRISON'S SHIP

The building of Morrison's ship began in November 1789. "On the 11th," he records in his Journal, "we began to cut down trees for our intended vessel, and having cleared a space near the square, under the shade of some trees, we laid the blocks, and, on the 12th, the keel was laid."

The plan, he adds, "was drawn to the following dimensions: Length of the keel 30 ft. Length on deck 35 ft. Length of the stern post 6 ft 6 ins. Stem 7 ft 2 ins. Breadth 9 ft 6 ins on the midship frame. Depth of the hold 5 ft. Breadth of the floors and timbers 4 ins to 3 1/2 ins; thickness 3 1/4 ins to 2 1/2 ins. Keel stem and stern post 8 ins by 4 ins." Although Morrison organised the building operation the plan would have been drawn by McIntosh, the carpenter.

Five days later, Morrison notes, "Having got some moulds made, I took part of them and got some of the natives to assist me when I procured three or four floors and some timbers. Churchill also took some and went to Oparre and Tettehah on the same errand, and returned on the 20th with some pieces of Poorou but only one answered to the moulds. In the meantime McIntosh superintended the cutting down trees and splitting them for plank, and I had collected several more pieces of Poorou which was the best to answer the purpose of timbering and the Bread fruit for plank."

Four days later, he records, "having collected several more floors, we set about trimming them for use, in which I assisted by doing part of the rough work while McIntosh and Norman [another of the ship's carpenters] fitted them. "In the meantime the rest were busy cutting down trees and splitting them for plank, which we laid up to season, but at this the progress was but slow, it being as much as we could do to trim one plank of 30 feet long in two days."

By the end of the month they found it necessary to erect a shed to work under because of the intense heat of the sun, and the approach of the rainy season. In December it rained incessantly for three weeks but they went on working in the shed fitting the timber they had on hand. When the weather improved, they set off in search of more timber. They had so few moulds to work from they had to alter them for every frame. Then some of the timbers they had trimmed and fitted "started" and became straight. After that they had to leave all the timbers to dry out thoroughly before attempting to finish and fit them. Dealing with the timbers which had started kept McIntosh and Morrison busy until Christmas while the others were busy making more planks.

In January, when the weather was fair, Morrison set off into the hills with some of Poeno's men in search of timber. "We sided them and left them to dry," he notes. "The natives frequently assembled about us to see our work, and seemed much surprised at our method of building. [They] always assisted willingly to haul the trees to hand, and hew off the rough. They are very dextrous at splitting, but, as they have no idea of working by rule, they could be of no use in trimming the plank.

"Among our visitors came a blind man, who they led to the place. He examined the work by feeling every part and asking the use and intention. [He] seemed amazed at the construction of the vessel of which he seemed to have a good idea and said to his countrymen, 'Our canoes are foolish things compared to this one'. He asked us many questions, and received answers, with which he went away well satisfied."

One of their major problems was the shortage of nails, or metal to make them. They were forced to use wooden dowels wherever that could be done with safety. Heidlbrandt, the ship's cooper, was given the task of making dowels out of Amai wood, which they found best served the purpose.

On the 11th of January, Morrison was off on another expedition in search of timber. "The business of searching for timber," he notes, "always took up a whole day, having several miles to go before any could be found to answer our purpose. When we found them we frequently had the misfortune to break them by tumbling them down the precipices, which we could not avoid, it being impossible to carry them along the steep cliffs. What we cut in one day would keep McIntosh and myself employed for three or four, having, as before observed, the moulds to alter for each frame. Nor was the making of planks less troublesome. Having no saws except handsaws the largest tree would afford no more than two thicknesses of plank. Some of the trees cut for that purpose measuring six feet round... took a deal of labour to reduce into plank of inch and a quarter with axes and adzes. We were forced to make the small trade hatchets (such as are sold in London at ninepence each) answer that purpose by lashing them to handles after the manner of the natives."

A good deal of trouble might have been saved by trimming the timber in the mountains to reduce the weight that had to be carried down to the improvised shipyard, but Morrison comments that he wasn't sufficiently experienced to do that successfully, and had to take the trees down in the rough so that the trimming was done under the supervision of the carpenters. This was clearly a substantial difficulty but Morrison says, "it was not sufficient to make us abandon our project."

There were other and more formidable problems. The work was interrupted by holidays; "state" visits; native celebrations; the theft of tools; quarrels stirred up by Brown; by arrests and punishments; by murder and even by civil war. Some of these events will be examined later, in so far as Morrison was involved in them. Fortunately there was also the occasional stroke of luck.

"On the 6th [of February 1790]," writes Morrison, "we received a visit from Eddea who was come down to visit her son the Young King at Oparre. She brought presents of cloth for each as did her sister Teano (wife to Vayheeadooa, Chief of Tyarrabboo) who accompanied her... When she saw the vessel, which now began to show in frame, she told me that she had got a handsaw from Captain Cox which she would give me. A man was sent away to Tyarrabboo to bring it. [He] returned in a few days and it proved to be a very good one. We supposed that it cost at least five shillings in London. It was quite new and had not been used, and was what we stood in great need of as our own were much the worse of wear."

Eddea's visit was a time for rejoicing. A space near the square was used for dancing, wrestling and throwing the javelin. The young men and women frequented the place for amusement whenever the weather permitted. "We were entertained with a dance almost every evening... without going from home to see it," Morrison records. When she left, Eddea gave orders that the shipbuilders were to be supplied with all the provisions they needed and "as everyone who came to visit us brought something... we never wanted for anything."

As the ship took shape the visitors multiplied. They were all "desirous of examining every part, and curious to know how every part was secured, but most of them were doubtful whether she would be finished, saying the job was too long, and wondering how we could keep at it without being tired."

Keep at it they did, although the difficulties multiplied as they improvised a blacksmith shop, sought substitutes for pitch and rope and canvas, and dealt with the distractions stirred up by others on the fringe of their enterprise. I dont suppose a Lewisman has ever superintended the building of a ship under so many and unusual difficulties. Yet, although the operation took place more than two hundred years ago, on an island in the Pacific, we have more detailed knowledge of it than we have of any vessel ever built in Lewis itself with the possible exception of the Sgoth being built for a television programme, as I write.

The first distraction was a dispute between Brown and some of the natives. Brown had gone visiting, as they all did from time to time, and he was entertaining his hosts with swordplay. His use of the cutlass became so dangerous the natives disarmed him for their own protection. One of them struck him across the hand with a piece of bamboo and cut him. In the scuffle Brown lost his loin cloth and his dignity! The loin cloth was part of the tick of a bed wrapped round his waist "in the country style." Brown demanded that the men from the BOUNTY should help him retrieve his possessions.

"On enquiry we found that he had been the aggressor," writes Morrison. "As we did not think the native to blame, we told him he must endeavour to live peaceably and not bring himself into trouble. Otherwise he must stand the consequences." Brown was given a plot of land by Poeno, to keep him occupied, but he continued to use the natives badly. They resented his behaviour but ignored it. They thought he was under the protection of their white friends.

The next incident was more serious. After a visit and entertainment, which I will refer to later in another context, it was discovered that the flag halyards had been stolen, along with a pair of trousers and three pigs from the sty. They were told the thief was in Oparre. "We followed and apprehended him," writes Morrison, "finding the halyards in his possession but the trousers and the pigs were gone. We brought him to Maatavye where we gave him a hundred stripes. Brown, having lost a hog, cut off his ears, though he could not be sure that he had stolen it."

The punishment meted out by Brown was barbarous. The hundred stripes was also barbarous, to our way of thinking, although it was the sort of punishment the sailors were used to themselves, for similar offences on board ship. Poeno did not think it severe enough. Nor did he think it would have a deterrent effect. He advised them to shoot the culprit. Otherwise he would now steal from everybody without fear. Morrison says he and his companions disregarded this advice and the man left the district, "amid the shouts and jeers of his countrymen." Ostracism from his own society was probably the most effective sanction of all, and the shipbuilders had little further trouble with thieves, although the natives had easy access to the tools. Also, as Morrison noted, "they knew that we would find them out as they cannot keep anything to themselves, and we began to get hold of their language so fast that we could understand everything they said, and make a good shift to discourse with them." Brown, however, made no attempt to learn the language, had no understanding of or sympathy with the local customs, and, in the end of the day, did his best to get Morrison hanged.

On a later occasion, when he was being feasted by Matte as an honoured guest, Brown demanded that his dog should be fed before some latecomers. It was explained by one of the Tahitians that the dog would be fed at the end of the feast. Brown was furious and struck at the man so violently he broke his own arm. He darted out for his pistol and would have shot the man, if he had not made a timeous escape.

Some time later there was an even more serious interruption to the work of shipbuilding. "The affair was this," writes Morrison. "Thompson who resided with Coleman at Point Venus had ill used a young girl, for which her brother, in revenge, knocked him down and fled. Coleman was at this time recovering from a fit of sickness, when Thompson came home vowing revenge on the first that offended him. A number of strangers had arrived at the point, where they generally stopped on their passage round the island, to take the opportunity of getting to windward in the morning before the sea breeze set in. [They] flocked round the house as usual to see the Englishmen. Thompson ordered them away. As he spoke English they did not understand him, and paid no regard to the order, on which he took his musket and, firing amongst them, killed a man and a child which he held in his arms. The shot passed through a woman's lower jaw, breaking both the bones and grazed another man on the back, at which they all fled."

Thompson was the AB who refused to give Morrison the navigation tables. Most of his shipmates were appalled at this new act of stupidity and malice. They had no doubt Thompson was guilty of child abuse and murder and refused to help him. Young Heywood, the midshipman, making one of his infrequent appearances in the story, tried to make peace with the natives by visiting the dead man's wife and giving her a white shirt. Churchill, the master at arms, an ambitious and disagreeable man, tried to turn the incident to his own advantage. According to Morrison, he had always aspired to take command and now thrust himself forward as the leader of a party to defend the little white colony against the expected retaliation of the natives. The others would have none of it. They trusted that their friends among the natives would see that they deplored the murder just as much as they did, and so it proved. No one but Thompson was blamed and the others were able to resume their shipbuilding for a time.

Later Morrison discovered that, in addition to his crimes of violence, Thompson had robbed his mate, Coleman, when he was lying sick in bed. Then Churchill developed itchy feet. He asked for canoes to take him to Tyarrabboo where he had special friends. He got the canoes and set off with his kindred spirits, Thompson and Brown. When Heywood went on a journey shortly afterwards, he was seized by some natives, who mistook him for Thompson. One of them was restrained, with difficulty, from bashing his head in with a huge stone. The others, fortunately, wanted to take him alive to the dead man's brother, so that he could have personal revenge. To their surprise, the brother greeted Heywood as the man who had come with gifts to the widow, expressed regret for his "arrest" and invited him home as a guest. Heywood declined the invitation but, when the natives asked him not to leave Maatavye, because Churchill, Thompson and Brown had come to live there, and might cause trouble, he readily agreed.

Although they were birds of a feather, Thompson and Churchill soon fell out. The quarrel was fostered in part by Brown but it came to a head when Churchill's friend, Vayheeadooa died suddenly without an heir, and Churchill, in Morrison's phrase, "was put in full possession of the Sovreignty of Tyarrabboo." Churchill assumed the name of Vayheeadooa and came down to the shipbuilders, in his new glory, offering them "large possessions in Tyrrabboo if we would go and live with him."

Morrison decided that Churchill wanted to make himself great at the expense of his shipmates. He told him drily that, for himself, he "would rather be one of Poeno's friends than Chief of Tyarrabboo." His assessment of the situation was quickly confirmed. A month later both Churchill and Thompson were dead, and Morrison was setting out for Tyrrabboo, in a new role as detective, to find out what happened to them.

The Tahitians were inveterate gossips and always on the move. Their news, however, was not always reliable. Morrison and his friends were distressed to hear that Heywood the young midshipman had been killed, but, as I have related, he turned up safe and well, although he did have a narrow escape. There was more substance in the report which reached them later of Churchill's arrogant rule in the "estate" he had inherited. When some of the natives frightened off the duck he was going to shoot, he shot the natives instead. A man was wounded in the back and a boy in the heel. The boy's wound mortified and he died a few days later. Then came a note from Burkett, one of the ABs to say that Churchill and Thompson were dead. This was followed by a visit from Brown, sent by Matte, to give details of the tragedy.

Thompson was jealous of Churchill's rise to power and threatened to shoot him if any distinction was made between them. Churchill heard of the threats and sent some natives in the night to steal Thomson's arms. They got his gun away, but he wakened when they returned to get the powder. Having no idea that Churchill was behind the theft, Thompson went to him for help in recovering the stolen gun. Churchill agreed and later returned the gun, saying it had been taken by some natives passing by, as they crossed the isthmus. At that point the man who stole the gun was beaten by Churchill for some unknown but, no doubt, trivial offence. In revenge, he went to Thompson and told him the truth. Shortly afterwards Churchill himself arrived. He had broken his collar bone on another duck shoot and Burkett had helped him home. Thompson feigned sympathy and welcomed them both. Over supper Thompson mentioned casually that he had found out who stole his gun. Churchill did not realise that he had really discovered the truth, but, in the morning, when Burkett was at the shore attending to their canoe, Thompson shot Churchill. When Burkett heard the shot, he hurried back and found Thompson at the door reloading the musket. He pointed it at Burkett but assured him he would not shoot "without you are angry." Burkett assured him he was not angry over Churchill's death, but decided it was no longer safe to stay with Thompson. He hurriedly buried the body and left. Before leaving, however, Burkett made another attempt to get the precious navigation books from Thompson but he still refused to part with them. Even if he could have read them the books would have been of little use to him. As soon as the natives heard that Churchill, their chief, was dead, they killed Thompson in revenge.

When Morrison and his friends heard this tale, they wondered whether Thompson had really been killed in punishment for his crime, or whether it was because he had taken over the "property" Churchill had inherited on Vayheeadooa's death. He doesn't spell it out, but clearly, if it was the latter, it might indicate a growing feeling against the white man's domination which could affect them all.

Morrison immediately set off to see the over-all chief, Matte, "as I wished to be particularly informed of the manner of their deaths." His inquiries confirmed the reports they had got from Burkett and from Brown. Matte quickly flushed out for him Patirre, the man who had organised Thompson's murder. Patirre made it clear he had no other motive than to avenge the killing of his friend and chief, Churchill, who, in his eyes, had succeeded Vayheeadooa and taken his name. A band of six or seven had gone to call on Thompson proclaiming him their new chief in succession to Churchill, conferring on him the name of Vayheeadooa, and flattering him with their attentions. When his guard was down, Patirre knocked him to the ground. The others pinned him with a plank across his chest and brained him with a large stone. Thompson's house was plundered. His body was buried. His head was cut off and displayed on the Morai, or ceremonial funeral platform.

"If I had a mind to see it [he told me] he would show it to me," writes Morrison. "I accordingly went to the Morai with him, when he produced part of the skull, which I knew by a scar on the forehead. I asked him why they had not brought [Thompson] to us at Maatavye. He replied, 'the distance is too great, our anger would be gone before we could get there. We should have let him escape when we were cooled so that he would not have been punished and the blood of our chief would have been on our heads.' I promised the man that he should not be hurt by me for what he had done, as I looked on him as an instrument in the Hand of Providence to punish such crimes," Morrison concludes.

Morrison was also interested to discover that the jealousy between Churchill and Thompson had been fomented by Brown, the incorrigible trouble-maker.

Despite all these interruptions, Morrison kept his eye firmly on the main task of building a ship to get back to Britain. As well as enquiring into the murders, he wanted to see Matte "about getting some rope and mats for sails." The vessel was not yet built but his mind was racing ahead to the problem of fitting her out with sails in an island which produced no canvas. Matte was afraid Morrison might stay at Tyarrabboo and assume the "crown" that Churchill had briefly worn. As a white man with weapons, he would have had little difficulty in taking over, and that would not have suited Matte, who wanted the succession for his own son.

Arrogant fools like Churchill, Thompson and Brown were undermining the status of the white man among the natives, but it still stood high, as was shown by a ceremony a few weeks earlier which caused the first interruption in the building of the ship. Two heivas, or feasts, were held on successive days. The second was an ordinary heiva, with feasting, dancing and the distribution of gifts. Morrison reckoned that during it Poeno, his own particular friend, had distributed nearly a hundred fathoms of cloth and matting among the BOUNTY'S crew. The first day's heiva was devoted to the worship of Captain Cook.

"Everything being ready," wrote Morrison, "Captain Cook's picture was brought by the old man who had charge of it and placed in front, and, the cloth with which it was covered being removed, every person present paid the homage of stripping off their upper garments, the men baring their bodies to the waist, Poeno not excepted, and the women uncovering their shoulders." Long speeches were made to the picture, acknowledging Captain Cook to be Chief of Maatavye, and a plantain tree and a sucking pig were placed before the picture as offerings.

Morrison, who by this time seems to have been fluent in the native language, translates the speech thus: "Hail, al hail, Cook, Chief of Air, Earth and Water. We acknowledge you chief from the beach to the mountains, over men, trees and cattle, over the birds of the air and the fishes of the sea &c &c." The "&c &c" no doubt indicates that the panegyric was as long-winded as these things tend to be even in our own day.

After the speech came dancing by "two young women, neatly and elegantly dressed, and two men." "The whole was conducted with much regularity and exactness, beating drums and playing flutes to which they kept true time for near four hours. On a signal being given, the women slipped off their dresses and retired and the whole of the cloth and matting, which was spread to perform on, was rolled up to the picture and the old man took possession of it for the use of Captain Cook." After that the BOUNTY'S crew were given fish, fruit and nuts. In return they were asked to fire the musketoon. They charged it with slugs and aimed it into a large tree The shower of fruit which resulted caused "much wonder" and the Tahitians departed "well pleased." With the memory of that demonstration of the white man's power still fresh in his mind, it is not surprising Matte was anxious that Morrison should not be a rival to his son for the succession in Tyrrabboo. Morrison assured him he had no such ambition and was returning immediately to his friend Poeno. Matte was relieved and promised to put in hand the making of all the matting they needed for sails.

Morrison got back to Maatavye on the 24th of April and noted, with pleasure, that "the work had gone very well" during his absence. "Both sides were planked up, the ceiling in and the beams secured." The others were not so deeply concerned as he was. "Norman and Heildbrandt left off work" at this point, "and did not return until the middle of May. However," he notes philosophically, "the heavy iron work was done and Coleman was now able to proceed by himself with making nails and small iron work." Morrison turned his attention to collecting bread fruit gum, which they boiled down into a good substitute for pitch. The ropes they had taken from the BOUNTY were teased into oakum to caulk the vessel.

The iron work for the rudder, bowsprit etc. had been one of their major problems. Coleman, the armourer, had been quite prepared to undertake it, provided the others would make him a forge and a bellows, and get "coal" to produced sufficient heat. A frame of plank filled with clay was used as a forge. The sides of the bellows were made out of bread fruit planks. The iron handle of a saucepan was used as nozzle. They had no leather, so they used canvas. This meant that, whenever the bellows was in use, someone was employed keeping it wet to make it reasonably airtight. Charcoal was made for the fire.

Most of the crew gave a hand at one time or another apart from the two midshipmen, who seem to have kept themselves aloof. The most consistent workers were Morrison and McIntosh, Norman, Millward, Coleman and Heildbrandt. They had a rest and an amusing interlude when one of the petty chiefs, named Mottooarro, arrived with a gift of baked hogs and some cloth. He had with him a dog which had been left behind by Capt Bligh. Although the dog had not seen any of the BOUNTY'S crew for over a year, it immediately recognised them, and, as Morrison puts it, "came fawning about us, at which the natives were much surprised." Bligh had left the dog, named Bacchus, along with a bitch, named Venus, with the intention of giving Tahiti a large breed of dogs. His intention was "in some measure frustrated", as Morrison puts it rather quaintly. Poeno's sister took a fancy to the bitch and kept it at Maatavye, while Mottooarro carried the dog to the other end of the island, so that Venus and Bacchus never met.

When it became apparent that they were going to have difficulty gathering enough gum to caulk the ship, Morrison organised a feast. Unusually it was open to "those of the poorer sort" and they were asked to contribute gum in proportion to the pork they received. The natives "did not fail to perform" so the invitation was repeated until they had sufficient gum for their purpose. As usual Morrison had calculated everything carefully. This method of procuring gum was dear according to conventional notions he notes, because it required a hog of two hundred pounds weight to produce fifty pounds of pitch. But the hogs cost nothing so, "the people were not overpaid for their labour."

To get the gum from which the pitch was made, they had to drive a wooden peg, using a stone as hammer, into the bark of a tree. The tree was left to bleed overnight. In the morning, when the gum had hardened, they scraped it off with a shell and made it into a ball. It took a man two days to gather a pound of gum. "No other tree affords this pitch but the breafruit," Morrison notes. "When it first runs [it] is as white as milk but it soon hardens and looks like white wax and, when boiled, becomes black and is in all respects like pitch extracted from pine, though this comes from the bark only and not from the tree."

By the 17th of May, they began to lay the deck and finished it on the 1st of June. Early in the shipbuilding operation they had taken a day off to celebrate Christmas, killing a hog for Christmas dinner and "reading prayers, which we never omitted on Sundays." Shortly after the deck was completed they had another celebration - the 4th of June, the King's birthday. They fired a volley, in lieu of a salute of guns, and drank a keg of cider prepared for the occasion "from the apples called vee." It is ironic that while Morrison and his shipmates were drinking a toast to the king, as loyal British sailors, the navy was already in hot pursuit of them, as dangerous conspirators and mutineers, destined for the gallows.

A great deal of ingenuity was required when it came to the working equipment of the vessel. They had to experiment with different woods to find out which suited a particular purpose. "The poorow answered for the shells of the blocks" he notes, "and the toa for sheaves and pins."

They had a setback when they started caulking and found that an insect called the hoohoo was already eating some of the timbers. The infested timbers had to be replaced but, he notes, "the rudder being fixed and the vessel caulked all over, we paid her with pitch and by the First of July she was ready for launching with masts, boom, bowsprit and gaffs complete." It was a truly remarkable achievement.

One of the greatest problems had been twisting the planks to fit the curve of the vessel's side. It sometimes proved "an overmatch for us", Morrison notes. "We broke several after spending a whole week's labour on them and being assisted by fire, water and a good workman who understood his business... Now we put up our tools and prepared for setting her afloat.

"With what ropes we could muster, we slung the masts on the sides, making a kind of cradle under her bottom, and, having done with most of the auger shanks, we made use of them as bolts and clenched them through the keel and keelson to strengthen that department. Being all ready on the 5th [of July 1790] we applied to Poeno, who told me that the priest must perform his prayers over her and then he would have her carried to the sea.

"The priest [was] sent for and a young pig and a plantain given him He began walking round and round the vessel, stopping at the stem and stern, and muttering short sentences in an unknown dialect. Having a bundle of young plantain trees brought to him by Poeno's order he now and then tossed one in on her deck. He kept at this all day and night and was hardly finished by sunrise on the 6th."

At that stage Poeno and Tew, Matte's father, arrived with three or four hundred men. When each of the chiefs had made a long oration the men were divided into two parties. One of the priests went on board and tossed a few plantain trees out from each side. He then ran fore and aft exhorting everyone to exert themselves. "On a signal being given, they closed in, and those who could not reach by hand got long poles. A song being raised, they all joined in chorus and she soon began to move. In half an hour she reached the beach and was called the RESOLUTION. Though several trees were cut down which stood in the way, she received no damage, except breaking the masts, in a passage of three fourths of a mile."

If the four hundred helpers carried the RESOLUTION three quarters of a mile in half an hour they must have been going at the double. What a magnificent sight it must have been. In any event, she was safely launched and towed round point Venus to "a good berth under the shelter of a point within the reef."

Point Venus was so called because it was there that the transit of Venus had been observed by a party of astronomers on one of Cook's expeditions. The smaller point, behind which RESOLUTION was anchored, was called Cockroach Point "according to its own name." By this phrase Morrison, presumably, means the English name he uses is a translation of the Tahitian name.

When the RESOLUTION was launched, Morrison and his friends turned their attention to the problems of equipping her for the voyage home. Almost everything had to be improvised. With an iron pot and a copper kettle in a "furnace of clay," they worked day and night boiling sea water into salt. So much fresh water flowed into the lagoon where they were based, they could only produce a pound per day. They had also to cut down more trees to replace the masts which broke as they used them to carry the hull to the sea. Heildbrandt, the cooper, was busy making casks while the others were killing, boning, and curing pigs with which to fill them.

The squabbles with Capt Bligh, over the quality and quantity of the food on the BOUNTY, is no doubt reflected in Morrison's insistence that only prime meat must be cured, and the portions, although the weight had to be guessed, must be kept as equal as possible at four pounds each. On a ship with a Captain and strict discipline, disputes over food could be sorted out, in the last resort by the use of the "cat", but on a ship with no obvious or accepted commander, where things were done by consensus, a quarrel over shares would have been fatal.

Then Morrison had problems with his watch. Time keeping could be important in the navigation of the RESOLUTION. He made a screwdriver out of a nail and "took her to pieces." "It cost me much pains and trouble to put the work together again," he notes, "which, however, I at last accomplished, and with such good success that Stewart would have me take his in hand and try what I could do. I took her to pieces and found about two inches of the main spring broke off. To remedy this, I softened the broken part of the spring and cut a new hole for the catch, and having put the work together found that she went very well."

Another task, although this does not seem to have been Morrison's, was to make a half-minute glass, for navigational purposes, by cutting a glass phial with a flint, fixing the two pieces together with a neck of lead, and filling one end with sand. To check it, they hung a musket ball from a thread and counted the number of times it swung while the sand trickled through the glass. Between this and the watch, he felt, they made it tolerably correct.

They then cannibalised the old azimuth compass which Morrison got from Fletcher Christian and for which, with his usual foresight, he had surreptitiously obtained cards and glasses. The box of the compass was too large for their purpose, so they made a new container out of a gourd and slung it in gimbals in the binnacle. They then made a lamp to light it while a supply of goat fat, which they had saved for the purpose, made a stock of candles for the voyage. McIntosh then built a cabouse, or galley, out of planks, lined inside with stones cut square "to contain the fire." While this work was going on, the ship was riding at anchor and they were pleased to see that "she still continued to be tight, nor did the sun hurt her, as she was continually covered."

The great, unsolved problem was getting sails. Matting was scarce and not very serviceable. They cut up all the clothes, which Fletcher Christian had made from sailcloth, when he put them into uniform, but they hadn't sufficient canvas "to make her one sail which would be fit to set at sea." While they were still wrestling with this problem, a messenger arrived from the Young King, asking for their assistance in quelling a rebellion. The people of the district of Tettahah, they were told, had made an inroad into Oparre "burning all before them." The Young King's aunt, Areepaeea-Waheine, had arrived from the island of Ryeatea, with reinforcements - "a numerous fleet which were all ready for war" - but they still needed the help of the white man's muskets. Morrison, and no doubt those with whom he discussed the matter, were reluctant to get involved in a civil war but, "as we did not know... we should ever be able to effect our purpose [of returning to Britain] we found it neccessary, for our own sakes, to assist them." Next morning a guard was placed on the schooner, while Morrison and the other "shipbuilders" marched off to war.

As usual everything was conducted with more ceremony than efficiency. The Young King's aunt welcomed her allies with a dressed hog and there was a feast before they set out. Having gone half a mile, they found the Marro Eatooa, or the signal for war. The signal was composed of several fathoms of cloth in one continuous piece, wound round several trees to block the path. A hog was tied to each tree the cloth passed around. The Marro Eatooa, notes Morrison, "is generally put up with some ceremony, and the enemy are defied to take it down."

"Our party", as Morrison calls their Tahitian allies, "ran instantly and seized on the Marro and the hogs, and the enemy, who lay concealed till now, made their appearance. A fray instantly commenced and several heavy blows [were] exchanged before we were observed by them. On our approach they fled, but this confused method of engaging prevented us from knowing our own people... and we were therefore of no use but to look on while the enemy retreated to the mountains and our party returned with a deal of plunder."

Morrison and his friends now gave "our party" an elementary lesson in tactics. They informed the chiefs "that they must alter their mode of fighting and bring their people under some command in case they should have occasion to go to war again." At the end of this encounter Morrison and his friends asked for mats to make sails for the schooner. The Young King's aunt, who seems to have been a formidable lady, took the matter in hand. In a short time they had sufficient mats to make three sails - main sail, fore sail and jib. She also saw that they were well supplied with provisions. The Young King sent them a double canoe 48 feet long, with a hog, a piece of cloth and a "bamboo of oil" for each of the BOUNTY'S men who helped them.

As soon as they were back to base, Coleman made two needles and began stitching the mats together for sails, using the bark of the poorow for twine, "quilting the mats, and seaming them at every foot distance to strengthen them."

They hadn't been long at this work when they were called to help again. The civil war had broken out with renewed violence. Eight of the BOUNTY'S crew were involved in this second expedition. They told the chiefs how they wanted it conducted, with the result that they set off in the cool of the morning and in good order. They found the enemy in a strong position, on the slopes of the mountains, commanding a narrow pass. By this time the heat was intense, but the Tahitians had provided plenty of coconuts "which we found very refreshing."

When they saw the strength of the enemy position, "our party" halted, but the BOUNTY men pressed on. They saw there was no way of getting at the enemy except through the pass. They struggled on in the blazing heat while stones rained down on them from the mountains. Fortunately no one was seriously injured except one Tahitian who was wearing "English

Clothes," which attracted the attention of the stone throwers. Once through the pass, the BOUNTY men marched up the hillside keeping up a steady fire. The enemy fled and "our party" set about gathering the plunder. They secured an "incredible number" of hogs, some of them so fat they couldn't carry their own weight and died with fatigue as they were driven down the mountain.

The fighting was by no means over, however, and the first voyage of the RESOLUTION was to Oparre, to join a large fleet of canoes which had assembled there. The line of battle consisted of forty canoes each paddled by fifty or sixty men, with pieces of painted cloth hoisted on the stern, drums beating, flutes playing, and warriors in feathered headdresses "cutting capers on their stages." This was serious war. A large area of foliage on the hillside was burnt, so that the enemy could not approach unobserved. In addition to this necessary precaution, the Young King's supporters rampaged through the territory of their opponents, firing the houses, and notching the bark of the bread fruit trees to stop their growth. Morrison and his friends did not approve of this and remonstrated with their allies for destroying the trees, which would be needed for food when the fighting was over.

Fortunately, after a few days they saw "a white flag coming down the hill" and peace was made on condition that everything was restored to the Young King. "Orders were now given for the fleet and army to return home," writes Morrison rather grandly. His own return home was also imminent but not, as he had planned it, in triumph on the RESOLUTION.

14
LOCKED IN PANDORA'S BOX

Morrison and his shipmates on Tahiti had no idea what happened to Fletcher Christian and his party after the BOUNTY left them. It was nineteen years before the colony on Pitcairn Island was discovered by a passing ship. By that time Morrison, and many of the others, were dead. For nearly two years they were equally ignorant of the fate of Capt Bligh and those set adrift with him after the mutiny. The reasonable assumption, if they speculated about it at all, was that Bligh and his party had perished.

Their boat was over-crowded, inadequately provisioned, and thousands of miles from any prospect of help. Bligh, however, was a consummate seaman. On the 12th of June 1789, he was within sight of the island of Timor, having sailed 3623 miles in 41 days under appalling difficulties. Two days later he was in the harbour of Coupang, arranging with the Dutch for his onward passage to Britain. He was well on his way home even before Fletcher Christian abandoned his attempt to found a colony on Toubai and returned to Tahiti where the party finally divided. He was back in Britain, on the 14th of March, on the very day on which Morrison celebrated the completion of the frame of his schooner, and the laying of the first planks.

Bligh's arrival in Britain caused a sensation. Only one side of the story was available - Bligh's - and he was a national hero. The mutineers were execrated, and feared. Apart from one or two whom Bligh specifically exonerated, all those who remained on the BOUNTY were regarded as dangerous and ruthless men, who had conspired together secretly to seize a British warship. At all costs, they must be found and hanged! Around the time the RESOLUTION was being launched in Tahiti, with high hopes of sailing to Batavia, where a passage to Britain on a larger ship could be obtained, HMS PANDORA was leaving Britain to scour the Pacific and bring the mutineers to justice.

If Morrison and his friends had been able to sail from Tahiti before the PANDORA arrived, and make their way back to Britain by their own endeavours, their subsequent history might have been very different. Unfortunately for them, however, long before PANDORA reached Tahiti, the plan of sailing home had to be abandoned.

Morrison records the collapse of his hopes in his usual laconic style: "December, 1790. Having got everything on shore by the 10th of December and expecting the wet season now to set in very shortly, we got the schooner hauled up and covered over to shelter her from the weather. Coleman having declared that he would not have anything to do with the schooner, and our finding that our hopes of reaching Batavia or any other place without sails, and finding that even mats could not be had, we dropped any further attempts that way and divided the pork."

Coleman's defection, although "defection" is perhaps too strong a word, raises some questions. He was the person one would have expected to be most anxious to make the attempt to get back to Britain. He took no part in the mutiny. Even Bligh agreed that he was detained on the BOUNTY against his will and at the court martial, he was completely exonerated. As amourer he had done much of the essential iron work on the RESOLUTION, as if he was keen to get home and, when the PANDORA arrived, he was the first to give himself up. In fact he boarded the warship before she dropped anchor.

There are two possible explanations of his change of attitude towards the RESOLUTION. The first is that he may have acquired family ties on Tahiti strong enough to make him wish to stay. That is not inconsistent with his alacrity in going aboard PANDORA once the navy had caught up with him. On the other hand, it may simply be that he had weighed up the risks of attempting an ocean voyage without proper sails, and decided that, although they could coast around the islands safely, they could not face the open sea. If that was the case, it would have reinforced, perhaps anticipated, Morrison's own doubts. Either way, it must have been a bitter disappointment to Morrison to abandon the project to which he had devoted so much time and energy.

Characteristically, he wastes no time on useless regrets, but applies his mind to a practical problem which caught his attention. The pork "on examination proved excellent meat, and superior to any that had been salted in the ship," he notes. But why, he asked himself, was it superior? After due deliberation, he "imputes" it "to a powder cask we had used to save the pickle in and by this means the saltpetre contained in the staves had been communicated to the whole of the pork."

Having solved the problem to his satisfaction, Morrison, sublimely unaware of the vengeance of the navy hurrying towards him on HMS PANDORA, turned his attention to the coronation of the Young King, if we can apply a western term like "coronation" to a very different and indeed a barbarous ceremony.

Eddea arrived from Tyarrabboo to thank them for their assistance in "the war which had proved very beneficial to her son." She brought presents for all and they were entertained with a boxing match by the men from Ryeatea, and wrestling and dancing by the men and women of Tahiti. Next day Morrison accompanied Eddea when she went to visit the Young King. In accordance with the local taboo Eddea had to change out of her own clothes into her son's, before she entered his house and she could not partake of any food under her son's roof. Surprisingly, the taboo was waived in respect of Morrison. He was permitted to enter in his own clothes, received courteously and given some pork.

There is no indication that Morrison was reluctant to comply with the taboo so far as his clothes were concerned. In fact he provides a good deal of evidence that he tolerated the native customs, even when he disagreed with them. The waiving of the taboo seems to have been a reciprocal acknowledgment by the Tahitians that the white men had their own customs which should be respected. Although he refers frequently to the local taboos, Morrison does not use the word. It had not yet come into common currency. In fact it was first used in English only a few years before the BOUNTY reached Tahiti.

Morrison explains that, until all the ceremomies connected with his installation were completed, the Young King was "restricted within particular bounds to prevent him rendering anything sacred which is not intended for his use. For this reason he was never permitted to come near the ship, as his presence there would have rendered everything sacred so far as to prevent, not only his own family but everybody else, from either eating on board or using anything that came from the ship."

A few days later Morrison went on to Papaara, where he became friendly with the local chief, Tommaree, "a handsome well made man of about 17 or 18 years and about six feet high." "He received me with every token of friendship... We soon became perfectly intimate and during my stay he feasted me every day and begged that I would be in no hurry to return home."

While Morrison was with Tommaree, the Young King's flag arrived. All the inhabitants hid themselves as it passed and all the fires were put out. The flag was taken, with great ceremony, to the Morai where the priests made peace offerings "with a long harangue." Tommaree also made a long speech declaring his allegiance to the Young King whom he called Toonooeaiteatooa! He ordered a feast to be prepared for the bearers of the flag, which was, in fact, a union jack, which the natives had got from Captain Cox, the man who left the troublesome Brown behind. It was no ordinary union jack, however. The Tahitians had decorated it with feathers, tassels and "breast plates." The British seamen who were present discharged their muskets in honour of the occasion and offered to circumnavigate the island with the flag "as it was composed of English colours."

While life in Tahiti went on in this rather idyllic fashion, Morrison was quite unaware of the two clouds gathering on the horizon.

The first and the nearest was that the ceremonies they were involved in were to end in human sacrifice on quite an extensive scale. The second was that Capt Edward Edwards on HMS PANDORA, who was reputed to be a martinet even by the standards of the time, was hastening towards them with orders, "to keep them as closely confined as may preclude all possibility of their escaping, having proper regard to the preservation of their lives so that they may be brought home to under-go the punishments due to their demerits."

Just after Christmas, 1790, one of the natives slipped into Morrison's house, unperceived, and stole a box containing his compass cards and glasses, his watch, and, most important, all his writing utensils and paper. The status of Morrison's Journal is a matter of much dispute among historians of the mutiny. It is clearly not a diary, but to what extent was it based on contemporary notes? This point will be examined later, in another context, but it is clear that the theft of his paper and writing materials was a serious loss for him at the time, and would have been a loss for us as well if they had not been recovered. Fortunately, next day, a young neighbour climbed a tree for coconuts, and, when he looked down, saw the box lying under a bush. It was discovered later that it had been taken by a visitor from Ryeatea who was later caught and given "a good smart whipping." Much as the BOUNTY'S crew had resented the regime of corporal punishment under which they lived in the navy, they resorted to the same methods themselves in similar situations. It would have been specially irksome for Morrison to lose his writing materials at that time because he was, no doubt, taking notes about the investiture of the Young King.

The climax was reached on 13th January 1791. This is what Morrison says in his Journal: "This day the ceremony of investing the Young King with the Marro Oora or Royal Sash took place. The sash is of fine network on which red and yellow feathers are made fast so as to cover the netting. The sash is about three yards long, and each end is divided into six tassels of red and yellow feathers, for each of which they have a name of some spirit or guardian angel that watches over the Young King while the Marro is in his possession. [It] is never worn but one day by any one king. It is then put into the sacred box and, with a hat or shade for the eyes made of wicker and covered with feathers of the same kind, and never used but on the same occasion. It is delivered to the priests, who put it carefully by in the Sacred House on the Morai where no person must touch it.

"The chiefs, or their substitutes, of Tipperroonoo and Morea attended, and Toonooeaiteatooa, the Young King, being placed on the Morai, a priest, making a long prayer, put the sash round his waist and the hat or bonnet on his head and hailed him 'King of Tahiti'." At this point the ceremonial took a grisly turn. "Three human victims were brought in and offered for Morea. The priest of Mottooarro [the chief of Morea] placed them with their head towards the Young King, and, with a long speech over each, he offered three young plantain trees. He then took an eye out of each with a piece of split bamboo, and, placing them on a leaf, took a young plantain tree in one hand and the eyes in the other, made a long speech holding them up to the Young King, who sat above him with his mouth open. After he had ended his speech and laid the plantain trees before the Young King, the bodies were removed and buried by his priests in the Morai and the eyes put up with the plantain trees on the altar.

"The rest of the chiefs then brought in their sacrifices in the same manner, going through the like ceremony, some bringing one victim and some two according to the bigness or extent of their districts, after which large droves of hogs and an immense quantity of other provisions, such as bread, yams, tarro, plantains, coconuts etc, were brought and presented to the Young King. Several large canoes were also hauled up near the Morai on the sacred ground. They were dressed with several hundred fathoms of cloth, red feathers, breast plates etc, all of which were secured by the priests and the Young King's attendants. The marro being now removed and taken care of by the priests, they all repaired to feasts prepared for them which lasted some weeks. The number of hogs destroyed on this occasion were beyond all conception, besides turtle, fish etc."

"I enquired the cause of the eye being offered and was thus informed: The King is the head of the people for which reason the head is sacred. The eye, being the most valuable part, is the fittest to be offered, and the reason that the King sits with his mouth open, is to let the soul of the sacrifice enter into his soul that he may be strengthened thereby, or that he may receive more strength or discernment from it. They think that his tutelar deity or guardian angel presides to receive the soul of the sacrifice.

"The human sacrifices offered this day were thirty, some of which had been killed near a month. These were the first that had been offered since our coming to the island. They never offer men but such as have committed some great crime, nor then but on particular occasions, but hogs, fish etc they offer without number and on every trifling occasion."

112

Morrison and his shipmates were now being sucked more deeply into the affairs of the islands. Before the installation of the Young King, Matte, his father, invited some of them to a feast. He told them he had been treated most uncivilly by the people of Tyarrabboo who had gone through the ceremonies because of the union jack, and their fear of the white men, not out of loyalty to the Young King. He asked for their assistance in punishing Tyarrabboo. If they went to Tyarrabboo under arms his son would be accepted as sole king. As an inducement he offered to provide men and canoes and meet the cost of the ammunition. To strengthen his argument he tried to persuade Morrison they had a right to punish the people of Tyrrabboo for killing Thompson. Morrison and his friends were reluctant to become involved. They said they would consider the matter, but in the meantime they wanted to go home to Maatavye. Some time after the installation of the Young King, the matter was raised again and this time they agreed to help.

Morrison does not explain how their reluctance was overcome. He simply records the arrival of McIntosh and Millward, "who having settled the matter relative to the war we determined to put it into execution." Tommaree then suggested that he should organise a great feast under cover of which men and canoes could be assembled. "The English would be there as partakers in the feast and when we were ready to attack them we could be in their country before they knew what we were at, and by this means make an easy conquest."

Morrison and his shipmates not only accepted the plan, they launched the RESOLUTION to carry it out. The vessel, which was to have taken them to Batavia and home, was now being used instead in a civil war in which they had no discernible stake. Stewart and Heywood, the two young midshipmen, took no part in the expedition. Nor did Coleman and Skinner. Morrison was there and with him Norman, Ellison, McIntosh, Millward and Heildbrandt. Even Byrn, the half blind fiddler, went with them. Later they met up with Burkett, Sumner, Brown and Musprat. Prior to setting out on their punitive expedition, they all sat down to breakfast together, at Tommarree's, but the meal was interrupted by the arrival of a messenger with startling news. HMS PANDORA had arrived at Maatavye. Stewart, Heywood, Coleman and Skinner were already in irons and the ship's boats were searching for the others.

A particular friend of Morrison's, Heeteheete, was engaged by Captain Edwards of the PANDORA as pilot for the search. He guided the PANDORA'S boats in the right direction, but took care that the messenger, whom he had sent off secretly to warn Morrison, got there first. The messenger brought "a very unfavourable account of the treatment of those who went on board from Maatavye."

The RESOLUTION hastily put to sea "with a fresh breeze at ESE, standing to the southward on a wind." As Morrison puts it, "We hoped, by keeping out of sight of the boats, to reach the ship and go aboard of our own accord, hoping thereby to have better treatment than if we stayed to be made prisoners." It proved to be a vain hope.

The arrival of HMS PANDORA had a dramatic effect on all the social relationships within Tahiti: between Brown of the MERCURY and the BOUNTY'S crew; among the BOUNTY'S crew themselves as mutineers, loyalists or neutralists; between the BOUNTY'S crew and different groups of Tahitians; even as between one group of Tahitians and another. Where relationships had rested on affection, or even friendship, they were little changed, but where they had rested on power, they were transformed.

In spite of distance and language difficulties news travelled fast and fairly accurately. When the RESOLUTION put to sea, after the interrupted breakfast, Morrison saw two vessels to leeward. "[We] could not discern whether they were boats or canoes, but as we left them apace, we thought they could be no other than fishing canoes. Soon after noon, we lost sight of them and about four o'clock we hove about and stood in, but it was Sunday the 27th before we could fetch in because of the contrary winds and light airs which prevailed."

As soon as they landed, they learned that Hayward, who had been a midshipman on the BOUNTY, commanded one of the search parties. They now knew for the first time that some, at least, of those who had gone with Bligh in the open boat had survived, and the Admiralty knew of the mutiny. Up until then it was possible that the PANDORA was merely seeking to unravel the mystery of why the BOUNTY had never completed the bread fruit mission.

Although he does not say so in his Journal, Morrison must have been acutely aware of the effect it would have on all of them that Bligh's account of the mutiny, rather than theirs, was first to reach the Admiralty. The message was driven home by their friend Tommarree who tried to dissuade Morrison from giving himself up. "If you do, Hayward will kill you, for he is very angry."

How the Tahitians pronounced the name Hayward we do not know, but we do know they had difficulty with some British names. Captain Cox of the MERCURY had been mystified, when he arrived at Tahiti the previous year, and was told the BOUNTY had been back under its new captain, Titreano: the nearest they could come to pronouncing Fletcher Christian's surname.

Morrison also learned from Tommarree that Brown had gone to the PANDORA, having first plundered Burkett's house and taken as much as he could carry. He probably felt it was safe to rob a man who was about to be arrested. On hearing of the robbery, however, Tommarree "sent everything back into the mountains." Morrison does not explain what "everything" includes, or what Tommarree's motive was. He might have been trying to protect the rest of Burkett's goods, or he might have been joining in the plunder himself. Either way, "everything" must have been of considerable value because Burkett, Sumner, Musprat, Heildbrandt, McIntosh and Millward went in pursuit of those who were carrying the goods into the mountains, leaving only Morrison, Norman and Ellison to take care of the RESOLUTION.

Tommarree tried to persuade Morrison to go into the mountains too, assuring him he would never be found there. When Morrison insisted on going to the PANDORA, Tommarree accused him of deceit, and threatened to prevent him. While this argument was going on, Morrison became aware of a commotion on the RESOLUTION. A large party of natives had gone aboard, under the pretence of delivering coconuts. Once on deck, they seized Norman and Ellison and threw them overboard. They then stripped the vessel of everything moveable. They even unbent the sails and unreeved the rigging. The ordinary Tahitians had been in awe of the BOUNTY'S fire power, but now another group of white men had arrived, whose power was even greater. The BOUNTY'S crew were "yesterday's men," and the Tahitians, apart from their special friends, treated them as such.

Morrison, who had been a considerable power in Tahiti, had now to plead with Tommarree for the lives of Norman and Ellison, and, by implication, his own. He reckoned there were more than a thousand natives swarming around the RESOLUTION. So many, in fact, that the vessel rolled over and threw them into the water.

"We asked Tommarree what was the meaning of this treatment... Seeing nothing of our companions and being unarmed ourselves we hardly knew what to think of our situation. He told us it was because we wanted to leave him. [He] told us we must go and secure ourselves in the mountains and keep away from the ship, and we should have our arms and everything restored and he would make good all our damages. "We still refused... He said 'then I'll make you go [to the mountains]!' His men seized us and [were] proceeding inland with us when we begged of Tommarree to let us see some of our shipmates before we went... He agreed and a guard was set over us till he should return. We were conducted to the house of Tayreehamoedooa where we had provisions prepared in abundance. We stayed here all night and next day, when we proposed to make our escape.

"A trusty friend who lived with me all the time I had been on the island, being one of Poeno's men, found us out and promised to have a canoe ready by midnight to carry us to Maatavye, where he said that Poeno waited with impatience to see us. As soon as it was night, he took his station on the beach and about ten o'clock brought Brown into the house. We asked him if he had any arms, when he produced a pistol which he said he had brought from the ship with two hatchets and a knife." Why Brown had returned after robbing Burkett and making off is not explained. He may have been looking for some more loot as the others were rounded up, but Morrison and the others seem to have accepted him at his face value. He gave them the two hatchets and the knife but retained the pistol himself. He was very anxious to discover where the others were but could give no information about the warship which had arrived beyond the fact that it was English. At the same time he produced a bottle of gin - Hollands Geneva, as Morrison describes it - so he must have been on board, or in close conversation with the crew. The inference is that Brown tried to make them drunk, perhaps to loosen their tongues, because Morrison comments, "the smell proved sufficient for me and the others drank but sparingly."

Any suspicion they had that Brown was spying on behalf of the PANDORA must have been increased when he told them he had been landed from one of PANDORA'S boats by Hayward and asked to deliver presents to Tommarree. "The canoe being ready, we armed," writes Morrison. "Norman and myself with a hatchet each and Ellison the large knife. [We] left the pistol with Brown, who fresh primed it, and we set forward. Having got to the canoe without interruption, we got in and paddled to Attahooroo, landing about six miles from Papaara on a sandy beach, which, being white was of some help to us in travelling [in the darkness]. [At Papaara] we left the canoe and proceeded along shore for 12 or 14 miles and reached Pohooataya's house at Tyetabboo about four in the morning of the 29th. Here we found a launch at anchor near the beach, and some canoes hauled up near the house. We hailed the boat but received no answer those aboard being all fast asleep, as were those who were on shore in the canoes. On enquiry we found that the canoes belonged to Areepaeea, who was with them and the officer commanding the boat was Mr Robert Corner, second lieutenant of His Majesty's Ship PANDORA, Capt Edwards. [Lieut Corner] being asleep in one of the canoes we waked him and delivered ourselves up to him, telling him who we were, and delivering the hatchets to Brown when he came up, also the pistol and ammunition which he had given to Norman by the way."

Lieut Corner immediately placed them under an armed guard and set off to find the RESOLUTION with Brown as guide. In the afternoon their old shipmate, Hayward, arrived with 20 armed men. It was a bleak reunion. Hayward ordered them to be securely bound. He asked them nothing except where the others were, and told them nothing. They were told by the PANDORA'S mate, on their way to the ship, that Bligh had been promoted Post Captain. Clearly his star was in the ascendant, which boded ill for them. They had a further indication of how they were regarded when they reached the PANDORA. "We were handed on board and both legs put in irons, under the half deck, after which our hands were cast loose. There being no marines, two seamen and a midshipman were posted over us with pistols and bayonets."

They found the two midshipmen, Stewart and Heywood, already in leg irons, together with Coleman, Skinner and Byrn, the half-blind Irish fiddler. They were told handcuffs were being made by the armourer for them too and next day they were put on. On the 8th of April, Morrison's schooner, the RESOLUTION, arrived, under the command of Lieut Hayward, with the rest of the prisoners.

"Orders were given to the sentinels not to suffer any of the natives to speak to us, and to shoot the first man who spoke to another in the Tahitian language," writes Morrison. "We remained under the half deck some days, during which time we had full allowance of everything except grog, which we did not then want, having plenty of coconuts provided by our friends. [Our friends, however,] were not suffered to speak or look at us. Any who looked pitifully towards us were ordered out of the ship. In the meantime a hammock was given to each to spread under us, and a shirt and trousers given to each of us, but these were of no use as we could not get them on or off, our irons being clenched fast.

"The carpenters were now set to work to erect a kind of poop on the quarter deck for our reception. The poop, or roundhouse, being finished we were conveyed into it, and put in irons as before. This place we styled Pandora's Box. The entrance [was] a scuttle on the top, of 18 or 20 inches square, secured by a bolt on the top, through the coamings. [There were] two scuttles of 9 inches square in the bulkhead for air, with iron grates, and the stern ports [were] barred inside and out with iron. The sentries were placed on the top while the midshipman walked across by the bulkhead. The length of this box was 11 feet upon deck and 18 wide at the bulkhead and here no person was suffered to speak to us but the master at arms, and his orders were not to speak to us on any score but that of our provisions.

"The heat of the place, when it was calm, was so intense that the sweat frequently ran in streams to the scuppers, and produced maggots in a short time. The hammocks, being dirty when we got them, we found stored with vermin of another kind, which we had no method of eradicating but by lying on the plank. Though our friends would have supplied us with plenty of cloth, they were not permitted to do it and our only remedy was to lie naked. These troublesome neighbours, and the two necessary tubs which were constantly kept in the place, helped to render our situation truly disagreeable.

"During the time we stayed [in Tahiti], the women with whom we had cohabited on the island came frequently under the stern, bringing their children of which there were six born - four girls and two boys - and several of the women big with child. [They cut] their heads till the blood discoloured the water about them, their female friends acting their part also and making bitter lamentations. When they came to be known, they were always driven away by the Captain's orders and none of them suffered to come near the ship. Notwithstanding [this] they continued to come near enough to be observed, and there performed their mourning rites, which, on the day the ship weighed [anchor], were sufficient to evince the truth of their grief and melt the most obdurate heart."

Best known to history of the women who mourned the arrest of the BOUNTY'S crew, or such of them as were still alive on Tahiti, was "Peggy" whom I have already mentioned as "wife" of the Orcadian midshipman, George Stewart. Their daughter was well known to the early missionaries to Tahiti, who, as we shall see, were helped in communicating with the natives by a list of Tahitian words compiled, in part at least, by Morrison. Whether Morrison also left progeny on Tahiti we have no idea. He writes of the "women with whom we had cohabited," not in any way excluding himself. But he writes so dispassionately of the parting that he appears to be speaking of other people's grief, rather than his own.

Byron, in a curious verse in "The Island" almost seems to confuse Stewart with Morrison, although there is no reason to believe that he knew that Morrison was a Lewisman:

"And who is he? the blue eyed northern child
Of isles more known to man, but scarce less wild;
The fair-haired offspring of the Hebrides,
Where roars the Pentland with its swirling seas."

Morrison's detached attitude to the parting may be purely a matter of temperament and style. It may also reflect the fact that, when the Journal was written in the form in which it has come down to us, his life in Tahiti, and any love affair in which he might have been involved, was a closed chapter: his main concern in writing was to vindicate himself from the charge of mutiny and expose Captain Bligh.

Continuing his account of the conditions in which they were imprisoned on the PANDORA, Morrison writes, "It being customary for the officer of the watch to examine our irons before he was relieved, McIntosh, happening to have a large shackle, had got one of his legs out in the night, which was reported to the Captain and a general examination took place. The leg irons were reduced to fit close, and Mr Larkin, the First Lieut, in trying the handcuffs, took the method of setting his foot against our breasts and hauling the handcuffs over our hands with all his might, some of which took the skin off with them. All that could be hauled off by this means were reduced, and fitted so close that there was no possibility of turning the hand in them. When our wrists began to swell he told us that 'they were not intended to fit like gloves.'

"However, Coleman's legs being much swelled, he was let out of irons as [were] also Norman and Byrn on their falling sick, but they were always handcuffed at night. McIntosh's and Ellison's arms being much galled by their irons had them taken off until they should get well, but their legs were still kept fast." Later, when some of the prisoners fell ill, the Surgeon, "a very humane gentleman," gave them all the assistance in his power but, adds Morrison, "at the same time informed us that Capt Edwards had given such orders that it was out of his power to be of any service to us in our present circumstances."

Morrison gives the surgeon's name as Mr Hambleton but it was actually Hamilton, and he has given us his own account of the PANDORA in his book, "A Voyage Round the World" which was published in 1793.

The Surgeon and the Second Lieut - Robert Corner - who also seems to have been more humane than Capt Edwards or Lieut Hayward, conspired to give the prisoners a copper kettle, in which they could heat their cocoa. "This," comments Morrison, "with the Divine Providence, kept us alive. As the place was washed twice a week, we were washed with it, there being no room to shift us from place to place. We had no other alternative but standing up until the place dried, or lying down in the wet. When the roughness of the weather gave the ship any motion, we were not able to keep ourselves fast, to remedy which we were threatened to be stapled down by the Captain, but Mr Corner gave us some short boards to check ourselves with, which he made the carpenter secure; and thereby prevented us from maiming each other and ourselves."

Such were the conditions in which James Morrison began the journey back to Britain on 19th May, 1791. They were far removed from the high hopes with which he joined the navy at Leith, twelve years before, or passed his examination as a gunner in December 1783. He must have found it specially galling to see his schooner, the RESOLUTION, now fitted with proper canvas, sailing proudly in their company, manned by his captors. Later, when they got to the Dutch East Indies, he would have found it even more galling to learn that the RESOLUTION had been sold, and the proceeds distributed as prize money among the PANDORA'S crew. All his efforts in Tahiti had only served to enrich his gaolers.

Morrison says no one was allowed to speak to the prisoners in PANDORA'S box, except the master-at-arms, and he was allowed to speak to them only about food. At the same time he gives a fairly detailed account of the PANDORA'S movements, which suggests that he must have had conversation with someone who had freedom to roam the deck. It may be that, in spite of Capt. Edwards prohibition, the crew did talk to the prisoners. It is also possible that the ban on conversation with the prisoners applied only during the time they spent at Tahiti, when the possibility of an attempt by the friends of the "wives" to rescue the prisoners was always present. Whatever the source of his information, he refers to a number of incidents as the PANDORA searched around the Islands, looking for the BOUNTY and the hard-line mutineers. On one of the islands they found the driver boom of the BOUNTY, but this gave no clue to the whereabouts of the mutineers: the boom had been lost at Toobouai before Morrison and his friends separated themselves from Fletcher Christian.

During the search, the PANDORA'S jolly boat was lost with five men on board, despite a diligent search by the PANDORA and the RESOLUTION. Morrison mentions that one of those lost was a son of the PANDORA'S boatswain. This implies an acquaintance with the crew, which he would not have had, if he were kept completely incommunicado. A few days later, off Chatham Island, the RESOLUTION was lost, or so it appeared. The PANDORA searched for ten or twelve days but no trace could be found of the missing schooner. If Morrison had any fears, at the time, that the vessel he and his friends built, with so much difficulty, had proved unseaworthy, he does not reveal them and, as I have already indicated, the schooner actually got to its destination, while the PANDORA did not.

Six years later, HMS PROVIDENCE, the vessel in which Capt Bligh made his second, and successful, voyage to Tahiti for the bread fruit, was sent to chart Nootka Sound, on the west coast of Vancouver Island. At Macao, on the way to Nootka, Capt Broughton of the PROVIDENCE bought a small schooner to assist with the work. According to John Marshall's "Royal Navy Biographies", published n 1825, Broughton discovered that the schooner was "the identical vessel built by some of the ill-fated BOUNTY'S people during their involuntary exile in the South Seas." The purchase was a fortunate one, says Marshall. When the PROVIDENCE struck a coral reef, off Formosa, and became a total loss, a hundred survivors were taken on board Morrison's schooner, which brought them safely to Canton. Among those saved was Lord George Stuart, a relative of the Marquis of Bute. He was then a midshipman but lived to become an admiral. To add another twist to the saga, 43 of the rescued men were transferred, from Morrison's RESOLUTION to HMS SWIFT, and lost their lives "under the command of an officer who was one of Bligh's companions, when turned adrift in the BOUNTY'S launch by Christian and his colleagues."

Some recent writers have argued that the vessel purchased by Capt Broughton at Macao was not the schooner built by the Lewisman and his friends, but Broughton's identification was made when these events were a good deal fresher in people's minds. His account of the incident was published in 1804, and he concludes with the comment, "strange as the coincidences may appear, what we have stated admits of no contradiction." Be that as it may, all the evidence is that the RESOLUTION was an excellent sea boat and was making her way to the agreed destination while PANDORA was carrying out a fruitless search for her.

In the course of the search, the PANDORA visited Annamooka for wood and water. The natives were not particularly friendly. According to Morrison the 2nd Lieut was knocked down by some of them, and his men stripped stark naked. Some of the natives, who got aboard the PANDORA and into the cabins, jumped out the port-holes, when discovered, taking some of the ship's property with them, including several of the Captain's books. "At Chatham Isles the natives were also very dexterous at thieving," writes Morrison. "One of them made a shift to get out of the port[hole] in the Lieut's berth, under the half deck, with a new uniform jacket belonging to Mr Hayward, which he put on as soon as he was astern of the ship and paddled off with it."

The PANDORA also visited some islands hitherto uncharted. Morrison comments that, "they seem to differ very little from the Friendly Islanders; their language seems to be the same, and the construction of their canoes is very near alike. They have hogs but they are remarkably small. These islands are high but do not appear to be very fruitful, and are about two days run to the N E by N of Annamooka." It is this sort of detailed comment which raises the question how Morrison could have come by his information, if he and his fellow prisoners had been kept in close confinement and not allowed to speak to the crew.

His next comment, that the Purser had purchased yams in lieu of bread and served them at the rate of 3lbs of yam for 1lb of bread, does not raise the same sort of question. His meals would have told him that yams had been substituted for bread, and the rate at which it had been done. That the Purser had purchased the yams would have been a simple matter of deduction. The ratio of 3lbs of yam for one of bread seems generous when one recalls that, on the outward voyage, Bligh, acting as his own purser, had given them only 1lb of pumpkin in lieu of 2lbs of bread.

It was at this point in the voyage, just after they left Annamooka, that Morrison heard the PANDORA'S destination was Timor. A few days later he knew she would never get there. They were approaching what we now know as the Torres Straits, between Australia and New Guinea. Let Morrison himself take up the tale:

"Finding no opening in the reef, we hauled to the southward, working to windward for some days, and on Sunday the 28th of August, the 2nd Lieut was sent to find an opening in the reef with the yawl and the ship hove to. On Monday the 29th, at 7 pm the ship went on the reef. Just at that time the boat returned within hail and warned them of the danger, but it was now too late. The current, running fast towards the reef, caused a heavy surf in which the ship was forced on to the reef with violent and repeated strokes and we expected, every surge, that the masts would go by the board. Seeing the ship in this situation, we judged she would not hold long together, and, as we were in danger at every stroke of killing each other with our irons we broke them that we might be ready to assist ourselves... and told the officers what we had done. When Mr Corner was acquainted with it, he came aft and we told him we should attempt nothing further, as we only wanted a chance for our lives, which he promised we should have, telling us not to fear. In the meantime the ship lost her rudder, and with it part of the stern post, and having beat over [the reef], between 11 and 12 she was brought up in 15 fathoms with both anchors, and the first news was nine feet water in the hold!"

At this point three of the prisoners, who had been given a good character by Bligh in his report of the mutiny, were taken out of Pandora's Box to help at the pumps. But Capt Edwards ordered that the others should be handcuffed again, and shackled with all the leg irons that could be mustered. "We begged for mercy and desired leave to go to the pumps, but to no purpose. His orders were put into execution though the water in the hold was increased to eleven feet and one of the chain pumps broke. The master at arms and corporal were now armed with each a brace of pistols and placed as additional sentinels over us, with orders to fire amongst us if we made any motion, and the master at arms told us that the Captain had said he would either shoot or hang to the yard arms those who should make any further attempt to break the irons. We found there was no remedy but prayer, as we expected never to see daylight, and, having recommended ourselves to the Almighty protection we lay down and seemed for a while to forget our miserable situation, though we could hear the officers busy getting their things into the boats, which were hauled under the stern on purpose and heard some of the men on deck say, 'I'll be damned if they shall go without us.'"

When the prisoners realised the ship was being abandoned, they began to loosen their chains again. The Master at Arms heard them and gave the order, "Fire upon the rascals." He was standing just over the scuttle on the top of the prison and Morrison called up to him, "For God's sake don't fire! What's the matter? There is no one here moving!"

Peering from their prison Morrison and his friends saw one of the ship's boats break adrift with only two men on board. The current was strong and they couldn't get back to the ship until another boat was sent to their rescue. They realised then that booms were being cut to make a raft. As the ship rolled on the reef, one of the topmasts fell into the waist and killed a sailor, who had been busy throwing the guns overboard to lighten ship. They could see that everything was in great confusion but could do nothing to help the ship or save themselves.

At daybreak they saw that the officers were all armed, and preparing to abandon ship. They called out asking not to be forgotten. Capt Edwards answered their plea in part - he sent Joseph Hodges, the armourer's mate, into the "box" to release Bligh's favourites, Muspratt, Skinner and the blind Irish fiddler, Byrn. They were in such a panic, Skinner was hauled out with his handcuffs still on, and the scuttle was slammed shut, trapping the Armourer's mate in the "box" with the prisoners. To his credit, Hodges then struck the irons off Stewart and Morrison. When the scuttle was opened again to let Hodges out, Morrison begged the Master at Arms to leave it open. "Never fear my boys, we'll all go to hell together!" he replied, and slammed the scuttle shut.

As he spoke the ship shuddered and the cry went up, "There she goes!" The Master at Arms and the other sentinels rolled overboard to swim for it. The small boats had cast off at the first sign of danger, leaving Capt Edwards on the sinking ship. Morrison could see him swimming after them.

Morrison and his companions were still locked in their prison. Two of them - Burkett and Heildbrandt - were still in irons. The ship was under water as far as the main mast, and the sea was now flooding into PANDORA'S box.

They heard Moulter, the boatswain's mate, scrambling over the top of the box, and shouted to him. He drew the bolt and threw the scuttle overboard. Immediately he had to jump overboard himself to get clear of the wreck.

"On this, we all got out, except Heildbrandt," writes Morrison. "[We] were rejoiced, even in this trying scene, to think that we had escaped from our prison, though it was full as much as I could do to clear myself of the driver boom before the ship sank.

"The boats were now so far off that we could not distinguish one from the other. However, observing one of the gangways come up, I swam to it and had scarcely reached it before I perceived Muspratt on the other end of it." The gangway, he adds, brought Muspratt up with it, but as it fell, it struck the heads of several swimmers and sent them to the bottom.

"I began to get ready for swimming," Morrison continues. "The top of our prison having floated [clear of the ship], I observed on it Mr P. Heywood, Burket and Coleman and the First Lieut of the ship. Seeing Mr Heywood take a short plank and set off to one of the boats, I resolved to follow him and, throwing away my trousers, bound my loins up in a sash or marro, after the Tahiti manner, got a short plank and followed... After having been about an hour and a half in the water, I reached the blue yawl and was taken up by Mr Bowling, the Master's Mate, who had also taken up Mr Heywood. After taking up several others, we were landed on a small sandy key on the reef, about two and a half or three miles from the ship. Here we soon found that four of our fellow prisoners had drowned."

Stewart, the Orcadian, whose love affair inspired Byron's poem, "The Island", was one of those struck by the gangway. Two of the others, Skinner and Heildbrandt, were still in handcuffs when they drowned. Surprisingly, Burkitt, although also in handcuffs escaped alive. Capt Edwards ordered that his handcuffs should now be removed. That was the first and only act of clemency Edwards showed to his prisoners, and it was unavailing. Burkitt was eventually hanged for his part in the mutiny.

Thirty-one of the PANDORA'S crew drowned in the wreck. None of them were officers.

Two tents were now pitched on the little spit of sand, or key, where they had landed. There was one for the officers and another for the PANDORA'S crew. No shelter was provided for the prisoners. "The Capt had told us we should be as well used as the ship's company," writes Morrison. "We found that was not the case for, on requesting a spare boat's sail to shelter us from the sun, being mostly naked, it was refused, though no use was made of it, and we were ordered to keep on a part of the island by ourselves, to windward of the tents, not being suffered to speak to any person but each other."

Capt Edwards, and those who felt like him, seemed to regard the prisoners - irrespective of their part, or lack of a part, in the mutiny - as if they had some virulent contagious disease, which might affect the PANDORA'S crew on the merest contact. It was the typical irrational fear of people clinging to power they cannot justify. The motivating force of harsh, repressive regimes. The violence of inner weakness.

The position of the whole party on the key - now known as PANDORA'S Key - was desperate. Their first meal was a mouthful of bread and a glass of wine. Water was so scarce "none could be afforded." "The sun took such an effect on us, who had been cooped up for these five months, that we had our skin flea'd off, from head to foot, though we kept ourselves covered in the sand during the heat of the day, this being all the shelter that the island affords, the whole of it being no more than a small bank washed up on the reef, which, with a change of wind might disappear, it being scarcely 150 yards in circuit and not more than 6 feet from the level of high water."

Without any criticism of Capt Edwards's navigation, Morrison adds that there were three

Destruction of H.M.S. 'Pandora' daybreak August 29th 1791,
(drawn by Peter Heywood) from The Mutineers of the Bounty -
Lady Belcher, London 1897.

keys together. They had landed on the middle one. Between it and the one to the south, there was a deep channel through which the PANDORA might have passed in safety.

"During the night we found the air very chilly, and, having no covering, we threw up a bank of sand to sleep under the lee of, which proved but an indifferent barrier as we had frequent flying showers of rain, sufficient to make our lodging miserable, though not sufficient to save any to allay our thirst which was very great." One of the PANDORA'S officers tried boiling sea water in a copper kettle and collecting the steam but, although he toiled all night, he collected only a spoonful. One of the seamen, "went out of his senses drinking salt water."

Next day a party was sent to the wreck to see what they could retrieve. They came back with one of the ship's cats, which they found, sitting in the cross trees above the waste of water. One of the ship's buoys went floating by, and, much to Morrison's surprise, no attempt was made to secure it although they were very short of vessels in which to store water - if they ever found any!

After two days on the key, the party sailed off in four boats, the pinnace, the launch, the red yawl and the blue yawl. "Ninety nine souls in all," with the prisoners shared among the boats. Morrison, who was regarded as one of the most dangerous of the "mutineers" because he was not afraid to speak up for himself, was one of three in the pinnace, directly under the eye of Capt Edwards. It was a daunting prospect. As Morrison sums it up, "we had a passage of between four and five hundred leagues to run before we could reach the Dutch settlement on Timor, with the scanty allowance of two musket ball's weight of bread, and hardly a gill of water and wine together, for twenty four hours, in a scorching sun, now nearly vertical." The first anxiety, when they set off from their temporary camp on Pandora's Key, which they called Wreck Island, was to find more water. When they sighted land, which they assumed was part of New Holland - Australia to us - the yawls were sent ashore. They came back with their vessels full. When the little flotilla stood into the bay so that they could all load up with water, eighteen or nineteen natives appeared on the beach. They were men, women and children, and appeared to belong to one family.

"They came off freely to the boats when we found that the colour of their skins was heightened to a jet black by means of either soot or charcoal. They were quite naked but their hair long and curling and matted like a mop. Some had holes in their ears which were stretched to such a size as to receive a man's arm. We made signs that we wanted water, which they soon understood, and a half anker being given to one of them, and some trifles by way of encouragement, he soon returned with it almost full."

The anker was poured into a "brecco" and given back to the native for a refill. This time he gave it to one of the women and sent her for the water. She came back shortly, accompanied by a man with a bundle of spears. The man, who had sent her, waded into the sea up to his waist, with the anker, and signalled to the boats to come in for it. The PANDORA'S crew were cautious and declined the invitation. Then they saw two of the men prepare their javelins. One was thrown and struck the pinnace. An arrow fell close by. At this, some muskets were fired. The native dropped the anker and fled, but when he realised he had not been hurt, he returned and went off with it. Capt Edwards decided not to follow the natives and ordered the other boats to follow him as he stood off to the westward where some other islands were in sight. The First Lieut seemed displeased they had given up the search for water so easily, and spoke his mind too loudly. The Capt heard him and roughly commanded him to keep his mouth shut or take the consequences.

The islands they had seen to the westward had no water, and nothing eatable, except a plum with a glutinous gum in it which stuck to their mouths and teeth. It was "by no means a delicacy" but they were so hungry they ate them. The only other food they had was some shell fish they had taken from the key - "cockles of the gigantic sort which measured about a foot the longest way of the shell" - and these they could not eat for want of water. Next morning they were luckier. They found an island where water could be got by digging. They filled all their vessels and boiled a kettle of portable soup, of which each man got a pint, with as much water as he could drink. It was at this point Morrison's comment about the buoy, which had been allowed to float away, was vindicated. Every vessel that could possibly hold water was brought into service, including canvas bags and a pair of boots, but the total amount of water they could store was less than 200 gallons for 99 men, on a voyage expected to take at least 14 days, with no knowledge of any intermediate point at which they could replenish their supplies. "The heat of the weather made our thirst insupportable and, as the canvas bags soon leaked out, no addition of allowance could take place, and to such extremity did thirst increase that several of the men drank their own urine, and a booby being caught in the pinnace, the blood was eagerly sucked... We kept a line constantly towing but never caught any fish although we saw several."

Morrison's concern with the general suffering of the party was diverted to a particular problem of his own when he got into conversation with McIntosh, who had built the RESOLUTION with him. "As I was lying on the oars talking to McIntosh, Capt Edwards ordered me aft, and, without assigning any cause, ordered me to be pinioned with a cord and lashed down in the boat's bottom... Ellison, who was then asleep in the boat's bottom, was ordered the same punishment. I attempted to reason and enquire what I had now done to be thus cruelly treated, urging the distressed situation of the whole, but received for answer, 'Silence, you murdering villain, are you not a prisoner? You piratical dog, what better treatment do you expect?' I then told him that it was a disgrace for the Captain of a British man-of-war to treat a prisoner in such an inhuman manner, upon which he started up in a violent rage, and, snatching a pistol which lay in the stern sheets, threatened to shoot me. I still attempted to speak, when he swore, 'By God! if you speak another word I'll heave the log with you.' Finding that he would hear no reason, and my mouth being parched so that I could not move my tongue, I was forced to be silent and submit, and was tied down so that I could not move. In this miserable situation Ellison and I remained for the rest of the passage, nor was McIntosh suffered to come near or speak to either of us."

The passage was shorter than they had anticipated, and they were soon sailing along the coast of Timor, although still searching for water. One morning they found a well near a beach and replenished their stock, but, by that time it was hardly necessary. The same evening, they reached the Dutch settlement at Coupang and anchored off the Fort.

If the prisoners expected that their conditions would be eased once they were clear of the small boats, they were disappointed. Let Morrison continue the tale: "In the morning the Captain went on shore to the Governor. About 10 we were landed and conducted by a guard to the Governor's house and from thence to the castle, where, notwithstanding our weak condition, we were put into stocks." The consequences of that form of confinement were horrifying when, after their long fast, they began to eat and drink in reasonable quantities. "Immediately on our landing, provisions were procured, which now began to move our bodies and we were forced to ease nature where we lay, which we had not done during the passage... Some were now so bad as to require repeated clysters but the surgeon... who visited us, could not enter the place till it had been washed by the slaves.

"We had laid six days in this situation when the Dutch officer commanding the fort, being informed of our distress, came to visit us, and, taking compassion on us, ordered irons to be procured, and linked us two and two, giving us liberty to walk about the cell." Immediately the men were given this relief by the Dutch, Capt Edwards, still terrified of his "mutineers" placed a guard of PANDORA'S men on the prison in addition to the Dutch soldiers. The prisoners, their spirit still unbroken, made the best of their situation. "As we were yet mostly naked," writes Morrison, "we got some leaves of the brab tree and set to work making hats which we sold to procure us clothing, but every article being dear we could purchase nothing... however we made shift to supply ourselves with tobacco and some little refreshments."

At this point, Morrison and his companions met up with another group of prisoners whose story was more extraordinary than their own. They were a party of twelve, seven men, three women and two children, who had escaped from Botany Bay and made their way unaided to Coupang. When Capt Bligh got back to Britain after the mutiny on the BOUNTY he was acclaimed for his great open boat voyage. People still write of it with admiration. It certainly was a remarkable achievement, even for trained seamen, led by one of the best navigators of his time. The world, however, has almost forgotten the anonymous convicts, who made an even more remarkable voyage by open boat, around the same time, taking with them two children, one of them a babe in arms, and having no navigational aids, and none of Bligh's previous acquaintance with the South Pacific.

The convicts succeeded for a time in persuading the Dutch authorities they were survivors from a ship, which they called the NEPTUNE. Unfortunately for them, they could not hold their tongues. The truth leaked out and they were arrested for the debts they had incurred in Coupang. Morrison shows little sympathy for these fellow prisoners of his. He wastes no words on their remarkable voyage, but merely comments that they were "discovered to be cheats and confined in the Castle till they should pay the debt they had contracted." The comment does not reflect a lack of compassion in his character, but rather an austere sense of right and wrong. In the next act of the drama in which he was involved his compassion was demonstrated in a very public manner in extraordinary circumstances.

15
A NARROW ESCAPE FROM THE GALLOWS

On the 5th October, 1791, Morrison and his fellow prisoners - including the party which had escaped from Botany Bay - were taken on board the Dutch ship the REMBANG. Before they were taken from their prison their hands were pinioned at their sides with cords. Lieut Larkan of the PANDORA, who was in charge of the transfer, took no chances. He tied the cords with his own hands and put his foot against the prisoners' backs, as he pulled them tight. Morrison complains their arms were almost hauled out of their sockets. Not content with this, Larkan tied the prisoners together, two by two, at the elbows. Only then were their irons removed. Before they reached the REMBANG some of the prisoners fainted. Their circulation was stopped by the cords. When they were on board the REMBANG, the lashings were taken off, but not until the leg irons had been put on again.

Over the next few days there was a modest relaxation in the regime. First of all, three of the prisoners, who had been given a good report by Capt Bligh, were released from irons and allowed to go on deck for air. The others, still anchored by the leg below deck, passed the time making hats for sale, from the materials they had brought with them from Coupang. Then the ship began to leak, and the prisoners were required to man the pumps. Two hours in the forenoon and two hours in the afternoon, pumping steadily with sentries standing over them.

When Morrison reported that he was not able "to stand the pump at spell and spell," because of his long confinement, Larkan taunted him, "You damned villain, you brought it on yourself and I'll make you stand it. If it was not for you we would not be here nor have met with this trouble." Morrison replied, philosophically, that trouble often comes unsought. He was told to shut up and get on with it. Events, however, justified his complaint. The prisoners collapsed under the strain. They had to be taken off the pumps and locked below decks again. The pumping was left to the Dutch seamen and Malay slaves.

Although Morrison suffered much through Capt Edwards harshness he was not blind to his qualities. The Dutch ship, he writes, "was badly found and worse managed. If Capt Edwards had not taken the command and set his men to work, she would never have reached Batavia having split most of her sails in passing the straits of Bali and, having none to bend in their stead, very narrowly escaped going on shore." Eventually they reached Samarang in Java and there, to everyone's delight, they found Morrison's schooner, the RESOLUTION. She had made the voyage without difficulty, reaching the rendezvous six weeks before the survivors from the wrecked PANDORA. Unlike the PANDORA, the RESOLUTION had lost no one on the voyage, although one of the men died after they anchored in Samarang.

While Morrison records the joy of the PANDORA'S men in being reunited with their shipmates, whom they had given up for lost, he expresses no pride in his own achievement in getting the vessel built, and no bitterness at the manner in which it had been seized as a "prize" by his captors. He simply records that, when they got to Batavia, the RESOLUTION was put up for sale. Capt Edwards purchased her, and gave her as a thank-you gift to the Governor. He then divided the money among the ship's company.

The prisoners' conditions eased slightly at Batavia. Three of them, - McIntosh, Coleman and Norman - were again permitted to walk the deck while the others remained confined but all of them were given ten shillings each to buy necessities over and above the food provided by PANDORA'S purser. "Nankeen cloth was here purchased and served to the ship's company," Morrison records. "As we had now recovered our health we commenced tailors as well as hat-makers, and, by working for the ship's company, got some clothes for ourselves which we stood in much need of." They didn't get very far with their tailoring enterprise, however. As soon as Capt Edwards heard what was going on, he put a stop to it! He was determined to make life as miserable as possible for his prisoners. They were at Batavia from the 7th of November until the 23rd of December, and in that time Capt Edwards permitted them to come on deck only twice - "for half an hour at a time to wash ourselves." Oddly, and without any explanation, Morrison adds, "here we enjoyed our health though the PANDORA'S people fell sick and died apace."

His greatest regret seems to have been that he did not have a chance to see Batavia properly. "With regard to the city of Batavia, I can say nothing, not having had a view of it, but it makes no show from the Road, the church and some storehouses being the only buildings that can be seen from the shipping. It is situated at the bottom of a deep bay or inlet and surrounded by low, and to all appearance swampy, land which has no appearance of cultivation. The small river, by which its canals are filled, empties itself into the bay and teems with such filth that the Road, where the large ships lie, is little better than a stagnant pool. During the night the dew falls very heavy and the morning is generally darkened by a thick stinking fog which continues until it is exhaled by the heat of the sun. As the sea breeze seldom reaches the road till afternoon, and sometimes not [at all] during the day, the weather is close and sultry, and the land wind coming off in the evenings brings with it a sticky disagreeable smell sufficient to breed distempers among Europeans. To prevent being affected by this, we applied for liberty to smoke tobacco, which being granted, all our leisure time was thus employed, but particularly in the mornings and evenings, which we found very beneficial and freed us from headaches etc which we supposed to be occasioned by the pestilential vapours.

"The climate of Batavia is by no means calculated for Europeans, and, together with the new arrack (a most pernicious liquor), carries off great numbers daily and such a havoc had death made within the last six months that the fleet now in the Road were forced to send to Holland for hands to navigate them, and even now they were not half manned, though the crews of the outward bound ships were put on board as fast as they came to anchor. It is said that 2500 officers and seamen had been carried off this season, exclusive of the inhabitants. The Chinese and natives of the island do all the labour in loading and unloading the ships as the Dutch seamen are mostly removed as soon as the ship is made fast.

"Provisions here are neither cheap nor good, the beef being all small and lean and rice is the only substitute for bread, at least all that can be the fare of the ship's company. Clothing of all kinds and especially the manufactures of Europe is dear also, and in fact I can find nothing cheap but arrack, which is as bad as poison, but nevertheless it is plentifully used by the Dutch, and it cost the PANDORA'S officers some trouble to keep their men from using it also."

Morrison was no doubt justified in his comments on arrack. The name occurs widely in India, Ceylon, Siam, Java, Batavia, China, Korea and even Mongolia for a variety of crude fermented liquors. In different places it was made from different substances, such as palm toddy, the flowers of the mahua tree, or the refuse of the sugar refineries. Even in modern times the manufacture of arrack has been very primitive and the resultant drink contains an unusually high proportion of unhealthy products, such as fusel oil and various acids. The injurious effects of the drink have been ascribed by some writers to adulteration with drugs, but that seems unlikely. The trouble lies in the crude process of manufacture. Even a hearty drinker of illicit whisky from a Highland bothy might look askance at the arrack being offered to the PANDORA'S crew in Batavia, but Morrison's objection to it I think, goes further. There are several indications in the Journal that he was very abstemious for a seaman. His one addiction seems to have been an insatiable thirst for information.

On 20th November 1791 one of the PANDORA'S lieutenants was sent back to Britain with part of the ship's company but it was over a month later before the main party, with the prisoners, began the long journey, divided among three Dutch ships. Morrison was on board the VREEDENBERGH on which Capt Edwards also sailed.

They dropped anchor for a couple of days at, "a small island in the entrance of the bay, called Onrest, on which the dockyard is, and to this place they send their convicts where they are employed making rope and careening the ships." By this time Morrison and his fellow prisoners were very hungry. They had been three days without food having fallen, not between two stools, but between two bureaucracies. As he explains it: "We weighed from this place on the 25th [Christmas Day, although he does not stress the fact!] tiding it out through the Straits. It was this afternoon before we got any provisions having been victualled no longer than the 22nd by the Purser of the PANDORA and when we got it, it was served after the Dutch method... Two drams of Arrack a day, equal to a third of a pint. Three pounds of flesh (beef and pork), one and a half of fish, ditto of sugar, ditto of tamarinds, half a pint of gee, half a pint of oil and a pint of vinegar with rice instead of bread to serve each man for a fortnight. The rice was little better than grains, most of it having the husks on it, and the oil and tamarinds were fit for no use that we could put them to. Such was our food, and two quarts of water a day gave us plenty to drink, but our lodgings were none of the best, as we lay on rough logs of timber, some of which lay some inches above the rest and which our small portion of clothing would not bring to a level. The deck also over us was very leaky by which means we were cntinually wet being alternately drenched with salt water, the urine of the hogs, or the rain which happened to fall."

The voyage to the Cape was uneventful apart from two more deaths among the PANDORA'S men, and several among the Dutch crew. The prisoners, once more, seem to have been healthier than the seamen, despite their incarceration. It is possible that the seamen, having more freedom to go ashore in the East Indian ports picked up infections from which the prisoners were protected by their captivity. Morrison does not speculate on the cause nor comment. He was too busy studying the manner in which the Dutch were cheating the British prisoners. "They made 'ranson', or fortnight's allowance, to serve us sixteen days, and by the time we had reached the Cape they had gained upon us nearly a fortnight's allowance."

March 14th, 1792, was a red letter day. Morrison records, "This day we were let out of irons, two at a time, to walk the deck for two hours each, but we were scarce able to stand on our feet we were got so weak by living - or rather existing - on our miserable allowance. This was the first and last indulgence of the kind we had during the passage, except one or two who had been let out for a few hours in a day by the intercession of the Dutch surgeon."

As they approached South Africa they began to feel the wind "sharp and cutting", after their long sojourn in the tropics and their debilitated condition, but at least things were beginning to improve. "Made the Cape of Good Hope [on the 15th March] and on the 18th came to an anchor in Table Bay, where to our inexpressible joy we found an English man of war was riding, which we were soon informed was His Majesty's ship GORGON from Port Jackson, and on the 19th we were sent on board her, where our treatment became less rigorous and 2/3rds allowance of provisions was now thought feasting. McIntosh, Coleman and Norman were here at liberty as before, and the rest of us had only one leg in irons and every indulgence given. Lieut Gardner of this ship, in the absence of Capt Parker, very humanely gave us a sail to lie on which by us was thought a luxury, and was indeed such as we had not enjoyed for 12 months before. Here, being supplied with shirts and trousers, we laid what trifle of cash we had out in refreshments and began to get our health and strength very fast, having the benefit of the fresh air, which for some time before we had been strangers to, being removed from between decks to sit on the forecastle for six or eight hours every day."

It is significant that this relaxation in the conditions under which the prisoners were held took place in the absence of Capt Edwards, who was living ashore until they sailed on the 4th of April. Even when he came on board, he was no longer in command, and when they were a few days at sea they were given a further concession. They were put on full rations like the rest of the crew.

On 18th April HMS GORGON sighted St Helena passing near enough to show the colours, a compliment returned by two vessels lying in the Road. St Helena did not have the associations for Morrison that it has for us. On 18th April 1792 Napoleon had not been heard of, although, in a sense he was already standing in the wings as the French Revolution was well under way. The Revolutionary Wars were not far in the future and, although Morrison could not have foreseen it at the time, he would soon be one of the minor players present at the very time and place when the Corsican made his first dramatic entry.

Four days later the GORGON reached Ascension Island where they took on supplies. They found an American schooner at anchor there. Of more direct interest to the prisoners and crew, they took on board 18 fine turtle to add a little variety to the menu. Shortly after they crossed the line, they spoke to another American brig, bound for Bengal and then a British brig, the PRINCE WILLIAM HENRY, presumably a whaler, "bound for the South

Fishery." On the 19th of June they arrived at Spithead.

Morrison gives no indication what his feelings were on reaching Britain. He must have known he would shortly be court martialled. He must also have known that, given the state of the law, and the temper of the navy and the nation, at the time, the risk of being condemned to death was high. The manner in which he had been treated on the homeward voyage, as compared with McIntosh, Coleman and Norman, was a clear indication that Capt Bligh had done him no favours in his account of the mutiny. He is equally reticent about the trial itself. So far as the modern reader is concerned the Journal ends in an anti-climax: "On the 21st we were removed to His Majesty's ship HECTOR, where we were treated in a manner that renders the humanity of her captain and officers much honour, and had beds given us and every indulgence that our circumstances would admit of allowed.On the 12th of September our trial commenced on board His Majesty's ship DUKE in Portsmouth Harbour and to the minutes of the Court Martial I refer the reader for a more particular account of that transaction. Meanwhile I shall endeavour to give some account of the Island of Tahiti, or King George's Island, and of the manners and customs of the Society Isles in general with an account of their language, such as I was able to procure during my short stay on shore there of nineteen months, exclusive of near five months which elapsed while the BOUNTY lay there under Lieutenant Bligh's command, and five months more which we expended after the taking of the ship before we landed, most part of which time we were conversant with the natives."

There follows a well organised and well written account of Tahiti and the customs of its inhabitants, running to just over a hundred printed pages in the Golden Cockerel edition. For us it has much less interest than the dry abbreviated official account of the trial to which he refers us.

Fortunately the official record contains a copy of the plea submitted by Morrison in his own defence: a remarkable document to have been compiled by a layman, without legal aid, or influential friends.

We also have an independent account of the manner in which Morrison conducted himself at the trial and afterwards, which adds greatly to his stature. It was published anonymously in the "Gentleman's Magazine" for December 1792 but it was written with first hand knowledge and authority. So far as I know, it has not previously been given the attention it demands in the vast literature about the mutiny and the main protagonists.

Ten prisoners were tried, on board HMS DUKE, before eleven post captains, presided over by Admiral Lord Hood, Commander in Chief of the Fleet at Spithead. Four of the ten were acquitted. They were McIntosh, Coleman, Norman and Byrn, whom Bligh had noted as people who wished to accompany him in the open boat but were prevented for valid reasons. Three were found guilty, condemned to death and hanged on HMS BRUNSWICK. They were Thomas Ellison, Thomas Burkitt, and John Millward, all of whom were proved to have been under arms, actively supporting the mutiny. Two, Peter Heywood a midshipman, and James Morrison boatswain's mate, were found guilty of mutiny, and condemned to death but strongly recommended by the Court to the Royal Mercy. The last, William Muspratt, was also found guilty and condemned to death but lodged a plea for clemency, because he was not allowed to call members of the crew, who were not mutineers, to give evidence in his defence. He was eventually pardoned, like Heywood and Morrison, despite the fact that the Court made no recommendation in his favour.

Heywood had many friends working for him, notably his uncle, Commander Parsley, who had considerable influence in the navy. Parsley pulled strings to have the trial expedited, so that it took place before Bligh's return from his second voyage to Tahiti. He also arranged to have those who made the open boat voyage with Bligh interviewed, to gather anything he could that might be used in Heywood's defence. He engaged a lawyer, with wide experience as judge-advocate in court martials, to appear for his nephew at the trial. In addition one of the captains who sat on the Court Martial - Capt Albemarle Bertie - was related by marriage to the Heywood family, and helped the young prisoner with money and in other ways, before he knew he was to be one of his judges.

With this influence behind him, Heywood was assured by well placed friends, almost as soon as he was convicted, that the chance of a Royal pardon was high, although he had to wait some weeks before it was officially confirmed. Morrison, on the other hand, had no influence with the court and no lawyer to defend him. He was on his own. He got no private assurances of clemency, when the sentence of death was passed on him, and had to wait, from the 18th of September until the 24th of October, before the news was brought to him that he was free. How then did he escape the gallows?

The anonymous writer in the "Gentleman's Magazine" has little doubt. "The boatswain's mate, who was pardoned," he writes, "stood his own counsel, questioned all the evidences, and in a manner so arranged and pertinent that the spectators waited with impatience for his turn to call on them and listened with attention and delight during the discussion." This tribute would have been of significance from any scribbler who had been present, but the author of the article in the "Gentleman's Magazine" was not a journalist. The internal evidence, from the article itself, is that he was the Captain, or one of the senior officers, of HMS BRUNSWICK. He was present throughout the trial, "from the opening of the prosecution to the passing of the sentence." He had ready access to the condemned men on the night before they died, and he was close to them, on the deck of HMS BRUNSWICK, when they were hanged.

The anonymous writer says he was "struck with horror and astonishment" at hearing Heywood and Morrison "included in the condemnation, as was everyone in the Court." That would seem to rule out the possibility that he was the Captain of the BRUNSWICK, who was one of the judges and would hardly have been struck with horror at the verdict. On the other hand, Capt Hamond of HMS BRUNSWICK is quoted by Sir John Barrow, in his authoritative account of the mutiny, published while many of the participants in the trial were still alive, as having referred to the behaviour of the condemned men, at their execution, in terms very similar to the writer of the magazine article. That the writer was either Capt Hamond, or one of his officers, is proved beyond question by the statement in the article, "on the receipt of the order for execution, the captains drew lots. The painful task was ours."

The author's tribute to Morrison is all the more notable because his purpose in writing had nothing to do with Morrison or his defence. He wrote to correct a number of misconceptions which were circulating among the public. The praise for Morrison was incidental.

First he disposed of the widespread belief that the three who were executed "protested their innocence to the last." On the day of the execution, he writes, "on the cat head, Millward addressed the ship's company, confessed the errors they had been guilty of and warned them, by his fate, to shun similar paths of impropriety." Millward, like Morrison, was "a man of education and capacity" and, also like Morrison, was deeply religious. The writer says he overheard Millward on one occasion read a sermon to his fellow prisoners, and, until he actually saw him in the act, thought he was listening to one of the chaplains "in the performance of his office." The second purpose the writer had was to quash the view held by "the vulgar" that those who were reprieved "bought" their lives "with money" while "the others fell sacrifice to their poverty." The amount of influence mobilised on behalf of Heywood gave some ground for the belief that there was one law for the rich and another for the poor, but, as the writer indicated, that did not apply to Morrison, who saved himself by his own exertions, nor to Muspratt. Finally he makes it clear that in his view, the three who were hanged "suffered justly, according to the articles by which they were tried," while there was no injustice in the pardon granted to the others.

It will be necessary later to examine, in some detail, the evidence against Morrison and the manner in which he extricated himself from the very tight corner he was in. In the meantime we can stay with the anonymous naval officer of the "Gentleman's Magazine" for a first hand account of the end of the affair.

Describing the last night in the condemned cell - a corner of the gun room - he writes, "not a ray of light was permitted to obtrude. All was silent, solemn and gloomy... In one corner of this wretched asylum was a small spot to which they were confined... In this small space they employed their night occasionally in devotions, conversation and sleep. Through a small opening in their cell, I, unperceived, observed them very minutely, and heard their conversation, which was cheerful, resigned and manly. Their faces were the cheerful indexes of serene and placid minds."

The behaviour of others was not as restrained as that of the three who were to die. The writer expresses the horror with which he saw the provost marshal steal the prisoners' night-caps as souvenirs. As the provost marshall came out from the condemned cell, he gloated, "the young one's a hardened dog." In the morning, boat loads of officers and men were sent from every ship in the fleet to the BRUNSWICK to witness the executions, as a solemn warning to others disposed to mutiny. The seamen were there under orders, but, quite apart from them, the river was crowded with craft of all sorts, carrying men, women and children "as if, instead of a solemn scene of sorrow, it had been a spectacle of joy." "Oh! how I wished for the pen of a Sterne," exclaims the anonymous naval officer, who was clearly shocked by the carnival atmosphere.

The writer then refers to Millward's address from the cat head, which I have already mentioned, and which was given in, "an open and deliberative manner, his speech nervous, strong and eloquent." Finally comes this astonishing sentence: "After half an hour spent in devotion, Morrison performed the last offices to his departing companions; the gun was fired; and their souls took their flight in a cloud [of smoke] amid the observation of thousands."

What exactly does that reference to "last offices" imply? Was the Admiralty so sadistic that the newly reprieved boatswain's mate was compelled to truss up his companions for hanging? Or does it mean that, after all he had been through himself; despite the fact that he had nothing to gain and much to lose in reputation by associating with the mutineers, having himself so narrowly escaped their fate; the boatswain's mate from Lewis, alone of all the BOUNTY'S crew, was man enough to stand beside his less fortunate companions, and give them such succour as he could, in the last fleeting moments of their lives?

16
"CONSCIOUS OF MY OWN INNOCENCE"

To secure an acquittal Morrison had to show, not only that he took no part in the mutiny, but that he had been actively loyal to Capt Bligh. Neutrality was not enough and the cards were stacked against him.

None of the witnesses called by the prosecution heard Morrison express a desire to go with Bligh. Some alleged he had called out, "If my friends enquire after me, tell them I am somewhere in the South Seas," which, they implied, showed acquiesence in the mutiny, if not active participation. Hayward, a most important witness, having been a midshipman on the BOUNTY and a lieut on the PANDORA, said complicity was written on Morrison's face, as Bligh and his party prepared to leave the BOUNTY. Another midshipman from the BOUNTY, Hallet, went even further. He declared that he had seen Morrison under arms. In addition there was the evidence of the PANDORA'S crew that Morrison's schooner had tried to evade capture. The Lewisman had a formidable case to answer.

The anonymous naval officer, who wrote to the "Gentleman's Magazine" tells us how well he conducted his defence and something of the cut and thrust which so aroused the admiration of the spectators comes across, even in the dry, factual and abbreviated minutes of the Court Martial. Morrison clearly knew exactly what he had to prove.

Fryer, the master of the BOUNTY, was a key witness, because Morrison had been in his watch on the night of the mutiny. As soon as he got a chance to question him, Morrison went right to the heart of the matter, "Did you ever see me under arms on the day of the 28th of April, patricularly on the taffrail, after the boat was astern, or know that I made use of any sneering expressions?" Fryer gave an emphatic "no."

Morrison then tried to get Fryer to confirm that he had been active in getting provisions and arms for Bligh's party in the boat. Fryer agreed that pork had been handed in but could not confirm it was by Morrison:

Morrison - Did you know there were such things as two gourds of water handed into the boat? — I know they were in the boat but I do not recollect seeing them handed in.

Do you recollect the cutlasses coming into the boat, by whom they were handed in? — I remember the cutlasses being handed down by a rope, but by whom I cannot tell.

As I was in your watch during the voyage, you must be a judge of my conduct, and you will therefore explain it to the court, giving my character at large? — A steady, sober, attentive, good man.

At this point the Court intervened to press Fryer on his assertion that Morrison had not been under arms, and had not used any sneering expressions. "Was your situation such that you must have seen and heard him?" he was asked. Fryer replied, apparently without hesitation, "I must have seen him if he had been armed, and, if he had made use of any opprobrious language, I must have heard him."

Morrison tried to press home the advantage:

You acknowledged in a former evidence that, had you remained in the ship, I should have been one of the first you would have called upon to assist you in your plan [to retake it], do you now confirm that evidence? — Yes.

Again the Court intervened to explore the matter further, asking what he meant when he told the Court that as he [Fryer] was escorted below by the mutineers, Morrison said to him it was now too late [to retake the ship]. Fryer replied, "It struck me at the time he was afraid of being overheard by the people who were under arms behind me, guiding me down, and that he did not speak it in a jeering contemptuous manner."

Cole, who as boatswain was Morrison's immediate superior, was not so helpful. When Morrison asked whether he had seen him under arms or heard him using any jeering expressions, he replied, not directly to Morrison, but to the Court, "I did not see him under arms. I heard him say that if anybody asked for him, to let them know that he was to the southward of the line, or something to that purport."

Morrison tried another tack:

Do you recollect the circumstances of the pork being handed into the boat, and, if it was not by me, can you point any person out who did hand it in? — I know the pork was put in the boat but by whom I cannot say.

Do you recollect that it was by the clumsiness of John Norton that two or three pieces of pork went overboard and that you damned his clumsy eyes and shoved him away from receiving any more of it? — No. I do not remember it. I know three or four pieces went overboard.

Do you remember the gourds of water being in the boat? — Yes. I do not know that there was water in more than one.

Do you remember that, previous to the mutiny there were two gourds in our berth, the property of myself and messmates? — I cannot say what they have in their messes.

Be pleased to give my character at large to the Court? — He was a man of very good character in the ship. He was boatswain's mate and steered the captain. He was attentive to his duty and I never knew any harm of him in my life.

Unfortunately for Morrison, he rather spoiled the testimonial by adding, immediately, in answer to the Court, that the comment about looking for him southward of the line was said jeeringly.

Hayward really put the boot in when Morrison cross-examined him. He could not say whether or not he had been under arms. He saw him emptying the long boat of yams, to make it available for Bligh and his party, but took the view that, in doing so, he was not obeying orders, but assisting the mutineers to get quit of Bligh as fast as possible.

During earlier questioning Hayward said that both Morrison and McIntosh were helping to get the boat out for Bligh but he deduced from this that Morrison was helping the mutineers and that McIntosh was helping the captain. Asked why he drew two different conclusions from the same set of circumstances, he replied, "The difference was in the countenance of the people. Though opinions may be ill grounded, the countenance of one was rejoiced and the other depressed."

Morrison pounced:

You say that you observed joy in my countenance, and that you rather inclined to give it as your opinion that I was one of the mutineers, can you declare before God and this Court that such evidence is not the result of a private pique? — It is not the result of any private pique. It is an opinion I formed after quitting the ship from the prisoner not coming with us, when he had as good an opportunity as the rest, there being more boats than one.

Are you certain that we might have had the large cutter to accompany you? — Not being present at any conference between you, I cannot say but perhaps you might.

Can you deny that you were present when Capt Bligh begged that the long boat might not be overloaded and that he did say that he would do justice to those who remained? — I was present at the time Lieut Bligh made such a declaration but understood it as respecting clothes and other heavy articles with which the boat was already too full.

Do you recollect that in consequence of such declaration I told you 'I will take my chance in the ship.'? — No. I do not remember such a circumstance.

Do you remember, when you handed your bag up the main hatchway and with it your fuzee [a short musket], that I was the person that received them from you and that Matthew Quintal came and seized upon the fuzee, and swore damn his eyes if you should have it? — I dont remember the person that took the bag and fuzee from me, and it might have been you, but remember the circumstances of Matthew Quintal's swearing that I should not have it, but from whose hands he took it I cannot remember.

Do you remember at any time on that day calling on me to assist you in any point of duty or to give my assistance to retake His Majesty's Ship? — I have a faint remembrance of a circumstance of that nature.

Questioned by the Court, Hayward said he had an idea that they might retake the ship using the Friendly Island clubs that were on board:

What answer did I give to you? — I do not remember.

Did I say, 'Go it! I'll back you! There are tools enough!'? — I do not remember.

Did you ever observe anything in my conduct through the voyage and particularly on that day that should give you cause of complaint? — During the voyage, not; and on that day I thought he was pleased, as far as I can judge of countenances. The prisoner assisted in preparing the boat for our departure but, as I have said before, I do not know his real intention.

Are you positive that there was a continual smile or appearance of joy in my countenance all the time that you observed me, or at the time only when you called on me for assistance? — I cannot say.

Hayward was clearly unwilling to say anything that would help Morrison but even his denials indicate that Morrison was speaking the truth. He agreed, for instance, that Matthew Quintal had taken the fuzee from him at a particular time and place, and had sworn at him, but he could not remember that Morrison was the other person present - the man who was helping him. How could Morrison have known the story in sufficient detail to question him about it, if he had not been the third man?

Morrison did not explain why he thought Hayward had a private pique against him, but his account of the voyage and the mutiny makes it clear that Hayward had the most natural of all reasons for trying to demonstrate his zeal in pursuing wrongdoers: he had been one himself!

When the BOUNTY was at Tahiti collecting the bread fruit, Hayward fell asleep on watch, enabling three of the crew to desert. Bligh clapped him in irons, bawled him out in front of the crew and disrated him. There were other incidents, not officially logged, but recorded by Morrison which show Hayward in an unfavourable light, in fact if Morrison is to be believed, Hayward, more than anyone else, was responsible for the success of the mutiny. He records, as the testimony of Fletcher Christian himself, that Hayward was one of those to whom Christian confided his first mad plan of deserting from the BOUNTY, alone, on an improvised raft. Some writers have questioned the accuracy of this, suggesting that Hayward would have run straight to Bligh with such a juicy morsel. But would he? Which was more to his advantage, to get a little temporary kudos from Bligh as a telltale, and live with Christian's animosity for the rest of the voyage, or to let Christian, who stood higher than he on the ladder of promotion, slip quietly out of the competition? More substantially, Morrison alleges that Hayward was again asleep on duty on the night of the mutiny. If he had been awake it would never have happened.

Hallet, the man who came closest to getting Morrison hanged, was on watch with Hayward on the night of the mutiny, or should have been: actually he failed to appear at all. He, too, by dereliction of duty, gave Christian the chance to seize the ship. It is no idle chance that the two men who had most to hide were the two most anxious to close Morrison's mouth for good.

Hallet gave the Court the names of eighteen men he saw under arms at the time of the mutiny. James Morrison was second on his list. In answer to the Court, however, he admitted that he had not made the record at the time - he made it "lately" - and he had not seen Morrison armed until after the ship had been seized and he was in the open boat, looking up at the crowded taffrail when it was impossible to be sure who was carrying what. The Court asked him to relate all he knew of the conduct of James Morrison on the day of the mutiny:

"When I first saw him he and Millward were talking together unarmed, but he shortly after appeared under arms."

The Court - How was he armed? — With a musket.

At what part of the ship was he when he was armed with a musket? — I did not see him under arms until the boat was veered astern and he was then looking over the taffrail and called out, in a jeering manner, 'if my friends enquire after me, tell them I am somewhere in the South Seas'.

Pressed by the Court to relate all he knew about Morrison from the beginning of the mutiny until that point, Hallet replied, "I have related the whole to the best of my recollection."

Morrison, cross-examining him asked, "Can you swear positively before God and this court it was me and no other person whom you saw under arms?" Unhesitatingly, and unequivocally Hallet replied, "I have declared it." Asked by Morrison to whom he made the jeering comment about the South Seas, Hallet replied that he did not "remark that the message was said to any particular individual." When Morrison took him over other events of the day, Hallet's memory was as vague on anything helpful as it had been precise on the two incriminating allegations:

Can you deny that I did lower down into the boat from the larboard quarter two cutlasses, two large gourds of water, and five or six and twenty pieces of pork? — I remember that four cutlasses were lowered and also the other things you mention into the boat, but by whom I cannot say.

Do you remember that I did personally assist you to haul one of your chests up the main hatchway and whether or not I was armed then? — The circumstances regarding the chest I do not remember and have said before that I did not see you under arms till after the boat was veered astern.

One curious incident, almost a bit of light relief, immediately followed. John Smith, who had been cook on the BOUNTY, told how he went round, in the middle of the mutiny, serving out tots of rum. The rum was taken from Bligh's cabin, on Christian's orders, to be served to those under arms. Morrison received a tot. Does that incriminate him? Not necessarily! Consider Smith's own position. He was Bligh's personal servant. He was loyal to his captain and went with him in the open boat. He was in the clear. If, however, he had been left behind because the boat was full, as other loyal seamen were, how would he have fared at a Court Martial, when it was proved that he took orders from the ring leader of the mutiny, "stole" the captain's rum, and served it to armed mutineers?

The story of John Smith, more perhaps than anything else, shows how confused and equivocal the whole affair was. Capt Edwards of the PANDORA, and many others, took the view that the mutiny had been long and carefully planned. The mutineers were dangerous criminals, capable of corrupting a whole ship's crew, even when they were prisoners in irons. In truth, the mutiny blew up spontaneously round one man's discontent, and succeeded almost by accident, because Bligh had lost the loyalty of his officers, and none of them was bold enough to lead an attempt to retake the ship.

Although with hindsight we can see the true significance - or rather the true insignificance - of Smith's action, his evidence presented Morrison with one of his most difficult moments. He had been offered and accepted a drink, ordered by the ringleader of the mutiny for those who were under arms.

He tried to make the best of it when he had the chance to cross-examine Smith:

Do you recollect when you came forward with the bottle that, abaft the windlass, Mr Cole and me were speaking together, that you gave Mr Cole a glass into a tin pot and said 'Morrison, you may as well have a drop though I am ordered to serve none but the sentries?'

The reply left him stranded: "I do not recollect a word of it."

Almost the only thing in Morrison's favour, and it had no direct bearing on his guilt or innocence, was a certificate of character from Charles Stirling who had been his Captain ten years before:

"I do certify that Mr James Morrison served as midshipman on board His Majesty's sloop TERMAGANT under my command during the year 1782, and I perfectly recollect his conduct met with my entire approbation, not only for his sobriety and attention to his duty, but I ever found he paid due respect to his superiors and that he was always obedient to commands."

With the certificate was a note to Morrison, in the Captain's handwriting:

"Captain Stirling encloses Mr Morrison a certificate of good behaviour while serving under his command on board the TERMAGANT; and he most earnestly hopes that as Mr M. at that time behaved well he will now be able to vindicate his character from the charge exhibited against him."

Despite the fact that it is formal and impersonal it is a very friendly message to pass between a captain and a boatswain's mate in the Georgian navy. But when all was said and done it was simply an expression of goodwill and had no bearing on the facts.

It was against this background that Morrison prepared his final submission to the Court. Heywood, who had legal advice, asked for an adjournment of a day to enable his advisers prepare his defence. The adjournment was granted. Morrison, no doubt, benefited from this breather as well, although his passionate defence of his innocence bears the marks of hasty composition.

So far as I know, it is the only document in his own handwriting that survives. His diary, journal and account of life in Tahiti appear to be copies made by others from Morrison's original. The text is his but not the handwriting.

The submission to the Court Martial is heavily underlined in many places, as if he were marking the words which should be emphasised. He had no opportunity, however, to read it to the Court in person. It was read by the Judge-advocate who, presumably, paid little attention to the writer's under scoring, and read it all in a colourless official voice. The reading certainly would have lacked the passion which is evident in the writing.

"Conscious of my own innocence of every article of the charge exhibited against me, and fully satisfied of my zeal for His Majesty's service, I offer the following narration, in vindication of my conduct, on the 28th day of April 1789:

"I was boatswain's mate of His Majesty's ship BOUNTY and had the watch on deck from eight till twelve on the night of 28th of April 1789. When I came on deck Mr Fryer, who was officer of the watch, ordered me aft to the conn, as Peter Linkletter, the quartermaster, complained that he could not keep his watch. There was little wind all the watch, and we were then near the island of Tofoa; I suppose about eight or nine miles off. I stayed at the conn until twelve o'clock; when I was relieved by John Norton, quartermaster, and went to my hammock and slept till daylight, when Mr Cole the boatswain waked me, and told me that the ship was taken, and that Mr Christian had made the Captain prisoner, and then said, 'I hope Morrison you have no intention to join Christian's party.' I answered, 'No sir! You may depend upon it that I will not. It is far from my intention.' He then left me and I hurried on my clothes, went up the fore scuttle, and into the head to look round about me, when I soon found the truth of what Mr Cole had said.

"I saw John Williams on the forecastle with a musket and fixed bayonet; William McCoy and Robert Lamb at the fore hatchway; Isaac Martin and William Brown on the after part of the booms and Henry Hieldbrandt on the quarterdeck, all armed in the same manner. Captain

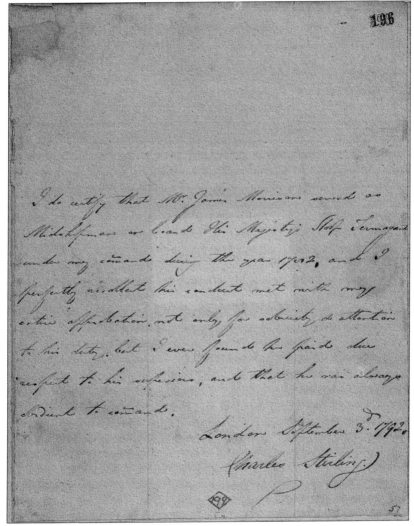

I do certify that Mr. James Morrison served as Midshipman on board His Majesty's Sloop Termagant under my command during the year 1782, and I perfectly recollect his conduct met with my entire approbation, not only for sobriety & attention to his duty, but I ever found he paid due respect to his superiors, and that he was always obedient to command.

London September 3d 1792

Charles Stirling

Copy of Captain Stirling's certificate in Morrison's favour submitted at the trial.

Bligh was on the larboard side of the quarter deck, between the guns, with his hands tied behind him and Mr Christian standing by him with a bayonet in one hand and the other on Capt Bligh's shoulder. The small boat was then out and some hands were clearing the large cutter, and Charles Churchill on the booms giving directions with a drawn cutlass in his hand.

"I stayed but a few minutes in the head when I came aft and met Mr Cole at the fore hatchway and asked him what was to be done. He told me he did not know, but desired me to assist in clearing the cutter. John Smith at the same time came forward with a bottle of rum and a glass, of which he gave me a glass, saying, 'You may as well have a drop Morrison though I am ordered to serve none but the sentinels.'

"I took the rum and went about clearing the cutter and got her out... Charles Norman who was then in the small cutter, complaining that he could not keep her free, she was got in... In the meantime Mr Christian ordered Charles Churchill to see Mr Hayward, Mr Hallet, Mr Fryer and Mr Samuel into the boat, telling them himself, at the same time, to get ready to go on shore with the captain.

"Mr Cole, Mr Purcell and some others then went to Mr Christian and begged for the long boat, which, after some hesitation, was granted and orders given for getting her out. I went about clearing her, and, while I was thus employed, Mr Fryer came to me and asked me if I had any hand in the mutiny. I told him 'No!' He then desired me to see who I could find to assist me and try to rescue the ship. I told him I feared it was then too late but would do my endeavour... John Millward, who stood by me and heard what Mr Fryer said, swore he would stand by me if an opportunity offered. Mr Fryer was about to speak again, but was prevented by Matthew Quintal who, with a pistol in one hand, collared him with the other, saying, 'Come, Mr Fryer, you must go down into your cabin and hauled him away.' Churchill then came and, shaking his cutlass at me, demanded what Mr Fryer said. I told him that he only asked me if they were going to have the long boat, upon which Alex Smith, who stood on the opposite side of the boat said, 'It's a damned lie, Charley, for I saw him and Millward shake hands when the master spoke to them.'

"Churchill then said to me, 'I would have you mind how you come on for I have my eye upon you.' Smith at the same time called out, 'Stand to your arms for they intend to make a rush.' This, as was intended, put the mutineers on their guard and I found it necessary to be very cautious how I acted... I heard Capt Bligh say to Smith, 'I did not expect you would be against me, Smith' but I could not hear what answer he made. However I proceeded in clearing the boat and, when she was hoisted out, I heard Mr Christian order Churchill to see that no arms were put into her, to keep Norman, McIntosh and Coleman in the ship and get the officers into the boat as fast as possible.

"While Churchill was putting his orders in execution I was employed in getting a tow line and grapnel and sundry other articles into the boat but she, in the meantime, was got so full and so deep that those who were in her began to cry out that she would sink alongside if any more came into her, upon which Capt Bligh said, 'You can't all go in the boat, my lads. Don't overload her. Some of you must stay in the ship.' Captain Bligh then asked Mr

Christian to let the Master and some of the men remain in the ship, to which he replied, 'the men may stay but the Master must go with you,' and ordered Mr Fryer to go into the boat immediately. Mr Fryer begged permission to stay, but to no purpose and he was forced to go into the boat.

"On seeing Mr Fryer and most of the officers go into the boat, without the least appearance of an effort to rescue the ship, I began to reflect on my own situation... Seeing the situation of the boat, and considering that she was at least 1,000 leagues from any friendly settlement, and judging by what I had seen of the Friendly Islanders but a few days before, that nothing could be expected from them but to be plundered or killed, and seeing no choice but of one evil, I chose, as I thought the least, to stay in the ship, especially as I considered it obeying Capt Bligh's orders, and depending on his promise to do justice to those who remained. [I] informed Mr Cole of my intention, who made me the like promise, taking me by the hand and saying, 'God bless you my boy. I will do you justice if ever I reach England.'

"I also informed Mr Hayward of my intention and, on his dropping a hint to me that he intended to knock Charles Churchill down, I told him I would second him, pointing at some of the Friendly Island clubs, which were sticking in the booms, and telling him there were tools enough. I was heartily rejoiced to think that any officer intended to make an attempt but was as suddenly dampened to find that he went into the boat without making the attempt he had proposed and now gave over all hopes and resolved to bear my fate with as much fortitude as I was able.

"As soon as Capt Bligh was in the boat she was wore astern. I went aft and, on hearing Capt Bligh request some provisions, I got all the pork which was in the harness casks, twenty five or six pieces and handed [them] into the boat. I also got two large gourds of water out of my own berth, which contained from 3 to 4 gallons each, these I also handed in, and, on Capt Bligh's desiring me to get him a musket or two I went to Christian and begged him to let me give one into the boat but was refused... On making further intercession, he ordered four cutlasses, two of which I handed in myself and Churchill brought the other two and said, 'There, Capt Bligh! You don't stand in need of firearms as you are going among your friends.'

"There being little wind Christian said, 'They will make better at their oars than wait to be towed.' Notice of this being given to those in the boat, Mr Cole asked for something to sling the mast over her side that they might be the better able to work at their oars. On hearing this, I obtained a bale of spunyarn and gave it into the boat. She was now cast off and Christian called me to hoist in the cutter. I heard Capt Bligh desire to speak to Mr Christian but he gave orders that no person should answer."

Morrison ends his direct account of the mutiny with that record of Christian's sullen response to Capt Bligh's last plea. It is of some interest that, although his own life was in peril, he went out of his way to put in a good word for four of those being tried with him. He asserted that Norman, McIntosh and Coleman were detained on the BOUNTY at Christian's express request. They were all acquitted by the Court Martial. More courageously he put in a good word for Millward, who had been associated with Churchill, one of the ringleaders of the mutiny, in the earlier abortive attempt to desert in Tahiti. Considering the atmosphere of the time, when mutiny was regarded almost as if it were a contagious disease, a man concerned primarily with his own safety would have suppressed any unnecessary reference to a shipmate whose record might help to drag him down. Millward in fact, was hanged, and according to the anonymous naval officer in the "Gentleman's Magazine", confessed his guilt from the gallows. Turning to the specific allegations made against himself Morrison continued:

"With respect to the evidence given against me, it has been said that from my alacrity in assisting to clear the boats and get them out, it would appear as if I rather favoured those in arms but it has been fully proved to this Honourable Court that the boats were only granted after much solicitation by the officers, who intended quitting the ship; and, if the launch had not been prepared with the utmost expedition the chief of the mutineers might have recalled his grant. I acted in this by order of Mr Cole the boatswain, nor can more guilt (if it can be deemed such) be imputed to me in this particular than to himself, who hoisted them out, or the carpenter and his crew who were also active in preparing them.

"My countenance has also been compared with that of another, employed on the same business. This Honourable Court knows that all men do not bear misfortunes with the same fortitude or equanimity of mind and that the face is too often a bad index to the heart. If there were no sorrow marked in my countenance it was to deceive those whose act I abhorred that I might be at liberty to seize the first opportunity that might appear favourable to the retaking of the ship. The Evidence who drew the comparison has admitted that it did not then appear to him that I was concerned in the mutiny and that it was only an opinion formed from not finding me in the boat. An opinion so founded will I trust have no weight with this Honourable Court, having no foundation whereupon it may rest.

"So uncertain is the judging of countenances that Captain Bligh declares in his letter; from the carpenter's sullen and ferocious aspect, he took him to be one of the chief mutineers; which unfavourable opinion was entirely overthrown by his having him company in the boat; but, had he chosen to remain in the ship, to an uncertain (and judging by appearance) inevitable fate in the boat, such conjectures would have been thought well grounded on him, though his innocence would have been equally strong, to a being who could have discerned his inward soul.

"It has been fully proved and owned that I was not the only person who bore no active part in the mutiny that wished to remain in the ship, had they been permitted, and I humbly conceive it is impossible to say who might have stayed had permission been granted. Let the Members of this Honourable Court suppose themselves in my then unfortunate situation and it will appear doubtful even to them which alternative they would have taken. A boat alongside already crowded, those who were in her crying out she would sink, and Captain Bligh desiring no more might go in, with a slender stock of provisions; what hope could there be to reach any friendly shore, or withstand the boisterous attacks of hostile elements and the perils those underwent who reached the island of Timor, and whom nothing but the apparent interference of Divine Providence could have saved, fully justify my fears and prove beyond doubt that they rested on a solid foundation; for by staying in the ship an opportunity might offer of escaping; but by going in the boat nothing but death appeared either from the lingering torments of thirst and hunger or from the murderous weapons of cruel savages, or being swallowed up by the deep.

"Mr Hayward saying there were other boats, which those who had chosen might have got into, tacitly acknowledges that the launch was then as deep as she could swim, and which also fully appears from Mr Fryer and the Carpenter's evidence to have been the case. As to the suggestion of having another boat, this Honourable Court is well informed that the small cutter, by reason of her defective bottom, would not swim; is it therefore in the least probable that Christian would have granted me the large cutter, the only boat then remaining; and the only one fit for service, or even should I go so far as to allow she would have been granted, it would have been madness for me to have got into a heavy boat by myself, without water or provision for, after having with much assiduity and entreaty, only procured so small a quantity for the number crowded into the launch, could I have expected anything for myself? And might not I have perished with hunger, thirst and fatigue, without getting one mile nearer the land, or if I had reached it, from the reception those met with in the launch, would not a cruel death have been my portion for such a disposition I conceive the natives to be of.

"It has also been said that, when the boat was veered astern, I appeared at the taffrail under arms. Amidst such a crowd, tumult and confusion, might not the arms in the hands of another man, wedged by my side, easily be thought to be in my possession; and might not the voice of another easily have been taken for mine? To what purpose would I have armed myself when all apprehensions of an attempt to retake the ship must have been over? Had I approved of the mutiny and wished to arm myself to assist in putting it into execution, I surely would not have deferred it until the officers and the men who accompanied them were placed in a helpless situation where they could have no recourse to arms and could make no effectual attack on those who had assumed the command. Had I approved of the violence carried into execution, would I have been so active in procuring subsistence for those [to] whom, by so doing, I gave perhaps the only chance they could have of reaching a European settlement and appearing against me at the bar of justice?

"I have endeavoured to recall to Mr Hayward's remembrance a proposal he at one time made by words, of attacking the mutineers, and of my encouraging him to the attempt, to back him with all the efforts I was capable of making. He says he has but a faint recollection of the business, so faint indeed that he cannot recall to his memory the particulars, but owns there was something passed to that purpose. Faint as the remembrance is (which is for me the more unfortunate) ought it not to do away all doubt with respect to the motives by which I was then influenced? If I offered to second the only attempt that was proposed for the recovery of the ship, and which to me appeared practicable if put into execution, could my heart be on the side of the mutineers? No! If I had wished them to succeed would I not immediately have left him and put them on their guard? Besides it fully proves by Mr Hayward disclosing his mind to me that he had unlimited confidence in my attachment to him; or he would not have expressed himself to one of whose intention he was doubtful in that manner.

"After the members of this Honourable Court have maturely weighed in their minds these circumstances, which to me are of the utmost importance, if any doubt remains in their minds with respect to my innocence on that fatal day, it has always been accounted the glory of justice in a doubtful case to throw mercy into the balance when I doubt not I shall be acquitted of so black a crime. Resting with entire confidence on the humanity and integrity of this Honourable Court, I humbly await its awful decision. I beg leave most humbly to remind the members of the Honourable Court that I did freely and of my own accord, deliver myself up to Lieutenant Robert Cornor of His Majesty's Ship PANDORA on the first certain notice of her arrival."

This eloquent plea for justice, and if not justice, for clemency, is signed in a firm hand, James Morrison. It must surely rank as one of the most remarkable documents ever penned by a Lewisman.

The following morning the Court decided, on grounds which can only be conjectured, that the charges against Morrison had been proved, and that he should "suffer death by being hanged by the neck" on board one of His Majesty's ships of war.

The naval method of hanging was specially barbaric. There was no trap door to open suddenly, breaking the prisoner's neck, and shortening his death throes, marginally at least. In a naval execution the prisoner was hoisted, choking and struggling to the yard arm of the ship, while the whole ship's company, and hundreds of civilian rubbernecks, looked on and gloated.

That was the prospect with which Morrison lived for six weeks until, as a contemporary press report records: "Portsmouth. October 28. Yesterday at noon Sir Andrew Hamond, the Commander in Chief at this Port, sent an order to Captain Montague of the HECTOR to release Mr Heywood and James Morrison, two of the unfortunate persons who were convicted of mutinously running away with the BOUNTY, armed ship, commanded by Capt Bligh, in the South Seas, who, at the earnest request of the Court Martial which tried them were pardoned by His Majesty.

"After reading the order, which he did upon the quarter deck, in the presence of his own officers and ship's company, Captain Montague pointed out to the prisoners the evil of their past conduct; and, in language that drew tears from all who heard him, recommended them to make atonement by their future good behaviour. They were both of them very visibly affected, and endeavoured in vain to make their acknowledgments for the tender treatment they had received on board the HECTOR."

7

KING OF A SOUTH SEA ISLAND

James Morrison disappears from the written record for a period after his reprieve. Lady Belcher in her book "The Mutineers of the BOUNTY" says he was given several months leave of absence because his "shattered health needed repose." As step-daughter of Peter Heywood, with access to the Heywood family papers, she was in a position to know and the presumption must be that he returned to Lewis. This is borne out by the fact that the oral tradition, half a century after his death, was that he had been "king of a South Sea Island." Such a tradition could not have arisen from the general literature on the BOUNTY. Nor could it have arisen from Morrison's own written account of his life in Tahiti because it had not then been published. It must have come *viva voce* from himself.

The principal identifiable transmitter of the oral tradition about Morrison's identity was Lillias, daughter of Kenneth Morison (Coinneach mac Mhaighstir Mhurchaidh) a merchant in Stornoway, and wife of Ensign Donald Morison, who was tacksman at Cross until he emigrated to America where he was embroiled in the American War of Independence, on the Loyalist side. Both Lillias and her husband were related to the mutineer. Ensign Donald kept a rough and rather disorganised letter book for some years after his return to Scotland at the end of the American War. The letter book survives in the archives of Stornoway Pier and Harbour Commission having, presumably, been left among the official papers by accident when the Ensign's grandson was an employee of the Commission. Although it is not conclusive, because of the gaps and general confusion in the order of the entries, the letter-book indicates that Lillias was not in Lewis at the time of the Mutineer's return, unless, of course, she paid a visit home which was not referred to in her husband's recorded correspondence. If not in Lewis she was resident in Edinburgh and might well have met the mutineer on his passage to or from Stornoway. Lillias was 28 years old at the time of Morrison's reprieve. She passed the story to her granddaughter, Margaret Morison, (Magaidh a' Chaiptein) who was nearly thirty when her grandmother died at the age of 100. Magaidh a' Chaiptein passed it to my aunt, Jessie Morison, who was 29 when Maggie died at the age of 66.

How much James Morrison told, how much he had time to tell in the "cèilidhs" he must have attended in the homes and inns of Lewis we can only guess. Certainly he had a plentiful treasury to draw on. In addition to the story of his adventure as told in the Journal he wrote, "An Account Of the Island of Tahiti and the customs of the Islanders," which runs to almost forty thousand words. It is well organised and written in a lively style. He observed every aspect of island life acutely and in great detail. He enquired into the meaning of customs he did not readily understand. He was well read in the travel literature of the period and knew when he was adding to the then existing knowledge of people in Britain about the Pacific islands. In places, for instance, he says he will not enter into further detail because the point has already been discussed by Captain Cook. The inference is that he believed the rest of his information was new. The fact that Morrison's Journal and "Account" were not published for more than a century after his death deprived them of that claim to freshness or originality. They were out of date before the general reader got access to them and survive only as curiosities of travel literature.

The "Account" does merit study for the light it casts, obliquely, on Morrison himself and it was not wholly without influence even in its own day. He concludes his book with these words: "Such is the best account that I have been able to collect of these islands and their inhabitants, who are without doubt the happiest on the face of the globe, and shall now proceed to give such a Vocabulary of their language as we were able to obtain during our stay among these islands." There is, however, no Vocabulary!

When the first missionaries from the London Missionary Society went to Tahiti, some years after the BOUNTY'S visit, they were armed with a Vocabulary which enabled them to converse with the natives. There is good reason to believe it was the Vocabulary missing from Morrison's book. Credit for the missionaries' Vocabulary is sometimes given to Peter Heywood, the midshipman tried and reprieved with Morrison, in whose family Morrison's papers remained for many years. That does not imply that Heywood stole the credit for another man's work. Morrison's use of the word "we" in describing the compilation of the Vocabulary, implies that it was a joint endeavour among the prisoners; no doubt helping to occupy the weary hours in captivity while they were awaiting the Court Martial. It is I think a fair assumption that Morrison took the initiative in organising the compilation, as he did with the building of the boat but others did much of the work.

So far as Morrison himself is concerned, the "Account" although it is in no way a personal apologia, reveals that he had a remarkable ability to understand, and imaginatively enter into, the feelings of other people, even when they were engaged in activities which he found repugnant. He was a deeply religious man but there is no intolerance, dogmatism or censoriousness - the three common sins of the devout! - in his attitude to the pagans of Tahiti. His devoutness is illustrated in a passage from the Journal where he says, "We kept the holidays in the best manner that we could, killing a hog for Christmas dinner, and reading prayers, which we never omitted on Sundays... We informed the natives of the reason of our observing these holidays, and especially Christmas Day; all of which [they] seemed to regard with attention, and readily believed all that we could inform them of, never doubting that the Son of God was born of a woman... They always behaved with much decency when present at our worship, though they could not understand one word... Several were desirous to have it explained to them and some of them wished to learn our prayers which they all allowed to be better than their own. Those who were constantly about us knew when our Sunday came and were always prepared accordingly. Seeing that we rested on that day they did so likewise and never made any diversions on it. One of them was always ready to hoist the ensign on Sunday morning and if a stranger happened to pass and enquire the meaning they were told that it was Mahana 'Atooa (God's Day), and though they were intent on their journey [they] would stop to see our manner of keeping it and would proceed next day, well pleased with the information."

The "Account" begins with a detailed description of the islands: the latitude and longtitude, extent, general appearance, climate, soil and produce, often illuminated with vivid little vignettes. "The highest mountains teem with innumerable cascades forming a delightful prospect. Thirty of these may be counted pouring from a high mountain behind Maatavye called Orafwhanna which water the neighbouring valleys and before it reaches the sea forms many small rivers and brooks all of which are excellent water, being produced by springs, some of which issue from the solid rock."

The comment that dogs "are here esteemed a delicacy and are allowed by former Voyagers to equal an English lamb," seems to imply that he did not sample dog's flesh himself but he does seem to write from personal experience, and with some feeling, about a root, "the leaves of which make excellent greens having a taste something like our asparagus," because he adds, "If they are not sufficiently dressed they cause an itching in the fundament for several hours after they are eaten." You can almost see him scratch!

He refers to other roots which are hot and biting, and describes how one in particular, "resembling a potato but bitter to the taste" is prepared in a process lasting five or six days to produce a "fine flour and makes excellent puddings and pancakes." The versatile bread fruit tree, which "grows to the size of an oak," provided the islanders with "food, raiment, timber for houses and canoes, and pitch for their seams... If [the fruit is] gathered before it falls its colour inside when baked is yellowish and its consistence like that of a potato though the taste is not like anything I recollect in Europe, America or India." That reference implies direct personal knowledge of India, and the point is reinforced a few pages later when he says of the fayee or mountain plantain "as I never saw any of them in the East or West Indies I suppose they are peculiar to these and the other islands in the South Seas." What is the significance of this? Is Morrison presuming a knowledge of the produce of India and the East Indies on the scraps of information he picked up as a prisoner on the voyage home to his trial, or does it, in effect, tells us that during the four missing years between the HIND and the BOUNTY he made a voyage to the East?

Among the curiosities he mentions are the nuts of the hootdoo tree "about the size of a sheep's heart, of a black colour, which have the property when put into the holes in the reef where the fish resort, to stupify them, so that they never attempt to escape but suffer themselves to be taken." He also mentions some of the plants newly introduced by Europeans such as tobacco and Indian corn, the latter "first introduced by the BOUNTY." The Europeans were delighted to find that the Indian corn grew luxuriantly with very little trouble, but the natives were rather contemptuous "alleging that they have plenty of food and it is therefore no use to labour for what nature has abundantly supplied."

Page after page is filled with descriptions of how they make all the articles in daily use: cloth of various kinds, matting, houses, thatch, canoes, scents, dyes, decorations for festive occasions and drugs, especially a concoction "from the stems of a coarse grass called mo'oo, something like hemp," which "almost immediately deprives them of the use of their limbs and speech but does not touch the mental faculty... They appear in a thoughtful mood and frequently fall backwards before they are finished eating. Some of their attendants then... chafe their limbs all over till they fall asleep and the rest retire and no noise is suffered to be made near them... After about a fortnight's constant use the skin comes all over with a white scurf like the land scurvy and the eyes grow red and fiery and the body lean and meagre but, on being left off for a few days, the scales fall off and the skin then becomes clear and smooth and they soon grow fat and wholesome to view. This gives me reason to think that this nauseous draught must be very wholesome as those who use it are seldom afflicted with disorders of any kind and those who use it regularly are some of the oldest men in the country."

The birds, the beasts and the fish are listed in the same detail as the plants and trees. Where fish are concerned there are descriptions of the tackle used to catch them and the manner in which it is made. "Every fisherman makes his own hooks, lines, twines and every article of his gear, which are not to be equalled by anything but their skill in using them... Their hooks are made of pearl shell, bone, wood & of different construction for the different fish, some being made to answer the double purpose of hook and bait. They make their hooks by grinding them into form with water and sand and with a drill made of a shark's tooth. They make a hole into which they introduce a sprig of the coral as a file and work out the inside part and, as they have no beard they make the point to round in towards the back of the hook, inclining downward, and seldom lose a fish after they get it once hooked." He describes their use of pots, seines and cast nets "both square and circular" and their method of following a shoal with a group of canoes until they surround it with nets when they sometimes dive overboard and catch the fish by hand.

"The most curious part of this fishery is that of taking the hedge hog fish and the sea cat - the one being so full of prickles that they can take hold no where but by the eyes... and the others adhere so close to the rocks that it is as much as two men can do at times to haul them off... This may seem an odd method of fishing but I have seen it attended with good success and the divers return in a few hours with large strings of fine fish. In the night they fish in canoes and on the reefs for different sorts of fish, which they draw round them by lighting bundles of reeds and have nets made to scoop them up and put into their baskets."

In the Golden Cockerel edition of the "Account" Morrison's description of fishing methods runs to ten large pages. The extent to which it is based on direct personal observation is shown by his account of "a kind of conger eel of a brownish colour with a green border round the fins from head to tail. These fish are of a poisonous nature to some and if eaten give the most excruciating pain while others who eat it feel no effects... As they have a remedy for it... I partook of one... without feeling the smallest effects from its poison while another who ate of the same fish was almost raving mad. His body and limbs swelled to an extraordinary degree and [were] covered with red blotches and at the same time the hands and feet [were] itching in such a manner as to be insufferable and burning as if on fire. The eyes [were] swelled and fiery and to all appearance fit to start from their sockets." The victim recovered after about eight days and a dose of medication by the priests. As well as the eel Morrison mentions a red crab "not bigger than a small horse bean which [they] say will kill a man instantly if he eats it." He drew the line at sampling that.

From natural resources the observant islander turned his attention to social economics. Trade he notes, "is generally carried on by making presents rather than by exchange of commodities." Cloth matting and oil were particularly important items of traffic "if it may be so called." His detailed account of the manufacture of fine white cloth from the cloth plant again has Hebridean overtones. He gives a lively picture of the women beating a piece of cloth to its proper breadth, accompanied by a song "given by one and chorused by the rest". The finished cloth, he tells us, was bleached in the morning dew to make it white or wrapped with leaves and notched bark "which makes it beautifully clouded with different shades of brown." Although the cloth was beaten out from the bark of trees some of it was so very fine that, at a small distance, it might be mistaken for "the labour of the loom." When a landed man - his phrase! - wanted a large quantity of cloth in a hurry as many as two hundred women might attend, "armed with beam and beetle... making as much noise as so many coopers." He goes into considerable detail on the dyeing of cloth, describing how they achieved "a beautiful red" from berries, various shades of brown from the bark of different trees, jet black from "a coconut tree which grows in swampy ground," yellow from roots and grey from the bark of the sloe tree. Sometimes they infused sweet scents with their dyes.

The women made matting and wove light baskets while the men made wicker baskets from a running vine called eayeeay. These, he says, were equal in workmanship to those of Europe. "Their platters, stools, chests &c are all neatly made and well finished and are the more admirable when we consider their tools which are no other than stone adzes of different sizes, shells, sharks' teeth, bones, sand to scour, and fish skins to polish."

Returning to the theme of trade or barter he explains how a man who needs more cloth than he can get from his immediate neighbours goes to "the people who inhabit the valleys" whose chief employment is making cloth. He takes with him a large hog or two and strikes a bargain with someone who is prepared to call his neighbours together to find out which of them are prepared to help. When that is known, the hogs are killed and there is a great feast, after which the women get round to making the cloth. If they fail to produce the goods on time, the owner of the hogs is free to plunder the home of the man with whom he made the bargain "as for a theft... If a man wants a house or a canoe built, he employs one or more carpenters, paying them beforehand one half of what shall be judged the value of the work they are to perform in hogs, cloth, oil, matting &c and finds them in provisions all the time they are at work... When the work is complete he pays the remainder according to agreement, but should he refuse or neglect [to pay] and the neighbours think the work worth the stipulated agreement, then they may plunder him of all that he is worth." Similar arrangements were made if a man wanted someone to supply him with fish for a period or cultivate a piece of ground for him, the whole or half of the stipulated price being always paid in advance. Their principal method of conducting trade, he adds is "by gifts and presents to each other, and it is not common to refuse the greatest stranger amything he stands in need of whether food raiment or anything else."

Morrison then turns his attention to the political structure of the island, as he understood it. The chiefs were supported by voluntary contributions and free gifts "which however the people must not refuse to make if they have the wherewithal to supply the demand; if they have not, it is not expected." Such a system was workable in a society where all the assets were tangible and everyone knew to the last cooconut how much his neighbours had. It is different in a world where the assets of the wealthy are concealed in Swiss bank accounts or laundered in the Cayman Islands.

He has a good deal to say about the intricate taboos which regulated the islanders' behaviour but he does not use the word; in fact it was first used in English only fifteen years before he wrote. He notes that the chiefs were "taller, stouter and of a different appearance from the common people and their women are also larger and fairer than the lower classes. They have in general a more serious and thoughtful turn and are more accomplished, they are always superior to them in all things either labour or diversion. Their only pride is in cleanliness and generosity for which they are remarkable." Many of the chiefs were over six feet and they had "no conception that a short man can be a chief... If any person speaks disrespectfully of a chief he is sure to suffer death, and should one chief speak ill of another it would instantly bring on a war." Here he was, as usual, drawing directly on his own experience having been reluctantly sucked into some of their conflicts.

"The people in general are of the common size of Europeans," he writes. "The men are strong well limbed and finely shaped; their gait easy and genteel and their countenance free open and lively, never sullied by a sullen or suspicious look. Their motions are vigorous active and graceful and their behaviour to strangers is such as declares at first sight their humane disposition... They are of an even and unruffled temper, slow to anger and soon appeased, and as they have no suspicion so they ought not to be suspected... An hour's acquaintance is sufficient to repose an entire confidence in them."

He goes on to describe in detail how the men dressed their hair and beards, suggesting that a painter might find among them an excellent model for a Hector or Achilles. The women took much pride in keeping their hair in exact order "and decorate their head with sweet flowers... They are careful to keep it free from vermin, and for that reason were exceedingly fond of our combs as they were also of scissors to trim it, a shark's took being the only instrument they have for cutting hair. Though the women hate to have vermin in their heads as much as we do yet the men are not so delicate and many eat them."

In an account of the Tahitians' method of making war he says a man who is wounded in battle is never esteemed a hero, however many of the enemy he has killed. "A man who suffers himself to be wounded does not know how to defend himself and it is more honour to return with whole than broken bones."

He must have spent many hours discussing religion with his Tahitian friends. He not only describes the practices he saw but attempts to interpret the thinking behind them, although one wonders at times how far he was importing into the explanations he got concepts from his own background rather than theirs. He thought of them as rather like some of the ancient Jewish tribes and their traditions reminded him of the Old Testament. Apart from their main gods he writes, "They have a number of inferior deities, every man and woman having a guardian angel whom they suppose to be the souls of their departed relatives who have been deified for their good works and whose business it is to watch and protect them while on earth. And as they believe that every man shall be rewarded with happiness in the next world so they take leave of this without any anxiety and when they die take leave of their friends with as much composure as if they were going on a journey... They say that when they dream the soul is absent, and talking of dreams they say 'My soul saw such a soul &c.'" "They believe that the sun and moon are the original parents of all the stars and, when they are in eclipse they say they are in the act of generation."

He found their ideas about creation "not unlike what we read in the Bible" and some of their accounts of the stars reminded him of Greek fables. "As they are superstitious in all their customs and think that every transgression against God and man is attended with punishment so they have but few that can be called real crimes among a people who have no other law but that of nature... Though they maintain that their method is right as they are taught, they allow that another is as good and are charitable enough to allow that every man, if he worships his God as he is taught, is in a fair way to happiness and will meet such reward as he deserves, but that this world is the sole place of punishment."

The relations between the sexes is commented on in several places. He notes that women take no part in religious ceremonies, have no place of worship for themselves and never enter one but at their birth but "they are no less in the eyes of the Deity than those who are permitted to be partakers of religious rites." He devotes a great deal of space to describing the Morai or sacred places, how they are built and the ceremonies conducted in them especially the fantastical decoration of the priests with red and black feathers "of which they suppose the Deity to be immoderately fond as he always makes use of birds when he descends on earth."

The marital habits in Tahiti would have been more foreign to James Morrison at the end of the 18th century than to us in the free and promiscuous years of the late twentieth. In some ways we almost seem to be regressing to the Tahitian standards. "When they marry they never join with their blood relations but a man may take two sisters and a woman two brothers at the same time if they are all agreeable. It is looked upon [as] a piece of great friendship for a man to cohabit with the wife of his adopted friend, if she is agreeable: the adopted friend being always accounted as a brother... If a man has a reason to part with his wife he informs her of it, to which she mostly agrees deeming it reproachful to remain after such notice. He then divides all his goods and chattels with her, and she leaves him and takes the female children with her, leaving him the males. If she lives single she always claims the rights of a wife, and though they do not cohabit, always look on each other as friends and apply to each other for any little property which at any future period of their separation they may stand in need of.

"If a man finds his neighbour, or one who is not his adopted friend, in the act of adultery with his wife, he has the law in his own hands and may, if he thinks proper, put one or both of them to death with impunity, or punish his wife with stripes and plunder the house of the offender. The latter is the most common but I have known two men killed who were taken in the act and no further enquiry made than the acknowledgment of the parties present to certify the fact."

Although he is a sympathetic observer, he is by no means uncritical. In an elaborate account of the ceremonies connected with marriage and childbirth, he says the honour and dignity of the head of the family is immediately transferred to the first born child, on the theory that the child is the fruit of both father and mother and therefore superior to either. Until the ceremonies connected with the transfer of power from parents to child take place, the child is sacred and surrounded, as we would say, with taboos. The ordinary folk carried out these ceremonies at once but those of high rank delayed as long as possible "under colour of it being grand to have their children in a sacred state, though in fact it is that they may continue longer in power [themselves]."

He has a great deal to say about marriage ceremonies and general social customs, like joining noses when they meet, after even a short absence, so that they can draw in each other's breath through the nostrils as a token of their great love. Sometimes, he says, this "embrace" is continued so long they almost suffocate each other. In different parts of the island the chiefs had houses in which they could shelter when they travelled. When a chief made use of one of these, he sent a message to the nearest person of his own rank and immediately he and his party were supplied with all the provisions they needed. Nothing produced by nature was regarded as a gift when given to someone else and no one was ever thanked for giving it. Indeed there was no word in the language to express thanks. A "thank you" was a deed not a word.

"It is no disgrace for a man to be poor, and he is no less regarded on that account, but to be rich and covetous is a disgrace to human nature. Should a man betray such a sign and not freely part with what he has, his neighbours would soon put him on a level with the poorest of themselves, by laying his possessions waste and hardly leave him a house to live in. A man of such a description would be accounted a hateful person and before they would incur such a name as that of covetous or stingy, they would part with the cloth off their back and go naked until they got more."

Even in such a paradise, however, there were jealously guarded boundaries to their land with little carved wooden images of men set up to mark them. In the absence of written records boundary disputes were decided on the say so of neighbours, a process assisted by the deeply held belief that a man would be afflicted with illness if he encroached on the property of a neighbour.

An account of their feasts and ceremonies, and descriptions of their buildings and building methods, is followed by a long account of the various types of canoe, their construction, their use, the manner in which sails are handled, their advantages and disadvantages compared with European vessels. It may seem strange he says, to European navigators how these people find their way at sea without the help or knowledge of letters, figures or instruments of any kind, but their judgment and their knowledge of the motion of the heavenly bodies enabled them to steer over long distances "with some degree of exactness."

The building of a large war canoe, or a canoe to be dedicated to the deity, began with a great feast. There were lesser feasts "at the finishing of every streak" and another great feast at completion when the vessel was dressed in cloth, fine matting, breastplates and red and black feathers. The final feast included a sacrifice, sometimes of a hog but often of a man. Again, as will appear, Morrison was writing of things he had actually witnessed.

"When men are wanted for such occasions the chief assembles the retirras [sub chiefs] at the Morai and a feast is made, at which none must be present but those who are by birth entitled to give their opinion. He then informs them of the business which they, however, know beforehand. They then agree among themselves about the fittest man and if any have been guilty of blasphemy or has been a most notorious thief and has escaped punishment, they fix on him and one of themselves undertakes to kill him. He watches his opportunity, the business being mostly kept a secret till he is killed, which is generally at night, when the man appointed to kill him, finding where he sleeps, knocks him in the head with a stone and gets his servants to make a large basket of coconut leaves into which they put the body... They are careful not to disfigure the face as that would make them unfit for an offering and another must be got instead, for which reason they generally strike them on the back of the head or the neck...

"If a man of property is found guilty of a crime which deserves death he is punished as well as the poorest in the island. An instance of this we saw at the time the young king was invested with the royal marro - one of the first men in Morea being sacrificed for attempting to stop the flag from passing through his land on that island. During the celebration of that ceremony numbers of human sacrifices were made and many who knew themselves guilty took sanctuary about our houses where they knew themselves perfectly safe, as they knew our aversion to such horrid practices, but we could not protect all although we often tried in vain to [persuade] the chiefs to drop their barbarous customs, who always gave the answer, 'If we do there will be no chiefs.' However we protected all who took sanctuary with us and though surrounded by the most notorious thieves on the island our property was always safe."

Turning his attention to food he says: "The men and women eat separately and for that reason each family has two houses except a man chooses to reside in his wife's house, then each takes one end... The women have their own particular trees for bread and can eat no other and must have particular people to catch fish for them. Should a shark, turtle, porpoise, albicore, dolphin or cavally, which are sacred fish, be caught by their fishermen they cannot eat of them but may dispose of them to whom they please. It has been supposed by most former voyagers that they were also forbidden to eat pork but in this they were most certainly mistaken, for if any woman has an inclination to keep her hogs penned and prevent them from feeding on any other ground than their own they may eat pork."

A great deal of detail follows about the manner in which meals are prepared and eaten, and the taboos surrounding food, although, as I have said, the word taboo is not used. They still got fire by rubbing two sticks and reciting a prayer. Without the prayer they thought there would be no fire. When they needed an oven they made a hole in the ground, filled it with wood and stones and set fire to it. When the wood was burnt and the stones were red hot, they wrapped the food in leaves and placed it on the hot stones covering it with grass and earth. When the oven was opened the food was removed so carefully that not a particle of sand or earth got into it.

From food he goes on to tatooing, describing the tools and dyes used, the patterns favoured, the parts of the body tatooed, or not tatooed, on men or women. It was a painful process, accompanied by loud lamentations which gave the impression that it was being imposed by force although it was always done at the "patient's" request. The young women were better than the men at bearing the pain but even they could not bear to have more than one side of the body tattooed at a time. A year might pass before they could face the second stage of the operation. The girls were generally attended by some of their female friends who held them when they struggled with the pain. "They are often in such a passion [with pain] as to strike even their own mother if she should happen to be performing that office, [but] she must not return [the blow] on pain of death."

He moves into more tranquil territory when he describes their games and diversions on land and sea: wrestling, javelin throwing, singing, dancing, swimming, but touches several times on the less happy effects of contact between natives and Europeans. Even that early in contact between the races the Europeans had introduced venereal diseases "for which death is their only remedy... As soon as anyone is known to have it no person will touch them nor theirs; nor will they bathe near them in the river. Their food is also carried to them, they not being suffered to touch any but what is for themselves. Their companions forsake them and they languish out the remainder of their days in a miserable manner. Though they want no food yet they pine at seeing themselves neglected and soon die."

The faults, however, were not all on one side. Those who make a trade of beauty," writes Morrison, "know how to value it and, when they come on board, bring with them their pimps or procurers, under the denomination of relations, to receive and secure the price, and these ladies are as well qualified to act their part as any of their profession in other countries and are no way bashful in making their demands... However the ladies who act these parts are not to be taken as a standard for the whole [any] more than the nymphs of the Thames or sirens of Spithead are to be taken as samples of our own fair country women."

This is a much abbreviated summary of Morrison's book: little more than an extended index to the whole. His "Account" ends with a passage which displays the extent to which he had established rapport with the natives, while so many others singularly failed:

"They never compare any kind of food to a man's head, for which reason the heads of animals have a different name, nor can they think of eating anything that has touched a man's head, and nothing can offend them more than laying a hand on their heads. Brown, who was left here by Captain Cox, was thought worse than a cannibal for carrying provisions on his head, of which none ever partook with him, though they were always ready to excuse him saying he knew no better which, in fact, was nearly the case, but it was his sole study to be contrary to them in everything and he took more pains that way than in conforming to their ways, which made him disagreeable to them all."

As one reads the "Account" one is continually reminded of the attitude and style, although not the content, of Martin Martin's description of life in the Western Isles written almost exactly a hundred years earlier and based in part, at least insofar as Lewis is concerned, on information supplied by John Morison of Bragar, the mutineer's great great-grandfather.

18

A TALE OF TWO GUNNERS

When James Morrison joined the BOUNTY Britain was at peace; thousands of navymen were 'on the beach' and he was glad to take any post that was available. After the trial, the situation was very different. Around the time the crew of the BOUNTY mutinied in the South Seas, opting for the perceived paradise of Tahiti in preference to the harshness of naval discipline, the people of France rebelled against their absolute monarch, Louis XVI, opting for the perceived paradise of a republic, guided by the principles of liberty, equality and fraternity, in preference to the grinding poverty in which they lived. The yearnings of the BOUNTY'S crew led to mutiny, murder and hangings. The yearnings of the French peasants led to the Reign of Terror and the battle of Waterloo.

On Sept 20th 1792, just two days after Morrison was condemned to death, the ragged levies of the nascent French Republic withstood the assault of an army of disciplined Prussian veterans at the historic battle of Valmy. Goethe, the German poet and philosopher, who was a witness of the battle, noted in his diary, "From this place and this day dates a new epoch in the history of the world, and you will be able to say; I was there." It would be surprising if a man of Morrison's courageous and independent mind, did not respond to the wave of enthusiasm which carried the doctrines of the French Revolution across Europe and around the world. At the same time, he was under naval discipline, and had just received a sharp lesson in the penalties of disobedience.

The hectic atmosphere which prevailed, and the erratic fault line the French Revolution opened up in Britain, are reflected for us in the pages of the "Glasgow Mercury". On the radical side of the fault line, the "Mercury" records the formation of an association dedicated to reform, with Thomas Muir of Huntershill as Vice-president. On the reactionary side, it records meetings of various incorporated trades in Glasgow - weavers, cordiners, maltmen, gardeners and wrights - all asserting that Britain was prosperous and any change in the constitution was undesirable.

Britain was not yet at war with France but was clearly drifting in that direction. In January 1793 the Government offered a bounty to every seaman who joined the navy. The Magistrates of Glasgow backed up the recruiting drive by offering an additional two guineas to every able seaman from the city who enlisted, and a guinea to every ordinary seaman. The magistrates or the compositor got things rather confused however, when they decreed that claimants of the bounty, "shall not be above the age of 15 nor under the age of 20." At the same time eight regiments of Fencibles were raised for home defence: one of them by Seaforth.

The main focus of attention in the preparations for war was the assembling of a great fleet at Portsmouth, led by HMS VICTORY. On January 9th the "Mercury" reported that, thanks to the great exertions of the officers and crew, the VICTORY, the most heavily armed ship in the navy, "will take in her guns tomorrow, and will go out to Spithead next week."

The following issue reported that HMS VICTORY had left the harbour and gone to Spithead. "The saluting batteries and platforms were crowded with people from all ranks to see this beautiful floating castle pass, and the Marine Band played "God Save the King" from the time she got abreast of the Powder Bridge till she saluted the broad pendant at Spithead." The same issue reported the execution of Louis XVI despite Tom Paine's plea for banishment rather than death. "I prefer an error occasioned by humanity to an error occasioned by severity. The mischief he has done has been the effect of prejudice and his condition. Had he been the son of a farmer, I am certain he would not have been a bad man." A fortnight later the "Mercury" reported that the Lord Provost of Glasgow had just received a letter from William McDowall MP saying: "I have this moment been informed that Mr Dundas has received a letter from Ostend that war was declared against Great Britain by decree of the [French] National Convention on the 31st of January."

It took twelve days, after the news of the French declaration of war was picked up by British agents in Ostend, before Glasgow heard the news. It was in that period James Morrison arrived back in Portsmouth and was drafted to HMS VICTORY. Although news of the declaration of war was not yet known in Glasgow, it would have been known in Portsmouth, when he reported for duty. The town was in a turmoil as the fleet prepared for sea. A few days later the press gang made a general sweep through the town at noon and picked up nearly a hundred reluctant seamen.

Two other items in the news, at that time, would have interested Morrison more than most people. Despatches had come to hand from the Pacific reporting that his old enemy, Capt Bligh, had got back to Tahiti, to complete the bread fruit mission interrupted by the mutiny. There Bligh learned that the shipwrecked crew of a South Sea whaler, the MATILDA, had recently reached the island after six days in open boats. The Captain of the MATILDA had left Tahiti before Bligh arrived, on a Bristol vessel bound for the west coast of America. The second mate and two seamen has also left in one of their own boats, in a courageous attempt to get to Botany Bay. The rest were still in Tahiti. Bligh persuaded most of them to return with him in his new command the PROVIDENCE or its consort the ASSISTANT. Four of the seamen, however, succumbed to the allurements of Tahiti and settled in with the natives.

Having been to Australia himself, Morrison would have been less excited than London was by the second item of news: the arrival of Governor Phillips from Botany Bay with two Australian aborigines, a man and a boy, four kangaroos, and a "number of other animals peculiar to the country." The "Mercury's" correspondent concluded that the aborigines, although skilled in catching fish and trapping kangaroos, were quite incapable of civilisation, and formed "a lower order of the human race."

There is a minor problem about Morrison's arrival on HMS VICTORY. His age is given correctly in the muster rolls but in one list his place of birth is given as Bandon, Cork. It should be noted, however, that the earlier list, which gives no place of birth, places Morrison as number 635. The second list, which gives the Bandon birthplace, lists him as 636. There are other Morrisons in the same area of the list, and it is possible that two entries have been confused. There can be no doubt the first entry relates to James Morrison of the BOUNTY because it is possible to follow his progress forward from that point from ship to ship until his death.

HMS VICTORY was flagship of a fleet of 22 ships of the line, and many smaller craft, preparing at Portsmouth. It must have given Morrison a wry smile when he learned that the Admiral, whose flag the VICTORY carried, was Lord Hood, who presided over the Court Martial which condemned him to hang. Morrison was a supernumerary on the VICTORY. As soon as the fleet reached Toulon he was transferred to HMS LUTINE as gunner's mate, and finally as master gunner, achieving the rank for which he had qualified by examination four years before joining the BOUNTY. The British navy had the free run of Toulon harbour at the time, because the south of France was still held by the Royalists. The city was closely beseiged, however, by a Revolutionary army, with which there served another gunner, from a very different island, who was about to emerge on the stage of history for the first time - the little Corsican, Napoleon Bonaparte.

We have no way of discovering the personal details of James Morrison's service during the Revolutionary and Napoleonic Wars. He was too small a cog in the machine. We can, however, reconstruct the circumstances in which he served, and, from his steady progress in the navy, we know that he must have done his duty competently in the situations in which he was placed.

When HMS VICTORY arrived off Toulon, in August 1793, France was even more deeply divided by the Revolution than Britain. Both fleets, in those years, were in a mutinous state. In the British Fleet seamen mutinied, but were subdued by the officers, and the ringleaders were hanged. In the French Fleet officers mutinied but the seamen subdued them and the ringleaders went to the guillotine. The Terror was raging in Paris but in the South of France there was a reaction against the bloodletting even in places like Marseilles, which had been fiercely Republican in the first flush of the Revolution. In Toulon, the Commander in Chief was a Monarchist: his deputy a Republican. Most of the sailors in the Toulon Fleet were Republicans but many of their officers, and most of the townsfolk were Monarchists. At the outbreak of hostilities, France had a powerful navy. It had probably never been so well placed to conduct a naval war with Britain. Toulon was the main base, where most of the ships of the line were built and where many of them were based. Three of the ships on which Morrison was subsequently master gunner - the LUTINE, the TONNANT and the GENEREUX - were French vessels, based at Toulon when HMS VICTORY arrived off the port. They came into British hands at different times, and in different ways, in a long drawn out naval war of fluctuating fortunes.

The LUTINE was captured in August, 1793, shortly after the VICTORY arrived at Toulon. She was a 36 gun frigate. She was lost on the Dutch coast six years later, with only two survivors, but Morrison had left her long before then. His stay on the LUTINE was relatively short as he was quickly promoted to a larger ship. One of the first changes the British navy made on vessels captured from the French was to instal a cannon in the captain's cabin. The French, being even more rank conscious than the British, regarded the captain's comforts as sacrosanct. The British took a pragmatic view and put guns wherever they could be used to advantage. This difference seems to have persisted, even during the early revolutionary fervour, when the French navy was democratised in other ways.

The arrival of the VICTORY completed the build up of British forces off Toulon. It had been a gradual process. Four separate squadrons, of varying strengths, had been sent to blockade the port, as ships became available. When Lord Hood arrived, with the main fleet, two commissioners came out from Toulon to treat with him for a joint effort to re-establish the Monarchy in France. Hood offered that, if the French ships were dismantled, and the British Fleet given access to the harbour, Britain would give all the support possible to the people of Provence to restore the monarchy. While the authorities in Toulon argued whether or not to accept the terms, the British negotiators slipped in and out in curious circumstances. To get to the Monarchists ashore they had to pass through the mainly Republican fleet. They went at night, hugging the shore so that their movements of their boats were hidden by the shadow of the cliffs. On more than one occasion, the British negotiators were arrested by Republican French sailors, and then liberated by the Monarchist mob ashore. In the end, the British Fleet got access to Toulon Harbour, which introduced an element of nationalism into the situation. Some French historians still maintain that Britain aimed to keep Toulon permanently, as they had kept Gibraltar. For a time, however, the uneasy alliance between the British and the French Monarchists kept Toulon open and the Austrian Emperor poured in troops, in a vain attempt to thwart the Revolution.

The French ships were ordered to go into the inner harbour and put their powder ashore. The officers complied but the sailors escaped into the interior and joined the French army closing in on the port. Footloose sailors, who continued to roam the streets of Toulon, were rounded up by the British, and, in what seems a quixotic gesture, were sent, under flag of truce, to Rochefort, Lorient or Brest, where they reinforced the French Revolutionary Fleet, in ports which offered a very much greater threat to Britain than did Toulon. British sailors were sent ashore to serve with the army. Whether Morrison was among them we have no way of knowing. Eventually the allies had 17,000 troops ashore but they were a strange mixture of British soldiers and sailors, French monarchists, Piedmontese, Neapolitans and Spaniards, squabbling with each other about the supreme command.

On the other hand, closing in, to raise the siege, were 30,000 Frenchmen, all fellow nationals, speaking one language, fired by revolutionary fervour, and led by five generals, including the newly promoted Napoleon Bonaparte, who had already identified the precise spot, on which he had to place his guns, in order to drive the British Fleet out of Toulon harbour, and who had devoted his organising genius to finding, or making, artillery for the task. He worked alongside his men, sleeping on the ground in his cloak when he needed rest. When he established a battery within pistol shot of the British lines, one gun crew after another was picked off by British marksmen. It looked as if the position would have to be abandoned: men were refusing to serve. "Call it 'the battery of the fearless,'" said Napoleon, and thereafter the position had its full complement of gunners. Even without the military genius of Napoleon the position of the Allies would have been hopeless. They were trying to defend a fifteen mile perimeter with inadequate numbers. The heights above the town were being captured one by one. The fleet was within gunfire and evacuation was inevitable. When Lord Hood took the decision to pull out, there was a scene of indescribable confusion shot through with threads of courage and extraordinary discipline. Retreating Neapolitans plunged into the sea and swam to their ships. The British fleet weighed anchor under heavy fire from red hot cannon balls. Some of the French ships, with Royalist officers and British crews, sailed out with Hood: among them the GENEREUX. Small boats, scurried across the harbour bringing wounded to the ships, or carrying demolition parties ashore. The French vessels which had been immobilised, or refused to sail with the British, had to be scuttled, but first their Republican crews had to be ferried ashore. Small parties of British sailors were employed transporting much larger numbers of the enemy ashore, while all around them Toulon harbour was ablaze. All the French stores along the seafront were torched. HMS VULCAN was set ablaze, with all her guns loaded, and aimed at the advancing Republican army. As the guns heated up, they went off, one by one, to delay the advance. Some French ships, which the Spaniards were to scuttle, were set on fire instead, with the result that they, too, blazed against the night sky, their cannon firing off at random, killing friend and foe alike. At one point there was a terrific explosion which, in the words of one eye-witness "awed into silence both beseigers and attacked." Other explosions followed and the retreating British fleet was showered with sparks.

What part Morrison played in this we do not know, or how he viewed the scene. It would be surprising if such an inveterate scribbler did not keep some notes but, if he did, they have long since vanished. We do know, however, that the other island gunner who was there, remembered the evacuation of Toulon to his dying day. Many years later, during his exile in St Helena, Napoleon wrote of the capture of Toulon: "The whirlwind of flames and smoke from the arsenal resembled the eruption of a volcano, and the thirteen vessels blazing in the roads were like so many displays of fireworks: the masts and forms of the vessels were distinctly traced out by the flames, which lasted many hours and formed an unparalleled spectacle." There is one thing missing from Napoleon's description: a reference to the panic-stricken Royalists - men, women and children - crowding the quays and crying for someone to take them from the city the Allies had abandoned. They had good reason for their fears. As soon as the battle for Toulon was over, the work of retribution began. Those suspected of collaboration with the British were sent to the guillotine in droves. Some French historians assert there were as many as two hundred executions a day, until the thirst for blood was sated.

When Lord Hood was driven out of Toulon, he based his fleet at Hyeres, an anchorage formed by a group of islands. His cousin, Sir Samuel Hood, arrived from Malta on HMS JUNO, without knowing that Toulon had fallen. The JUNO sailed boldly into the middle of the French Fleet and, in the darkness, ran aground. While her crew were struggling to get her off, a boat drew alongside and some heavily muffled figures boarded the JUNO. They said they were the port authorities and ordered the JUNO to sail into the inner harbour for quarantine. At that moment, the moon came from behind a cloud, revealing the Revolutionary tricolour on the port officials' hats. The crew of the JUNO realised they had sailed into a trap and were now prisoners of the French. The third lieutenant of the JUNO, feeling a faint night breeze on his cheek, whispered to his captain, "I believe we can fetch out, if we get her under sail." Sir Samuel immediately arrested the port officials, ordered them to be imprisoned below decks, and the JUNO sailed out to safety, with the French fleet and the shore batteries blasting at her as she went.

The incident must have aroused considerable talk throughout the fleet but, however interested Morrison might have been, he could not have foreseen the local connection. Exactly ten years later, Sir Samuel Hood married Seaforth's daughter, Mary, who later succeeded to the Seaforth estates. Sir Samuel, who was much older than his wife, died before she became proprietor of Lewis, but her marital, and financial history, would obviously have been very different, if the JUNO had been sunk by French guns, when Sir Samuel made his famous dash for freedom from the harbour at Toulon. With only one landlord, of almost unlimited power, and generally an absentee pursuing other interests, Lewis was particularly vulnerable to remote, haphazard events, affecting the individuals who had power over them, but completely unrelated to the island's needs or aspirations.

Another event which must have been of special interest to James Morrison, while he was gunner on the LUTINE, was the terrible accident which happened on HMS ARDENT. The ARDENT and the LUTINE were often engaged on the same duties after the fall of Toulon, when Admiral Hood was trying to secure control of Corsica, and help the Austrian forces who were opposing the French in the north of Italy. In April 1794, for instance, ARDENT and LUTINE were engaged together in a small battle off the town of Oneglia "with the help of the inhabitants, firing muskets." Oneglia, a small seaport, near Genoa, was a main supply route for the French Revolutionary Forces in Italy, where Napoleon was on the general staff, rapidly rising in rank and influence. The French army was living from hand to mouth, according to Robespierre, because of the British navy and the corsairs of Oneglia.

While engaged on a later operation of the same sort, the ARDENT caught fire and blew up. There were no survivors and the vessel vanished in smithereens. Nothing was found to identify her afterwards but a fragment of the quarter deck with the gun locks still attached to the beams. Another British vessel, HMS BOYNE, caught fire around the same time while lying at anchor with the rest of the fleet. It was assumed either that the ward room funnel which passed through the decks became overheated, or that a piece of lighted paper was carried by the wind into the Admiral's unoccupied cabin when the marines were practising musketry. As the fire flared up the whole fleet scattered. The BOYNE'S guns were loaded and went off in all directions as the fire got to them. Most of the crew got away safely, but when the ship finally blew up, one of her masts was seen soaring into the air above a plume of black smoke. After Morrison transferrred to the ROMULUS there was still another incident, which serves to underline the importance of the work of a master gunner in the British navy at the end of the 18th century. Taking part in a long sea chase of the French fleet in company with the ROMULUS, the ILLUSTRIOUS was sailing with her guns inboard but loaded, ready for instant action. Pitching in a heavy sea the shot rolled back and fore, setting up friction and creating heat, until the powder ignited in one of the guns. The explosion blew away the gun port and the ILLUSTRIOUS shipped so much water through the gap, she had to leave the line of battle and make for sheltered water. In the curious situation of the time, when no one was quite sure which side anyone was on, the Captain of the ILLUSTRIOUS accepted the guidance of a man who was on board the vessel in unexplained circumstances, but who claimed to be a pilot for the coast between Spezia and Genoa. The "pilot" ran the vessel aground and the sea was "making a fair breach over her" when night fell. In the morning the ILLUSTRIOUS made an attempt to get a hawser ashore, in the hope that it would be possible to get the crew away on rafts. This failed and the situation of the crew was extremely perilous when HMS ROMULUS, Morrison's ship, arrived on the scene, rescued the crew and the stores, and set the wreck on fire to prevent anything of value falling into enemy hands. One can imagine a man of Morrison's enquiring mind pondering on the manner in which the friction of loose shot in a loaded cannon had generated enough heat to destroy a ship, and the implications for his own position as a master gunner, responsible for the safety of the powder magazine and the guns.

During his service on the ROMULUS, Morrison was involved in two very controversial naval engagements. Hood had gone back to Britain and was succeeded by Admiral Hotham, who, despite his name, seems to have lacked the fire of some of those who served under him, like Nelson and Troubridge. Hotham twice sighted and chased a French fleet without bringing them to decisive action. He scored a victory of sorts in that the French fled, but he did nothing to diminish their growing strength in the Mediterranean, and was much criticised by some of his own subordinates for his lack of vigour. In the second chase, he flew his flag in the slowest vessel in the fleet, with the result that everyone was held back, in case they completely lost touch with their commanding officer. At times Hotham was seven miles astern of the vessels which headed the chase. He showed a good deal more energy, after his recall, when, as one naval writer puts it, "by dint of sheer interest he got himself made an Irish peer."

Morrison's ship the ROMULUS was more closely engaged in these two half-hearted naval actions than the Admiral himself. The first action took place after the French Fleet made a successful sweep of the Mediterranean, capturing a number of small warships and 25 heavily laden merchantmen. They also captured the British 74 gun ship BERWICK, which had been left behind in Corsica for repairs, when the rest of the fleet sailed. Hotham was cruising in the Gulf of Genoa when he picked up the French Fleet, sailing from Toulon with 5000 troops to retake Corsica, which Britain had occupied. The two fleets were fairly evenly matched. The French had fifteen ships of the line. Hotham had fourteen. There were two days of fruitless manoeuvring after the French fleet was sighted. Then the French 84 gun vessel CA IRA fouled another French vessel, and fell astern with her foremast and topmast gone. She was captured by the British and taken in tow by Morrison's ship. Two other French ships, on which he served after they were captured by the British, the GENEREUX and the TONNANT, were also involved in the running fight.

In 1796 the whole situation changed. The Spanish, who had been allies of the British at the capture of Toulon, and then neutral, re-entered the war on the side of the French. This presented the British Fleet with a vast new coastline to patrol, and they were forced temporarily to withdraw from the Mediterranean altogether, maintaining a blockade of the French and Spanish ports, as well as they could, from Gibraltar and the Tagus. In the three years from Lord Hood's arrival at Toulon until the British were driven out of the Mediterranean, Morrison, serving on three different ships - VICTORY, LUTINE and ROMULUS - was almost continuously at sea. He was involved in two important, if inconclusive, battles and numerous minor skirmishes afloat and ashore. He took part in the capture of Toulon, and then in the evacuation, when Napoleon's star first rose in the European sky. He got to know the Mediterranean and its islands even more intimately than he knew the West Indies and the South Pacific. With the troubles of the BOUNTY firmly behind him, he made steady progress in his chosen branch of the service, and was on the threshold of promotion to be master gunner on a ship of the line: the highest post open to a gunner in the Georgian navy.

19

MORRISON GOES TO CULLODEN

In the spring of 1797 James Morrison was transferred to HMS CULLODEN. It was one of the most important moves of his career; second only to his joining the BOUNTY. More important than the BOUNTY perhaps, in that it led inexorably to his death.

HMS CULLODEN was Morrison's first 74-gun ship as master gunner. He was now in charge of the armament of one of the most formidable vessels in the British navy of that time, under one of its most famous Captains. The name CULLODEN appears frequently in the naval histories of the period and also spills over into the popular fiction which has grown up round it. In Patrick O'Brien's novel "Post Captain" there is a reference to the CULLODEN'S pet crocodile. O'Brien is generally regarded as the best of contemporary historical novelists, but I do not know whether the reference to the crocodile is based on fact, or is simply a flourish of the novelist's imagination. It is of some interest that this particular novel has passing references to three of the ships on which Morrison served, at a time when he was the master gunner on each, which shows in an odd, reflective, roundabout way, that his career took him right to the heart of the action.

It would be wrong, I think, to assume that the name of his new vessel had the same resonance for Morrison as it has for us, although he was very much nearer the battle of Culloden than we are. We can enjoy the luxury of making judgments on the quarrels of the 18th century without any consequence for ourselves. Morrison had to choose between harbouring hatred for Cumberland's butchery after the battle, or making his peace with the new order, and pursuing his personal career according to its rules. At that time it was forbidden to speak Irish (or Gaelic) in the navy. Even in the middle of last century islanders were not accepted for the naval reserve unless they could speak English. The evidence is that Morrison sloughed off his Gaelic background and promoted an English-speaking identity, which was the "progressive" stance for a Highlander at that time.

The most important fact about the CULLODEN, so far as Morrison's subsequent career is concerned, was that the Captain - Thomas Troubridge, who later became Admiral Sir Thomas Troubridge - took a personal interest in Morrison's career. James Ralfe, in his massive book of naval biographies, covering the reign of George III, writes of Troubridge, "We believe him to have been in no respect inferior to the greatest and most admired commander that the British navy ever produced," thus making a direct comparison with Nelson himself. Troubridge did not belong to one of the old English naval families, nor to the aristocracy. His background was in some ways similar to Morrison's own. Morrison was the son of a tacksman and merchant. Troubridge was the son of a baker. He had none of the influence then almost essential for progress in the navy, and had to be content with a berth as cabin boy on a West Indian trader when opportunity unexpectedly beckoned. A relative of Troubridge was housekeeper to Sir Charles Saunders who had been a naval companion of Anson and was, at the critical moment for Troubridge, First Commissioner of the Admiralty. One of the housekeeper's duties was to massage the Admiral's feet, to ease the pain of his gout. One day when she was unwell, Troubridge's young sister stood in for her. The gouty old Admiral took a fancy to the girl, found out about her brother, and promptly had him accepted as a midshipman on HMS SEAHORSE. The Admiral died not long after Troubridge entered the navy, and the patronage which had given him a flying start came to an abrupt end. He had another lucky break however, when HMS SEAHORSE captured a very much larger French vessel. The Captain, when he was congratulated by the Commander in Chief confessed with unusual generosity, that his success had been entirely due to the gallantry of a young midshipman named Troubridge.

With this background Troubridge had a rather different attitude towards his subordinates from those who believed they were born to be obeyed, and there were two other incidents in his career, which might have made him more understanding of a man who had been accused of mutiny, like Morrison, than many captains of the time would have been. Early in the French Revolutionary War, Troubridge's ship the CASTOR was captured and he became a prisoner. The CASTOR was later recaptured by the British, along with the French vessel on which Troubridge was being held. Troubridge was court martialled for the loss of the CASTOR and, although he was acquitted, and immediately appointed to command CULLODEN, a much bigger ship, he knew something of the ordeal Morrison had endured at his own trial. He also had direct experience of a naval mutiny, which may have given him a better understanding of Morrison's predicament on board the BOUNTY. CULLODEN was lying at Spithead when, late one night, the greater part of the crew burst into open mutiny, removed the ladders and barricaded themselves below decks, taking the petty officers prisoner. Troubridge was ashore at the time, but his officers armed the marines and alerted him to the mutiny. For three days all the admirals in the port successively reasoned with the mutineers and eventually they agreed to return to duty. The ship's company was then mustered, and ten of the ringleaders seized. The prisoners were spread among the vessels of the fleet, so that they had no contact with each other until they were court martialled. Eventually two were acquitted and eight were hanged. The mutiny took place some years before Morrison joined the crew but the year in which he did join CULLODEN - 1797 - might well be described as the year of mutinies. There was a mutiny at Spithead on HMS ROYAL GEORGE. There was a mutiny off Cadiz. There was a general mutiny at the Nore. There was a mutiny on the convict ship LADY SHORE. There was a mutiny on HMS HERMIONE and there was a mutiny in the squadron at the Cape of Good Hope. These mutinies were caused by the harsh conditions in which seamen worked, the arbitrary conduct of officers, and the air of freedom which was wafting across the Channel from Revolutionary France.

When the ROYAL GEORGE was ordered to sea the men scrambled up the shrouds but instead of setting sail gave three cheers for their freedom. Their motivation was not primarily political, however. They had substantial grievances. They wanted, for instance, a 16 ounce pound. When food was measured out to them, they got only 14 ounces to the pound. The fault lay not with the pursers as individuals but with the system. The pursers were held accountable for all the stores on a ship and had to have some margin to cover natural wastage and loss by theft or spoilage. The mutiny on the ROYAL GEORGE was what in civil life would be a trade union matter. Petitions were addressed to Parliament and the Admiralty "couched in respectful language." Requests were made for better food, more vegetables, better attention for the sick, and leave to visit their families when the fleet was in port. The authorities offered an increase in pay. It was rejected by the men. The offer was increased. The men said "thank you" for the concessions offered, but stood out for more. Even when all their material demands had been met, the seamen refused to return to duty, until the King and Parliament issued a proclamation embodying the agreement and giving a blanket pardon to the ringleaders. Throughout the negotiations, the seamen made it clear that they would return to duty immediately, if the enemy fleet put to sea. At one point in the negotiations, however, an Admiral seized one of the seamens' delegates by the collar and shook him, swearing that he would have all the delegates hanged and every fifth man from the whole fleet for good measure, whereupon the delegates returned to the ROYAL GEORGE and hoisted the red flag. The bloody flag, as they called it. Immediately the men throughout the fleet loaded all the guns, and mounted watches, as if they were at sea. No violence was done to the officers, but they were not permitted to go ashore. The dispute was not settled until Lord Howe arrived from London with the text of an Act of Parliament granting the seamen's wishes, and extending the King's pardon to the ringleaders. It all ended with the seamen carrying Lord Howe shoulder high through the port. Most of the captains and officers immediately returned to their ships, but a few refused to resume their command and had to be replaced. Would it be stretching the probabilities to suggest that the bullies identified themselves in this way by an act of cowardice?

The significance of these events for James Morrison's career is that, against that background what happened on the BOUNTY, or at any rate his part in it, was of little significance, and must have been readily understood by the new breed of more tolerant officers, who were slowly transforming the ramshackle Georgian navy into the formidable fighting force which is generally associated with the name of Nelson. When James Morrison stepped on board the CULLODEN to take up his new post the only thing that mattered was his skill as a master gunner and that was soon put to the test.

The battle of Cape St Vincent, in 1797, was of crucial importance. It prevented the conjunction of a large Spanish fleet with the French fleet, assembled at Brest for Napoleon's planned invasion of Britain. A few days before the battle, HMS CULLODEN was in collision with HMS COLOSSUS. Masts and the bowsprit were so badly damaged that, in normal circumstances, the vessel would have been sent to the nearest port for repairs. Instead she was repaired at sea. At daybreak the ship had seemed an unmanageable shambles; by afternoon she reported ready for action. Sir John Jervis, who led the British fleet, had fifteen vessels under his command. The Spaniards had twenty seven, many of them more heavily armed than any vessel in the British fleet, and some of them much faster and more manageable than the British ships of the line. The British fleet had the advantage in the quality of the crews, discipline and seamanship, and general preparedness.

It was the rule in British warships of the period to have every gun manned and loaded, before daybreak, and every seaman at action stations. If, in the hours of darkness, a British vessel came close to an unseen enemy, it was prepared for instant action, when daylight revealed his presence. A generation which has watched man's first landing on the moon, in the comfort of our own homes, at the very moment it took place, must make a great effort of imagination to appreciate the utter blindness of a fleet at sea, when knowledge of an enemy's movements was restricted to the horizon visible from the crow's nest of a ship. The Spanish vessels were crewed mainly by soldiers, unused to shipboard, and seamen hurriedly conscripted, when Spain entered into alliance with France. They were just as brave, just as good fighting men, as the British, but they weren't sharpened and honed for the task in hand.

On the 13th February, a Portuguese frigate, commanded by a Scot, Captain Campbell, reported that the Spanish fleet was only five miles to windward. The Spanish fleet became aware of the presence of British ships at the same time but took little notice, as they thought it was a convoy of merchantmen. Even when they realised the vessels were British men-of-war, they were misled, by a passing American vessel, into thinking Sir John Jervis had only nine vessels with him, instead of fifteen. Early on St Valentine's day, 24 miles south west of Cape St Vincent, the south westerly tip of Portugal, HMS CULLODEN reported five sail. By 9.30 the CULLODEN, BLENHEIM and PRINCE GEORGE were giving chase, followed by the rest of the British fleet.

The day was hazy and, when the morning mist began to lift, the Spaniards were astonished to see fifteen British ships of the line sweeping down to cut their fleet in two, separating the five stragglers spotted by the CULLODEN from the main body. Because she had been the first to spot the enemy and give chase, CULLODEN led the British van, when the order was given to pass through the Spanish line, and cut the fleet in two. A broadside from the starboard guns of CULLODEN marked the start of the engagement. At one point there was a possibility that the whole British fleet would pass through the Spanish line, doing only superficial damage, and giving the enemy an opportunity to withdraw safely. Nelson, who was commodore of part of the British fleet on HMS CAPTAIN, saw the danger, and, without waiting for orders from the Commander-in-chief, changed course to cut off the Spaniard's retreat. HMS CULLODEN, under Troubridge, gave Nelson close support and these two vessels bore the brunt of the action. The CULLODEN was closely engaged by the SAN-YSIDRO and the SALVADOR-DEL-MUNDO. The SAN-YSIDRO was a 74 gun ship like the CULLODEN. The SALVADOR-DEL-MUNDO was an even more formidable vessel, mounting 112 guns. In fire power, the CULLODEN was out-gunned by more than two to one.

By the end of the action, the CULLODEN had sustained damage to the fore mast and main mast. Her rigging and her boats were shot to pieces. The hull was riddled both above and below water. She was leaking badly. Several of her guns had been put out of action. The casualties were out of all proportion to the rest of the fleet. The CULLODEN was one out of fifteen British vessels engaged in the Battle of Cape St Vincent, but she sustained a seventh of the fatalities, and a fifth of the wounded in the whole fleet. The official list of casualties seems small compared with the battles in our own time. The CULLODEN reported a lieut of marines, seven seamen and two marines killed, and 39 seamen and eight marines wounded. The official return, however, counts only those killed outright, and those suffering obviously from serious wounds. Many of those reported wounded, died shortly after the battle. Many of those not even listed as wounded, suffered injuries which later suppurated, leading to amputations, and frequently to death.

After the battle, four prizes and 3000 prisoners were taken into Lagos and then on to Lisbon. The sailing qualities of the Spanish fleet are attested by the fact that the prizes, with skeleton crews, arrived in the estuary of the Tagus before the British fleet. Most naval histories give Nelson the major credit for the victory at Cape St Vincent, although Sir John Jervis was Commander-in-Chief. Jervis himself singles out Troubridge and the CULLODEN for special praise. In a private letter to Lord Spencer, Jervis said Troubridge, on CULLODEN, had led the fleet "in a masterly style... That gallant officer opened his fire on the enemy ships to windward, which effectually separated the sternmost and leewardmost from the main body, then tacked, and prevented their rejunction. As soon as he had succeeded in passing through the enemy's fleet, he gave his starboard broadside to the nearest of their ships as he threw in stays: his example was followed by the van of our fleet and thus the action became nearly general."

News of the victory was received in London with something approaching delirium. Sir John Jervis was made Earl St Vincent. Two of his admirals were made baronets, and a third given a lucrative post abroad. Nelson was given the Order of the Bath and promoted Admiral. The fleet was thanked by both Houses of Parliament and gold medals were struck for all the flag officers and captains. All the first lieutenants in the fleet were promoted commander.

If James Morrison was master gunner on board HMS CULLODEN at the Battle of Cape St Vincent, he was right at the heart of the action in one of the great battles of British naval history. But was he? J. E. Chandler, whose book about Capt Bligh, "Beloved, Respected, and Lamented" is published by the Tradescant Trust, on behalf of the Museum of Garden History in Lambeth, where Capt Bligh is buried, says categorically that James Morrison fought in all four of Nelson's great victories: Cape St Vincent, the Nile, Copenhagen and Trafalgar. He is correct is saying Morrison was at the battle of the Nile. He is definitely wrong in saying Morrison was at Copenhagen or Trafalgar. One can only assume that he found one of the innumerable James Morrisons in the navy on the muster lists for these battles, and did not bother to check his real identity. So far as Cape St Vincent is concerned, there is an element of doubt.

The battle of Cape St Vincent was fought on February 14th, 1797. The warrant appointing Morrison master gunner of CULLODEN is also dated 14th February, 1797. He definitely was master gunner of CULLODEN very early in March, but the weight of evidence, as far as I can read the muster rolls and log books of the period, suggests that he was still on board HMS ROMULUS, at Gibraltar, on the day of the battle, and did not join HMS CULLODEN until the 2nd of March. He was formally entered on CULLODEN'S muster roll on 5th March.

I am reluctant to accept that he missed the battle although the evidence points that way. The idea of a Lewisman, on a ship named CULLODEN, at the battle of Cape St Vincent is suffused with so much irony and so many contradictions. Like most Highlanders of my generation I first heard of the Battle of Cape St Vincent through Robert Browning's poem "Home Thoughts, from the Sea":

> Nobly, nobly, Cape St Vincent to the North-west died
> away;
> Sunset ran, one glorious blood-red, reeking into Cadiz
> Bay;
> Bluish 'mid the burning water, full in face Trafalgar
> lay;
> In the dimmest North-east distance dawned Gibraltar
> grand and grey.
> "Here and here did England help me: how can I help
> England," say...

I was conscious, even as a child, of the anomalous use of the word "England", meaning Britain, but I had no idea then, and the history lessons in the Nicolson did nothing to tell me, that the events of the period involved so many fellow islanders both on sea and on land. I became conscious around the same time of the contrast, indeed the conflict, between Browning's jingoistic celebration of the might of the "English" navy, and his sneer at Wordsworth as "The Lost Leader" - "just for a handful of silver he left us!" - because he repudiated his early republicanism when the French Revolution finally spawned Napoleon. The complexity, and ambiguity, of Browning's attitude to the events of his own time, helps us, in a way, to understand the complexity and ambiguity of our own attitude to the history of a period in which many Gaelic-speaking islanders were involved in Imperial adventures, in which they had no very obvious personal stake and from which we have derived an inheritance of intermingled pride and resentment.

Whether James Morrison took part in the battle of Cape St Vincent or not, the CULLODEN'S first mission after the battle involved him in an adventure which reads like something out of one of the Hornblower novels: an abortive attempt to seize the Island of Tenerife.

The squadron detached for the task was commanded by Nelson and consisted of three ships of the line, four frigates and some smaller craft. One of the frigates, HMS ZEALOUS was commanded by Capt Samuel Hood who, some seven years later, as I mentioned in another connection, established a tenuous link with Lewis by marrying Seaforth's daughter. When Nelson got to Tenerife, he decided to land a mixed naval and military force to storm the defences of Santa Cruz. The main party consisted of a thousand men, seamen and Royal Artillery men, commanded by Troubridge. A gale thwarted the attempt to land, but the Spaniards were alerted, and the next attempt was even more hazardous.

Nelson led the second attempt himself, but everything went wrong for him. The rough seas and the darkness of the night made a coordinated assault impossible. Before the landing party even reached the shore, alarm bells were ringing through the town and the shore batteries were keeping up a steady fire. Nelson was wounded in the arm, and had to have an amputation. The various landing parties were separated widely from each other and no one knew where anyone else had got to - or not got to! Troubridge succeeded in making a landing but his boats were swamped, cutting off his retreat and dowsing most of the ammunition with water. Despite this, he marched boldly into the prado, the great square in the centre of the town, where he found himself in a trap, from which he extricated his little force with consummate effrontery.

As he told the story himself in a letter to Nelson: "From the darkness of the night I did not immediately hit the mole, the spot appointed to land at, but pushed on shore under the enemies battery, close to the southward of the citadel. Captain Waller landed at the same time, and two or three other boats. The surf was so high, many put back; the boats were full of water in an instant, and stove against the rocks, and most of the ammunition in the men's pouches was wet. As soon as I had collected a few men, I immediately advanced with Captain Waller to the square, the place of rendezvous, in the hope of meeting you and the rest of the people, and I waited about an hour; during which time I sent a sergeant, with two gentlemen of the town, to summons the citadel. I fear the sergeant was shot on his way, as I heard nothing of him afterwards. The ladders being all lost in the surf, or not to be found, no immediate attempt could be made on the citadel; I therefore marched to join Captains Hood and Miller, who, I had intelligence, had made good their landing to the SW of the place I did. I then endeavoured to procure some account of you and the rest of the officers, but without success. By daybreak we had collected about 80 marines, 80 pikemen and 180 small-armed seamen: these I found were all who remained alive of those who had made good their landing; and with this force, having procured some ammunition from the Spanish prisoners we had made, we were marching to try what could be done with the citadel without ladders, when we found the whole of the streets commanded by field-pieces, and upwards of 8000 Spaniards and 100 French under arms, approaching by every avenue. As the boats were all stove, and I saw no possibility of getting more men on shore, the ammunition wet, and no provision, I sent Captain Hood with a flag of truce to the governor, to declare I was prepared to burn the town, which I should immediately put in force if he approached one inch further; and at the same time I told Captain Hood to say it would be done with great regret, as I had no wish to injure the inhabitants, and that, if he would come to my terms, I was willing to treat, which he agreed to."

The courage and effrontery of the CULLODEN'S captain is breathtaking. Trapped in the centre of the town, his retreat cut off, his men wet and dispirited, with inadequate ammunition and no food, outnumbered more than twenty to one by a force which commanded all the narrow streets with field artillery, he gave the Spanish governor ten minutes to accept his terms, and got away with it. Few men can have played poker with such success from so weak a hand.

In concluding his report Troubridge is almost apologetic for his failure to take the town: "From the small body of men, and the greater part being pike and small-armed seamen, who can only be called irregulars, with very little ammunition in the pouches but what had got wet in the surf at landing, I could not expect to succeed in any attempt upon the enemy. The Spanish officers assured me they expected us, and were perfectly prepared, with all the batteries, and the number of men already mentioned, under arms. This, with the great disadvantages of a rocky coast, high surf, and in the face of forty pieces of cannon, will show, though we were not successful, what an Englishman is equal to; and I have the pleasure to acquaint you, that we marched through the town on our return with the British colours flying at our head."

Troubridge was not only permitted to leave with colours flying, but was provided with boats, by the Spaniards, to get his men back aboard ship. They were also given a ration of biscuits and wine, to refresh them for the journey, and were told that, if they sent their wounded ashore, they would be cared for in the local hospital. It may be that the Spaniards felt that, although Troubridge and the small landing party were in their power, the island was still at the mercy of the British squadron lying off shore. It is more likely, however, that the authorities on the island regretted their monarch's decision to enter the war on the side of France, and would have preferred to remain neutral, trading with both sides, as the Dutch were doing so profitably in St Eustacia, when, as a clerk on HMS SUFFOLK, at the start of his career, Morrison had been a minor cog in the capture one of the greatest treasures ever seized (and lost!) by a British fleet. The second explanation of the Spaniard's accommodating attitude is supported by the fact that they not only offered to care for the wounded, but to replenish the stores of the British Fleet. That clearly was dictated by commercial prudence rather than humanitarian concern for the enemy's hunger and thirst.

I do not know whether James Morrison was one of the "Englishmen" who, in the abortive attack on Santa Cruz, showed what they were "equal to" or whether he was one of those languishing on board the CULLODEN, wondering what was happening to their captain and their shipmates ashore. Either way, he would have shared in the general relief that the landing party had succeeded in extricating itself from an impossible situation. Unfortunately, he has not left us an account of the incident to match his Journal of the BOUNTY and his adventures in Tahiti.

The Spanish offer of succour for the wounded was not unique. After the battle of Cape St Vincent, the British surgeons were dismayed to find that the medicine chests on the Spanish ships they captured were without the basic necessities, so the Spanish wounded were transferred to British ships for treatment. Before leaving Tenerife, Nelson thanked the Spanish governor for his treatment of the wounded. They also exchanged gifts, and Nelson offered to carry the governor's despatches as he had no vessel of his own to send. This unusual offer was accepted with the result, as Southey puts it, Nelson "became the first messenger to Spain of his own defeat." In military terms the assault on Santa Cruz was not only a defeat but a fiasco. Yet, like many another disaster, it aroused more pride at home than a success. In a odd way, the fact that Nelson, the great hero, lost his arm, in an escapade he should never have got himself involved in, added as much to his reputation as his part in the victory at Cape St Vincent. With 141 killed or drowned, 105 wounded and 5 missing, at Santa Cruz, the casualties were almost as high as in the earlier engagement. Among officers they were actually higher. And, on the other side of the account, no serious damage was inflicted on the enemy.

Following the affair at Santa Cruz, Nelson returned to Britain to recuperate from the loss of his arm. There he found the bureaucrats at the Admiralty a good deal more difficult to handle than his Spanish enemies in Santa Cruz. When he tried to collect his arrears of pay, a petty clerk in the Admiralty refused to settle because he had not produced a certificate from a surgeon, confirming that he had lost the sight of an eye. Nelson was back next day, armed with two certificates, one certifying the loss of an eye, the other the loss of an arm. He couldn't trust them to accept the evidence of the empty sleeve pinned across his chest.

Meanwhile, the CULLODEN returned to the wearisome watch off Cadiz. At sea continually. Always on the alert. Beating back and fore, irrespective of wind or weather. At all costs it was necessary to make sure the remnants of the Spanish fleet did not slip out of Cadiz to rendezvous with the French at Brest. When, at last, in May of the following year, Morrison and his shipmates were given orders to sail from Cadiz, it was to join Nelson again, now back on duty, maintaining a similar tedious watch on the French fleet at Toulon.

When HMS CULLODEN joined Nelson's squadron off Toulon in the summer of 1798, James Morrison was back in the waters where his rehabilitation began, after the court martial of the BOUNTY mutineers. The circumstances, however, were entirely different. In 1793, when he went out on the VICTORY, and was posted gunner on the LUTINE, Britain had access to Toulon harbour, and a foothold ashore. In the south of France Royalists and Republicans were still at war with each other. Britain commanded the Mediterranean. Now Napoleon was at the height of his power. The British had no secure foothold anywhere in the Mediterranean. The watch on Toulon was an uneasy vigil, with the fleet continually at sea, trying to discover the purpose of the frantic activity in Toulon, Marseilles, Civita-Vecchia, Genoa and Bastia, where some great enterprise was clearly being prepared.

On May 3rd, Napoleon left Paris and, on the 8th, he arrived at Toulon. There a fleet of 72 war vessels had been assembled, with 400 transports. There were 10,000 seamen and 36,000 soldiers in the port. Napoleon was in supreme command, and under him were 20 generals and 4 admirals. His flagship which had been the SANS-CULLOTTE, celebrating the French Revolution and the proletariat, was renamed the ORIENT, signalling Napoleon's ambition to outmatch the conquests of Alexander the Great.

Nelson had only 14 sail of the line to thwart the great French adventure and he had no idea where the enemy were heading, when eventually they sailed. Was it an attack on Naples or Sicily? Was it the conveyance of an army to the coast of Spain, for a joint attack by France and Spain on Britain's oldest ally, Portugal, without whose harbours the British fleet would be gravely crippled? It was even thought possible Napoleon planned to sail through the Straits of Gibraltar for a descent on Ireland. British intelligence, perhaps deliberately misled, thought a passage through the Straits most probable. Nelson, with a seaman's instinct, sniffed the breeze and decided that a fleet, which left Toulon with a north west wind, was heading up the Mediterranean. But he didn't know where.

As Nelson swept eastward looking for clues, HMS CULLODEN was sent to Naples, where Troubridge went ashore to see the British Ambassador, Sir William Hamilton, husband of Emma, who later became Nelson's mistress. Hamilton was able to tell him the French had passed to the southward, probably heading for Malta. Before they got there, the British fleet fell in with a brig from Ragusa, the wealthy satellite of Venice from whose name the word argosy is derived, and which we now know as Dubrovnik. The brig reported that Napoleon had been to Malta but had already left. Nelson decided Napoleon was heading for Alexandria, and pushed on after him with all sail. When he reached Alexandria, however, the harbour was empty, apart from a few Turkish vessels, and an angry Turkish governor declaring he would resist a landing by either the French or the British.

Puzzled, Nelson withdrew to Syracuse, in Sicily, where he got the whole fleet safely into harbour, despite the intricate entrance and the fact that none of his captains had ever anchored there before. The fact was that the British fleet, unencumbered with transports, had outsailed Napoleon and reached his destination before him. The two fleets had passed, not very far apart, without ever sighting each other. British intelligence was hampered by Napoleon's ruthless policy of sinking every ship he met, irrespective of nationality, or mission, to make sure there were no blabbing tongues, to tell the British navy what they had seen. While Nelson was at Syracuse cogitating, Napoleon was at Alexandria, getting his forces ashore in spite of the angry Turkish governor. As Napoleon himself was going ashore, to assume the surpreme command, a sail was sighted to the westward. "Fortune, will you desert me now?" he asked, assuming the British fleet had arrived, while he was still disembarking on a hostile shore. The vessel, however, was one of his own, with despatches from Malta, and, long before Nelson arrived on the scene, Napoleon had got all his troops safely ashore, subdued the Turkish resistance, and made himself master of Alexandria.

At this point, James Morrison was on his way to Greece. The CULLODEN had been sent to Coron to see if the Turkish governor there had any information of Napoleon's whereabouts. Coron, in the south of Greece, is known to us today as Kalamata. It is not likely that Morrison, despite his enquiring mind, had time or opportunity to study ancient history as CULLODEN raced from point to point in search of the elusive Napoleon, If he had he would have enjoyed the irony. Here he was in an ancient Greek port, now occupied by the Turks, where the empire of Alexander the Great had finally disintegrated, more than two thousand years before. After Alexander's death, his great empire had dissolved in a series of civil wars, known as the Wars of the Diodochi - the Successors. Alexander's successors included some of the great generals of history, selected and trained in his extravagant campaigns, but, once the restraining hand of Alexander was removed, they destroyed each other in exactly the same way as the hard line mutineers of the BOUNTY destroyed each other on Pitcairn Island.

Morrison and his shipmates however, were more interested in the fact that the Turkish Governor confirmed Nelson's guess that Napoleon's aim was the conquest of Egypt. The news was urgent but as CULLODEN hurried back to Nelson she had the added fortune to capture a stray French merchantman with a cargo of wine, of which the British fleet was running short. Nelson moved quickly, when he got the news, and on the 1st of August, the British Fleet could once more see the minarets of Alexandria. The flag of the angry Turkish commander had been removed from the citadel and in its place was the French tricolour. There was a mystery, however. The harbour was crowded with shipping, but they were all transports, or small naval vessels. Nelson's quarry, the French battle fleet, had vanished. A few hours later, a British frigate found the French ships of the line in Aboukir Bay, twenty miles to the east north east.

As master gunner on one of the leading British warships, Morrison must have felt his heartbeat quicken, as the British fleet bore down on the anchored French, but whatever excitement he felt at the prospect of another great sea battle, was quickly swallowed up in the anguish of frustration. It was late afternoon. The French fleet was anchored in shoal water, intersected by hidden sandbanks. Their admiral reckoned that Nelson would not attack, in failing light, in such treacherous waters and with luck, he might slip away under cover of darkness. His instructions from Napoleon were precise: to avoid a general engagement, and keep the fleet intact, as cover for the army. Nelson, however, had other ideas. Each vessel was ordered to show four lights horizontally at the mizzen peak and fly the St George's Cross, because the large area of white would be more easily seen at night. With these precautions against the dangers of what we now call "friendly fire" Nelson sailed into Aboukir Bay and so deployed his ships that their fire would be concentrated on a group of French warships, whose destruction would tear the heart out of the fleet.

HMS CULLODEN moved cautiously in with the rest, taking soundings as she went. At one moment she had eleven fathoms of water, but, before the lead could be swung again, she was aground. While the rest of the fleet fought with the French, Morrison and his shipmates fought with the sea. There was a heavy swell. The CULLODEN was pounding on a spur of rock. The rudder was gone and the vessel badly holed. With the assistance of one of the frigates, she was finally worked clear but, by that time, she was taking in a hundred and twenty tons of water every hour. A sail was passed under the vessel's keel to restrict the inrush. A spare topmast was rigged to serve as a rudder. The CULLODEN was able to limp away from the scene, but she had taken as little part in the battle as if she were still at Syracuse.

Although Morrison did not know it at the time, however, his fate was being shaped by the battle he missed. Among the vessels captured from the French was the TONNANT, a large vessel carrying eighty guns. Some years later he became her master gunner, under another famous admiral, Sir Edward Pellew, who became Lord Exmouth. Morrison served Pellew as faithfully as he served Troubridge, but it was a personal quarrel between the two which sent him to a premature death.

The naval records are almost inexhaustible in number, but, for the purposes of following the career of a humble individual, tantalisingly scanty and incomplete. We can only guess at the quality of James Morrison's service from the fact that he was highly regarded by

Troubridge, who was himself highly regarded by Nelson. When the Government distributed awards after the Battle of the Nile, every first lieutenant in the fleet was promoted, except the first lieutenant on HMS CULLODEN. The bureaucrats at the Admiralty decided that the CULLODEN had not taken part in the battle. Nelson wrote to Lord St Vincent, "For Heaven's sake... get it altered... Troubridge... deserves every reward which a grateful country can bestow on the most meritorious sea-officer of his standing in the service. I have felt his worth every hour of my command." In another despatch, Nelson asserted that Troubridge, with his vessel ashore, was better than many captains afloat. "It was Troubridge," he told the Admiralty, "who equipped the squadron so soon at Syracuse; it was Troubridge who exerted himself for me after the action; it was Troubridge who saved the CULLODEN, when none that I know in the service would have attempted it." Lord St Vincent agreed in this assessment of Troubridge, pointing out that, although the CULLODEN did not get into the Battle of the Nile, the promptness of the crew's response to the grounding had saved two other ships from the same fate, enabling them to take part in the engagement. He also pointed out that, while the crew of the CULLODEN were struggling to keep the ship afloat, they were also organising stores for the vessels engaged in the action, taking care of the wounded, conducting the exchange of prisoners, and helping to repair the damage on other ships. Eventually the matter was solved with naval pragatism. The first lieutenant of the CULLODEN was not included in the list of promotions, but instructions were issued separately that he was to get the very first vacancy that occurred.

An insight into the attitude of Troubridge and his crew is given by a letter he wrote to Lord St Vincent, while his ship was still taking in seven feet of water an hour: "I shall use every exertion to patch the poor CULLODEN up again; and I flatter myself I can still fight a good battle in her, if opportunity offers. I am now fagging hard at the leak, and in the first harbour we make I must and will patch the old ship up, and make her last as long as your Lordship has the command. Two pumps going I shall not mind; we are fully equal to that. I endeavour, and I believe succeed in making my men believe that the leak is nothing, for they dance every evening as usual."

Nelson's victory at the Nile was overwhelming. Of thirteen French ships of the line, nine were captured, and two destroyed by fire. Of four frigates, one was sunk, and another destroyed by fire. Only four French ships escaped capture or destruction. On Nelson's orders, a service of thanksgiving was held on the British ships. To many of us today there is something hypocritical in thanking God, in effect, for the destruction of human life; and arrogance in assuming that God is on our side. At the time, however, the French prisoners regarded things very differently. They were astonished to see the crews of the British ships assembled for a religious service "at a time of such confusion." They believed it was the basis of the discipline which prevailed in the British navy. Attitudes then were very different from ours. One of the Captains, after the battle, had a coffin made from the mainmast of one of the captured French ships, which he sent to Nelson, so that, when the admiral's time came, he could be buried in one of his own trophies. Macabre as the idea may seem to us, we might all be better, if we were reminded, in moments of hubris, of our own impermanence.

Nelson accepted the gift in that spirit. He had the coffin set up against the bulkhead in his cabin, behind the seat in which he sat at dinner.

The Turks were even more delighted at the setback for Napoleon's plans of conquest than the British. Priceless gifts were showered on Nelson but, more relevant to the story of James Morrison, was the rejoicing among the common people. Thousands of Arabs and Egyptians watched the battle from the rooftops, as if they were spectators at a great game of football. Seldom has a decisive naval victory been won so close to the shore, in full view of a vast body of civilians. That night, and for three nights following, bonfires burnt along the Egyptian coast. In Morrison's nearly thirty years of naval service he saw many remarkable sights, but it is a fair assumption that one, clearly etched on his memory, would have been that line of bonfires along the Egyptian coast, while they were still struggling to keep the CULLODEN afloat, and the crew were dancing nightly on the deck, as if they hadn't a care in the world.

Morrison's skill as a gunner was tested to the full, early in the following year, when Nelson sent the CULLODEN back to Alexandria to destroy the French transports. "If it can be done, Troubridge will do it," he wrote to Lord St Vincent. The fact was that it couldn't be done. Alexandria had been heavily fortified after the battle of the Nile and it was no longer possible to attack it successfully from the sea. But Troubridge, and his Lewis gunner, pounded at it, despite the danger, until all the mortars had burst, and the fire-ships were lost in a gale.

Between these two visits to Egypt, Morrison's service on CULLODEN took him to several places with which Lewis folk of later generations have become familiar in other ways. Hebridean sailors in the two world wars of this century got to know Malta well. James Morrison got to know it two hundred years ago, when the CULLODEN blockaded the French there, in co-operation with a Portuguese fleet. The CULLODEN was also involved in the final capitulation of the French force which had occupied the island. In February 1799, the CULLODEN was part of a squadron blockading the port of Naples. Troubridge decided first to secure the islands in the Bay, and so Morrison became the first Lewisman on record to visit Capri. It was a very different island then from the glittering holiday resort we know today. The inhabitants were miserable peasants close to starvation. Troubridge tried to get supplies to relieve their hunger, from their own government, but the Sicilian authorities were so incompetent and corrupt it proved impossible. The navy had to distribute food from their own resources. It was a confused situation. Officially the Sicilian Government was fighting on Britain's side. Actually many Sicilians were helping the French. Troubridge and his men were engaged in feeding the starving, but even more urgently in tracking down spies, informers and saboteurs.

It was during this time an incident occurred on board CULLODEN which must have sent a roar of laughter resounding through the ship. A Sicilian lieutenant colonel, ostensibly an ally of Britain, sent a messenger to ask for two sloops with which to attack a small fort. Troubridge promised him the sloops. The lieutenant colonel sent the messenger back immediately arguing that sloops were inadequate. He must have frigates. Again Troubridge agreed. Still reluctant to attack the forts, the lieutenant colonel arrived in person, asking for two ships of the line. This last request was made, on board the CULLODEN, in the captain's cabin. Suddenly the cabin door burst open, the lieutenant colonel shot out, with Troubridge in hot pursuit, kicking him along the deck and shouting, "First sloops, then frigates, then ships of the line. Damn you! You're afraid to fight!" While this incident reached its climax in full view of the crew, news of another incident would have seeped round the ship less dramatically. During the bombardment of Alexandria, Troubridge intercepted a vessel which had been permitted to leave the harbour, ostensibly as a neutral. He suspected there was a spy on board. He took the captain to his cabin on the CULLODEN. There he showed the captain a firman - an edict or letter of authority from the Turkish government - without giving him time to read it. He explained that the firman related to a spy on board the vessel, giving Troubridge authority to execute as traitors those who harboured him. The firman related to quite different matters, but to save his own skin, as he thought, the captain admitted there was a Frenchman on board disguised as a Turk. When the spy was produced, Troubridge waved the firman in the captain's face once more, and he persuaded the spy to reveal where Napoleon's despatches were hidden on the ship. The spy had the equivalent of six hundred pounds concealed on his person. Troubridge let him keep the money, but sent him to Rhodes, commenting, a little cynically, that "the grand seignor would do this fellow more justice than I could." Just to make sure he "recommended him strongly for decapitation."

While still serving with Troubridge on the CULLODEN Morrison was involved in a number of shore expeditions. Notably there was an attempt to reduce the fort of St Elmo, near Naples, for which it was necessary to take the ship's guns ashore, and to cut down a wood, under enemy fire, to open up a line of attack. St Elmo was a hard nut to crack. "It is difficult to make approaches, the castle stands in so commanding a situation," Troubridge reported to Nelson. Still "several of the shells fell well, and I hope broke some of their shins." The gunners were working under very great difficulties. The civilian labourers, engaged to help them, fled at the sound of enemy musketry, even when it was not fired in their direction. CULLODEN'S crew was depleted at the time because Troubridge had to send eighty of his best men to try to restore order in Naples, where the magistrates were making a fortune, taking bribes from local Jacobins, who supported the French. Even more importantly, the guns were beginning to wear out. "Four of our mortars are nearly done up," he reported. "Their touch-holes are as big as a half crown." Morrison, his master gunner, clearly had his problems. At last the British force got close enough to begin to mine the fort. Intrigued by the thought that it was occupied by Neapolitan nobles as well as French republicans, Troubridge wrote to Nelson, "I am a strong advocate, if we can accomplish that, to send them, hostages and all, to Old Nick and surprise him with a group of nobility and republicans" arriving together. That, however, proved unnecessary. St Elmo finally capitulated after "a few hours sharp cannonade."

Reporting to the Government at home, Nelson praised "the fortitude, perseverance and ability" of the forces under Troubridge, in capturing a fort "of very great strength" and in a formidable position. He added, "We have but one idea - to get close along side. None but a sailor would have placed a battery only 180 yards from the Castle of St Elmo. A soldier must have gone according to art and the [roundabout] way; my brave Troubridge went straight, for we had no time to spare." If "brave Troubridge went straight," those who served under him must have done the same, including the master gunner from the Western Isles.

A little later, the CULLODEN was engaged in a similar action against a fort at Capua, 15 miles from Naples. On this occasion it was necessary to build a pontoon bridge across the river Volturno. At Capua, Troubridge faced most of the problems he had at St Elmo, with an added problem of particular concern to the gunners - the local powder was so bad the shells fell short, He pled with Nelson for "ten casks of our own powder" for the mortars. "If you comply," he added, "it will be necessary that some person belonging to us should accompany it, or they will steal one half and change the other." He also had problems with the Neapolitan mortars. The metal was poor and they were liable to blow up. It was necessary, he said, to get their own ten inch mortars taken ashore from the ships and set in land beds. "Pray lend us all the spades and shovels from the ships; the tools these country people have work too slow for us," he pleaded. A few hours after sending that appeal, he accepted the capitulation of the garrison. He had been closer to victory than he imagined. By the time he was ready to make the next attack, at Gaeta, the garrison capitulated without a fight.

Following the capitulation of Gaeta, Troubridge had to deal with the sort of dilemma which arose at the end of the Second World War, and of which we are still feeling the repercussions. The French who capitulated at Gaeta were straight-forward prisoners of war. According to the practice of the period, they were repatriated on parole, having promised they would not serve again for the duration of the war. Along with the French, however, were large numbers of Neapolitans who had rebelled against their King. They were repatriated as well, although it was well known they would be treated as traitors and probably executed. Troubridge was well aware of the dilemma. He had a very simple view of things, in one way. Rverything Britain did was right, while everything other people did was wrong. But he also had a strong humanitarian streak. His letters contrast the feasting at the Neapolitan court in Palermo with the sufferings of the poor in Rome and other cities. He anguished over the fate of political prisoners held by Britain's ally: "At present there are upwards of forty thousand families who have relations confined. If some act of oblivion be not passed, there will be no end of persecution; for the people of this country have no idea of anything but revenge, and to gain a point would swear a thousand false oaths. If the king knew as much as I do, he would certainly come to Naples. The property of the Jacobins is selling for nothing, and his own people, whom he employs, are buying it up, and the vagabonds pocket the lot. I should not be surprised to hear that they brought a bill of expenses against him for the sale."

At the same time, Troubridge was worried by Nelson's involvement with Emma Hamilton, which clouded his judgment and kept him in Palermo, when he should have been elsewhere. Troubridge was immensely loyal to Nelson but his letters are full of carefully guarded advice. In January 1800, in a poignant letter, Troubridge wrote, "I have this day saved 30,000 people from dying; but with this day my ability ceases. As the government [of Naples] are bent on starving us, I see no alternative but to leave these poor unhappy people to perish, without our being witness to their distress. I curse the day I ever served the Neapolitan government. We have characters, my lord, to lose; these people have none. Do not suffer their infamous conduct to fall on us." In another letter he warned, "I pray your lordship be cautious; your honest open manner of acting will be made a handle of."

In such a confused situation, involving many nations, and factions within each, there was a great deal of diplomatic activity, if one can dignify such blatant horse trading with the name of diplomacy. Some of the most important negotiations took place in Troubridge's cabin on the CULLODEN. The crew would have been aware of the coming and going of gold braided and be-ribboned men, but how much of what went on behind closed doors became known to others, we can only guess. A man with Morrison's interest in all around him would certainly have picked up whatever scraps of information, or speculation, there were. Unfortunately, however, he has not left us an account of the misery of Capri and Naples, to match his account of the tropical abundance of Tahiti.

This chapter in his adventurous career came to a close in the summer of 1800. By that time he had been seven years in the Mediterranean, four of them on HMS CULLODEN, continuously on board ship and almost continuously at sea: considerably longer than the total duration of either the First or the Second World War. On Hogmanay 1799, the CULLODEN was off Valetta, in Malta. In June 1800 she was moored in Mahon Roads, in Minorca. On the 7th July 1800, she was off Cape St Vincent, back to the scene of the first great battle of the campaign. Ten days later, the CULLODEN log gives the ship's position as "811 miles off the Lizard." Everyone's eyes were now on home. When the battle of Cape St Vincent was fought and Morrison joined the vessel Britain had not a single foothold within the Straits. When CULLODEN returned home, five years later, the Mediteranean was almost a British sea.

As soon as CULLODEN docked, Troubridge was appointed to command the Channel Fleet, under Earl St Vincent, but a few months later he was appointed one of the Lords Commissioners of the Admiralty. CULLODEN went into dry dock to make good the ravages of a long campaign, and the near shipwreck at the Battle of the Nile. James Morrison had little or no leave, on his return to Plymouth: certainly not long enough to visit Lewis. The CULLODEN arrived late in July 1800. In August Morrison was gunner on HMS AMBUSCADE, commanded by a Scot, the Hon John Colville. His association with Troubridge was interrupted but not broken. It was renewed in April 1805, when Troubridge was appointed to a command in the East Indies, and asked for the Lewisman as master gunner on his flagship: a rare tribute from a great admiral to one of his subordinates.

20
BACK TO THE WICKEDEST TOWN

On the AMBUSCADE James Morrison returned to the haunts of his early years in the navy. The ship was sent on convoy duty to the West Indies, and, in August 1801, he was back in Port Royal, the British naval base in Jamaica, just across the bay from the capital, Kingston. Port Royal was legendary among seafaring men. Before Britain occupied Jamaica, it was the haunt of buccaneers, including the notorious Henry Morgan. It was reputed to be "the wickedest town on earth." In Morrison's day it was one of the great slave markets of the world. The slave trade to Jamaica, and the carrying of slaves by British ships, were abolished in 1807, the year of Morrison's death. Although that brought the traffic in new slaves to an end, it took another quarter of a century before existing slaves were emancipated. There were something like 400,000 slaves in Jamaica at the time of the AMBUSCADE'S visit.

We have no means of knowing whether Morrison was interested in the slavery question, or what his views were, if he was. It was an issue, however, which touched his native island, peripherally at least. There is at least one occasion on record when the Captain of an American vessel - the FRIENDSHIP of Philadelphia - touting for emigrants in Lewis, was accused of planning to sell them as slaves, once he had them in his power. That accusation may just have been anti-emigration propaganda, but W. E. Gladstone's father, whose wife was born in Stornoway, had extensive interests in the mainstream slave trade, and the Seaforths, who owned Lewis, had a plantation in Berbice called Brahan, after their Ross-shire home. As late as 1804, just three years before the abolition of the trade, the Earl of Seaforth was in correspondence about the possible purchase of thirty or fifty slaves. On the other hand, it must be added that, as Governor of Barbadoes, Seaforth enacted a law imposing the death penalty on anyone who killed a slave, including the owner. Previously the maximum penalty for killing a slave was a fine of fifteen pounds and that was rarely exacted. Seaforth's law was restricted in effect by the proviso that the killing had to be proved by white witnesses, but, even so, it was bitterly resented by slave owners at the time. On the other side of the account, Zachary Macaulay, (father of Lord Macaulay, the historian) who ranked probably next to Wilberforce in the emancipation movement, was a third cousin of James Morrison's father.

The old town of Port Royal was devastated by earthquakes on several occasions, long before and long after, James Morrison's visits, and, like so many of the other places to which his naval service took him, it is now a tourist resort. In one of the very old churches, which survived the first great earthquake, silver plate is on exhibition which the exhibitors, but not the historians, are persuaded was a gift to the church by Henry Morgan, the great buccaneer himself. The quayside, where Morrison would have stepped ashore, is now given over to seafood restaurants, and is known as Henry Morgan Marina. The fame of a blackguard is more enduring than the power of an empire!

Whenever Morrison's name appears on the muster roll of the AMBUSCADE there is the mark # beside it. I have got no authoritative explanation of the significance of the mark, but the AMBUSCADE was a 36 gun ship and consequently a step down for a man who had been master gunner on a ship of the line. The mark may indicate that Morrison was seconded to the AMBUSCADE temporarily.

After the voyage to the West Indies the AMBUSCADE was in and out of Plymouth for a time, presumably engaged in the never ending watch on the Channel ports in the years before Trafalgar. In 1802 Morrison's ship was transferred to St Helens in Lancashire, 12 miles NE of Liverpool. In 1803 the Captain, who later became Lord Colville, Admiral of the White, was appointed to command the Sea Fencibles on the coast of Cumberland, which suggests that the AMBUSCADE was employed on coastal defence when stationed at St Helens; the easiest billet Morrison had in the whole of his naval career. His luck didn't last for long. In March 1802, a warrant was issued appointing him master gunner on HMS GENEREUX, a warship captured from the French. The GENEREUX was ready for sea when he went aboard and he was soon on his way back to the Mediterranean.

The GENEREUX was based for some time at Port Mahon, the capital and principal seaport of Minorca which had just been ceded by Spain to Britain. There he had an unexpected meeting with a large party of fellow Gaels. In June 1802 the GENEREUX embarked the men and baggage of the 79th Regiment - the Cameron Highlanders - for the voyage home to Britain. The Camerons had taken part in a strenuous and bloody campaign in Egypt, under Sir Ralph Abercromby, for which they received the honour of bearing the figure of a sphinx with the word Egypt, on their colours and appointments. They were returning to Britain to fill up their much thinned ranks.

Shortly after the Camerons returned to Britain, the Highland Regiments were threatened with the loss of their kilts. This provoked a memorable letter from Col Alan Cameron to the War Office protesting against "the degrading" proposal "to strip us of our native garb... and stuff us into harlequin tartan pantaloons." In the course of the letter, he made the point that "Highlanders" and "Scotchmen" are not synonymous terms, and protested against the practice of "adulterating" Highland regiments "with every description of men" and appointing officers "unacquainted with the language and habits of Highlanders." Col Cameron, it is interesting to note, also made a fierce attack on "rack-renting Highland landlords" who were destroying the source from which the Highland regiments drew their strength.

This is not wholly irrelevant to James Morrison's career. It underlines the point I made at the beginning that Highland soldiers, whether recruited or pressed, generally retained their territorial and cultural identity, under officers who spoke their language, and were recognised as kinsmen and leaders, while those pressed into the navy, and, indeed, those who joined voluntarily, like Morrison himself, were atomised and dispersed among a multitude of ships, which had no territorial or cultural connection with the Highlands, so that it is impossible to establish their numbers, or follow their careers, except in the rare case of a man like Morrison, who was plucked out of obscurity by his trial for mutiny, and the record he left us in his Journal.

There are other elements in the story of the Cameron Highlanders which, inferentially, have a bearing on Morrison's career. When Alan Cameron of Erracht was granted letters of service in 1793 for the raising of a regiment, he was allowed no bounty by the Government, as other Highland regiments were. The men were recruited solely at the expense of their officers. After a tour of duty in Flanders they returned to Britain. They were ordered to raise the strength to 1000 men and embark for India. While the officers were still trying to comply with the order, they were told the regiment was to be dispersed and the men drafted into four other regiments. This was deeply resented and Col Cameron sought a meeting with the Commander in Chief. Jameson's "Historical Record" gives us an account of the interview, which is almost certainly apocryphal but deserves to be true. According to Jameson, Col Cameron told the Duke of York, "To draft the 79th is more than you or your Royal father dare do." The Duke replied, "The King, my father, will send the Regiment to the West Indies, if he chooses." Col Cameron retorted, "You may tell the King, your father, from me, that he may send us to hell if he likes, and I'll go at the head of them, but he dare not draft us."

It is a matter for military historians, but it looks to the layman as if there is a pattern behind the refusal of bounty for the raising of the Camerons, the attempt to disperse the regiment at the first opportunity, and the proposal that they should lose their kilts. No clan was more closely associated with the Jacobite Rebellion of 1745 than the Camerons. Is it possible that, nearly half a century later, elements in the military establishment were still more suspicious of the Camerons than of other Highland clans? HMS CULLODEN, the third of the name, still figured prominently in the navy list. Morrison had served on her, and we will meet her again before the story is finished. It almost looks as if the Rebellion was still motivating diehards in positions of power in London long after the people of the Highlands had accepted the inevitable and were getting on with their lives as loyal citizens. If this interpretation is correct, it helps to explain why Morrison gives no hint of his Highland provenance in his Journal, and why it is difficult to find an unequivocal indication of his birthplace in the naval records which survive.

In August 1802 the GENEREUX returned to Britain and paid off. The unstable Peace of Amiens had been signed, and James Morrison seems to have been without a job for several months. War broke out again, early in 1803, and, in May, he was appointed master gunner on another warship captured from the French, HMS TONNANT. He would have known her well by sight: she was one of the French Fleet at Toulon, when the port was still held by French Royalists against the Revolutionaries, and he was there on the VICTORY and the LUTINE. The TONNANT was a ship of the line, mounting more than eighty guns.

The Captain of the TONNANT was Sir Edward Pellew, a distinguished sailor and Parliamentarian, who became the first Viscount Exmouth. The TONNANT was attached to the Channel Fleet, keeping a close watch on the French ports where Napoleon was building new fangled "gunships" for his projected invasion of Britain. Shortly after Morrison joined the TONNANT'S crew, however, she was detached from the main fleet, with five other ships, under Pellew as Commodore, to keep a special watch on the Spanish port of Ferrol.

Ferrol, which has always been one of the main Spanish naval bases, has a fine natural harbour, deep and safe, concealed from the sea by hills, and with a narrow entrance through which only one sailing ship could pass at a time. It was nominally a neutral port, when Pellew was sent to blockade it, but it was a handy bolt-hole for the French. The British aim was to see that no vessels, belonging to France or her allies, which got into the port, could venture out again. Closing the trap effectively meant constant vigilance, and weary days at sea, beating back and fore along a dangerous coast. The long vigil at Ferrol began, however, with a sea chase which would have given Morrison an opportunity to show his skill as master gunner. A Dutch squadron, on passage to India, left Ferrol the day before Pellew arrived. The TONNANT, and her accompanying vessels gave chase, under full press of sail, as far as Madeira, where the Dutch squadron was overtaken and destroyed. While Pellew pursued the Dutch, a French fleet of five sail of the line arrived from St Domingo, and anchored in Ferrol. They were still there when Pellew got back on station, neatly trapped. Pellew's own situation, however, was far from comfortable. Apart from the necessity of being almost continuously at sea, he now had to face the prospect that the French might slip down from Brest and catch him between two squadrons, each more powerful than his own. The situation was so tense, that Pellew, although he was a considerate commander, kept his crew at quarters all through the night. Frequently the TONNANT and her little squadron were driven out to sea by tempestuous weather. Food and even water became scarce, as the prevailing westerly gales prevented the arrival of supplies from home. Eventually Pellew, surveying the coast from a cutter, found a little cove between Ferrol and Corunna, which he considered safe, although it had been condemned by a celebrated Spanish cartographer. There the squadron rode out many a heavy gale. One of the attractions of the cove for Pellew was that, from a windmill on an eminence above it, he could see the harbour of Ferrol and keep the enemy under surveillance. The French also, sometimes, used the mill as an observation post, and officers of the two opposing navies played hide and seek with each other, on neutral territory, as they scrambled up and down the hill, from opposite sides, to the same point of vantage.

Because of the shortage of supplies from home, Pellew tried to live off the countryside. He sent his purser ashore to buy beef, but the territory was so poor he had to go inland forty miles for a little fresh meat and wine. Two attempts were made to assassinate the purser as he did his "shopping", but whether by the French or the Spanish does not appear. It was well into the New Year before supplies arrived from Britain, by which time Morrison and his companions were feeling the pinch. The TONNANT'S log gives little detail. After all, it was routine for the British navy to be almost continuously at sea while the threat of invasion remained. Nelson records in his diary, around that time, the day he stepped ashore from the VICTORY for the first time in "two years, wanting ten days."

Although detail is lacking, the log does give us the feel of the duties in which Morrison and his shipmates were involved:

7 June - off Cape Prior chasing brigs and schooners with Portuguese colours.

13 June - on a foray into the Mediterranean.

26 Nov - a battle off Cape Ortegal.

28 Nov - signalled SPENCER and ARDENT to see if they agreed prize money.

24 Dec - Off Cape Ortegal. A great gale and heavy seas. The jib split.

7 Apr - His Excellency the Captain General of the Kingdom of Galicia came alongside.

13 Apr - Agreement for sharing prize money was answered by MARS, NORTHUMBERLAND, SPENCER, DRAGON, GANGES, PHOENIX and MALTA.

The visit of the Captain General of the Kingdom of Galicia was no doubt a glittering occasion. Despite the hardships of long weeks at sea, the top ranks in the Georgian navy maintained a great deal of magnificence. Pellew had a reputation as a *bon viveur*. His blockade of Ferrol, and his style of living, have both passed into naval folklore, and use is made of this by C. S. Forester in his novel "Hornblower and the Hotspur," in which he describes an imaginary Council of War on board the TONNANT, when she was still with the main Channel Fleet, before the shortages at Ferrol imposed leaner rations, even on the Commodore. It is fiction, but it is based on historical research, and it gives us a feel of life on board the TONNANT, when Morrison was master gunner, although at a very different level in the naval hierarchy from the Commodore:

"The deck of the TONNANT seemed incredibly spacious after the cramped deck of the HOTSPUR, for the TONNANT was no mere seventy-four. She was an eighty-four, with dimensions and scantlings worthy of a three-decker. She was a reminder of the era when the French built big ships in the hope of over-powering the British seventy-fours by brute force instead of by skill and discipline." Clearly the armament under the Lewisman's supervision was unusually formidable, even for a British ship of her line!

"The great poop-cabins had been thrown into a single suite for Pellew, in the absence of a flag-officer permanently on board," writes Forester. "It was incredibly luxurious. Once past the sentry the decks were actually carpeted - Wilton carpets in which the foot sank noiselessly. There was an ante-room with a steward in dazzling white ducks to take Hornblower's hat and gloves and cloak... The cabin was finished in some rich material - damask, Hornblower guessed - with a colour scheme of nutmeg and blue unobtrusive yet incredibly satisfying to the eye. Daylight poured in through a vast stern window, to glint upon the swaying silver lamps... On the far side were two large masses so draped as to be shapely and in keeping so that no uninitiated person could guess that inside were two eighteen-pounder carronades. 'This must take you a full five minutes to clear for action, Sir Edward,' said Cornwallis. 'Four minutes and ten seconds by stop-watch, sir,' answered Pellew, 'We strike everything below, including the bulkheads. 'Another steward, also in dazzling white ducks, entered at this moment and spoke a few words in a low tone to Pellew, like a well trained butler in a ducal house, and Pellew rose to his feet, 'Dinner gentlemen,' he announced. 'Permit me to lead the way. 'A door thrown open in the midships bulkhead, revealed a dining room, an oblong table with white damask, glittering silver, sparkling glasses, while more stewards in white ducks were ranged against the bulkhead."

In spite of the glitter, there were some signs of the prevailing shortages. There was no flour to make the duff. The Commodore apologised because it was made with crushed ship's biscuits. The biscuits also provided the maggots which fed the Commodore's chickens. Clearly the Commodore and the gunner from Lewis moved in very different circles, but there was at least one point in which their paths converged: the Commodore was interested in education. As his biographer puts it, "With that care for the improvement of his young officers which was always such a prominent feature of his conduct, he advertised for a superior schoolmaster for the TONNANT, to whom he offered 50 pounds per annum, in addition to his pay, that he might obtain for them better instruction than the regulations of the service would afford." The stewards, in dazzling white duck, who lined the Commodore's dining room in Forester's tale, were really the sons of gentlemen, signed on as midshipmen and learning navigation under the schoolmaster Pellew provided. According to the normal practice in the navy at the time, these youngsters were placed in the general care of the master gunner and lived in the gunroom. If Pellew had a special interest in the education of his midshipmen, he must inevitably have discovered that his gunner was "a person, from talent and education, far above the situation he held," to use the phrase applied to Morrison by Sir John Barrow, who was the Second Secretary (or as we would say now, the Permanent Secretary) at the Admiralty for 41 years, and is generally regarded as the man who first established the great British tradition of the non-political civil servant. It is speculation on my part, but I do not think I am stretching the probabilities too far, when I see a connection between Pellew's interest in education and the fact that, when he was promoted rear admiral in 1804 and sailed for the East Indies, Morrison was transferred from the TONNANT to the CAMBRIDGE, as a gunnery instructor, stationed at Plymouth.

21
LOST WITH ALL HANDS

Whether or not I am right in my guess that Admiral Sir Edward Pellew, later Viscount Exmouth, was responsible for Morrison's appointment as a gunnery instructor, it is certainly true that another great seaman, Sir Thomas Troubridge, winkled him out of the gunnery school because he wanted his old gunner from the CULLODEN in his flagship, HMS BLENHEIM. Troubridge was promoted rear-admiral in April 1805, and given command of the Indian seas, east of Point du Gallo, in the Island of Ceylon, which we now know as Sri Lanka. He sailed for his new station at the end of the same month so he must have moved fairly quickly to get the gunner he wanted.

Because of the new appointment, it is clear that neither Troubridge, nor Morrison, took part in the battle of Trafalgar, in October of that year. There were, however, at least two Lewismen in the battle, who had made the navy their career, in addition to the anonymous multitude of pressed men who cannot be traced. According to his tombstone in Ui cemetery, John Morison, who was later tacksmith of Aignish, took part in the battle of Trafalgar and James Robertson, a Stornoway man, was a midshipman on HMS VICTORY, standing not far from Nelson when he died.

HMS BLENHEIM had its own little spat with the French, on her way to the Indies. Troubridge was shepherding a convoy of ten East Indiamen, and a body of troops bound for Madras. Off Madagascar the British convoy was sighted by the French Admiral Linois, who had been sent out by Napoleon to prey on British merchant shipping, in the Indian Ocean, much as the German pocket battleships preyed on British shipping in the Second World War. Many Lewis seaman learned, by bitter experience, the damage such a raider can inflict on merchant shipping, and how difficult it is to track it down, even with sophisticated modern equipment. Linois, in 1805, was even more elusive, and in the words of J. H. Rose in his "Life of Napoleon" "he was destined to be the terror of our merchantmen in eastern seas." His reputation was so fearsome, in fact, that he passed into the folklore of the period and still survives in modern naval stories. One of the highlights of Patrick O'Brian's novel "HMS Surprise" describes an encounter between his hero Captain Jack Aubrey and Linois, in the waters the BLENHEIM was traversing.

"Who is that old fashioned fellow who carries his mizzen- topmast staysail under the maintop?" asked Stourton, one of the imaginary SURPRISE'S imaginary officers.

"Stourton, Stourton" cried Jack "it is Linois. Haul your wind! Hard a-port, hard over. Let fall the maincourse there. Strike the pendant. Forestaysail; main topgallant. Marines, Marines, there; clap on the mainbrace. Bear a hand, bear a hand. Mr Etherege, stir up your men."

Although all that was happening only in O'Brian's imagination it may give us a flavour of the excitement on board the BLENHEIM, when the French warship MARENGO, named after one of Napoleon's great victories, was seen bearing down on the BLENHEIM, accompanied by two frigates, and a British vessel, the BRUNSWICK, which Linois had already captured and adapted to his own use. Linois, at that stage, must have felt that he had stumbled on a great prize. Four miles away, on his lee bow, were ten large, richly laden Indiaman, guarded by only two British warships. The French fleet had a considerable advantage in fire power. The MARENGO matched the BLENHEIM gun for gun. The BRUNSWICK, with a French crew on board, had been converted into a formidable fighting ship and, in addition, there were the two frigates, the BELLE POULE and ATLANTE, each carrying 44 guns. The BLENHEIM was accompanied only by a brig. In addition, there was a heavy swell running, which prevented the BLENHEIM from opening the lower deck gun ports, while the French, firing from the sheltered side of their ships, could use their full armament.

In a sentence, which is very relevant to the story of James Morrison, one naval authority puts it succinctly: "The British 74 had only a battery of 18-pounders with a few nines and carronades to oppose the whole united broadsides of the French 74 and the frigates. Notwithstanding this, M. Linois did not remain long within gunshot" of the BLENHEIM. A passenger on the BLENHEIM was killed by a piece of wood. Some of her sails were torn. Another man was killed on one of the ships of the convoy. That was all the damage sustained by the BLENHEIM and her convoy, in an exchange of gunfire, lasting half an hour. The French vessels, on the other hand, were forced to break off the engagement because of the serious damage inflicted on their masts and hulls. During the engagement Troubridge succeeded in holding his convoy together in close formation and, although the French made another reconnaissance, they did not venture to renew the engagement. In the words of Ralfe, in his biography of Troubridge, "The BLENHEIM sailed too ill to attempt the pursuit." The order was given to set topgallant sails. The convoy also made more sail, and continued on their voyage to Madras.

In Madras Troubridge was involved in a battle of another sort with a fellow admiral, and the government at home. It was a battle in which James Morrison would have been very interested. He had served under both the admirals involved, and had been master gunner on both their flagships. The commander in chief on the East Indian station was Sir Edward Pellew, who commanded the TONNANT when Morrison was master gunner just a few years earlier. His flagship, now, was the CULLODEN, on which Morrison had served under Troubridge.

Three weeks after Sir Edward Pellew's promotion and appointment to the East Indian station, there was a change in the government at home. Appointments were then given to political friends even more shamelessly than they are today. Pellew had supported the outgoing government. Troubridge supported the incoming one. Even before he left home, Pellew knew he was liable to be ditched by the new ministry. He warned his brother, who was also a ship's captain, to be circumspect in all his conduct, so that he gave the ministry nothing they could use to discredit him. He even warned him never to sleep out of his ship, in case someone else commanded it by the time he got back. In his very first letter home from India he wrote, "Probably my successor is already on his way to supersede me." He wasn't quite right. The government had decided merely to cut his command in two, but they bungled even that.

Sir Edward was to retain control of the seas west of Ceylon, where there was little to do but protect Britain's possessions in India, and British merchantmen crossing the Indian Ocean. The seas east of Ceylon, which included all the rich Dutch colonies, then at war with Britain and so offering an active commander great opportunities of prize money, were transferred to Sir Thomas Troubridge.

On his arrival, Troubridge went on board his old vessel the CULLODEN, to present his letter of appointment to Sir Edward. It was not a pleasant task and he did not relish it, even although he was to be the gainer. As it turned out things were even more difficult than he had expected. Pellew read the letter then held out his hand and asked for his own letter of recall. Troubridge explained there were no letters of recall. Pellew was to remain with the western part of his command:

"On no" said Pellew, in effect. "If the Admiralty have not recalled the letter appointing me, I am still in command of the whole area, and you control the seas east of Ceylon as my subordinate."

Apart from the slight to Troubridge's dignity, this arrangement had important practical consequences. It meant that Pellew, as commander in chief, would share substantially in any prize money Troubridge picked up in the rich East Indies. Tempers rose. The two men shouted at each other. At one point Pellew asked the Captain of CULLODEN to join them as a witness to the argument. When Troubridge refused point blank to serve under Pellew, Pellew called his bluff by writing out an order immediately and handing it to him. At last Troubridge accepted the logic of Pellew's argument. No doubt he felt his friends at home would quickly make good their oversight and send Pellew the essential letter of recall. Having won the argument, Pellew magnanimously gave Troubridge a squadron of his own and the best part of the station.

Both men wrote home drumming up support. At first the Admiralty took the view that Pellew had committed an illegal and unprecedent act of resistance to lawful authority. On reflection, however, it was decided that he had been right. He still held the King's commission as commander of the whole East Indian station. Rather than admit that they had bungled the matter, the Admiralty sought a way out by appointing Troubridge to the command at the Cape of Good Hope, well clear of Pellew's territory. It was a decision which had fatal consequences for Troubridge, himself and for the Lewis gunner he had chosen for his flagship.

It takes only a few paragraphs to describe the row between Troubridge and Pellew over the East Indian command, and only a few minutes to read them. The quarrel and the uneasy truce which followed were, however, spread over many months. While ships sailed back from India to Britain with the two Admirals' conflicting arguments; while the Government at home dithered over its bungling of the appointment; while ships sailed back to India again with news of Troubridge's transfer to the Cape of Good Hope, the worthy admiral and his Lewis master gunner were busy hunting down rich prizes in the seas east of Ceylon. According to Pellew's biography, Troubridge's command was "most lucrative." "In addition to its general advantages, some prizes of immense value were taken."

"On the 26th of July, 1806, the GREYHOUND frigate and HARRIER, sloop of war, fell in with two large armed [Dutch] Indiamen, richly laden with spices, and protected by a frigate and a corvette. The British gallantly attacked them, and captured, with little loss, the frigate and both the Indiamen. To add to the gratification of the Admiral, it was his son, Captain Troubridge, who commanded the HARRIER." Young Troubridge was an able seaman but, as his father's son, he had enjoyed greatly accelerated promotion.

The BLENHEIM does not seem to have been involved directly in the capture of the Indiamen "richly laden with spices." As Admiral, however, Troubridge would have had his share of the prize money, and so would Pellew, as Commander in Chief, thus rubbing salt in Troubridge's wounds.

If the BLENHEIM was not involved in the action it is not likely that James Morrison shared in the prize money, but, as we shall see later, there is at least a presumption that he did earn considerable prize-money on his tour of duty in the Far East, and that, years later, after much haggling, some of it reached Stornoway, and possibly saved his father from bankruptcy. The one thing certain is that, whatever prize money he earned as master gunner on Troubridge's flag ship, did not enrich him personally.

Just as his career followed Admiral Troubridge's, at a distance, like the shadow of a bird marking its flight along the ground, so they died together, in February 1807, in circumstances which no one knows for a certainty but, concerning which, there can be little doubt.

Early the previous year they had a dry run - more appropriately, perhaps, a wet run - of the final disaster. The BLENHEIM, in the words of Troubridge's biographer, writing in 1828, "had got on shore in the Straits of Malacca, where she had received so much damage as to render her unfit to cross the Bay of Bengal; but, having repaired her at Pulo-Penang, and rigged jury-masts, Sir Thomas, whose pride was to overcome difficulties, proceeded in her to Madras, where he arrived in safety. Here the defects of his ship became daily more apparent; her back was broken in a most extraordinary manner, and her beams and riders showed that she was falling to pieces, while the labour of the crew at the pumps barely sufficed to keep the water from gaining on her as she lay at anchor. Captain Bissell commanded the ship, and, as was his duty, represented her state to the rear-admiral. Sir Thomas, however, persisted in his purpose of sailing in her to the Cape [to take up his new command]; and such was the confidence reposed in his talents, that many passengers from Madras embarked with him."

The extent of the damage to the BLENHEIM can be gauged from Admiral Troubridge's log which tells the story of the incident which caused it, in spare, unemotional, telegraphic language. Under date 7th April 1806, the log records: "Shoaled on sandbank." "HARRIER in company." "The ship much over on her broadside."

April 8th: "Throwing wood, stores, empty casks and shot overboard." "Ship nearly on her beam ends." "Cut away the masts." "Losing battle with the pumps." "All provisions, stores, wood etc overboard." "Guns, gun carriages, iron ballast, and a large quantity of ballast thrown overboard."

By the 10th, however, the BLENHEIM was off the shoal, and stores were being taken back on board. Presumably some of the stores thrown overboard were salvaged by the HARRIER. The ship, however, had sustained fatal damage, despite Troubridge's efforts to have her repaired and his determination to sail, in her as his flagship, to the Cape.

His biographer continues the tale: "He sailed on the 12th January; the JAVA of 36 guns, an old Dutch prize frigate, commanded by Capt George Pigot, and the HARRIER, brig, of 18 guns, Capt. Finlay, being in company. On the 1st of February... not far from the S.E. end of Madagascar, they were caught in a tremendous gale of wind, and forced to lay-to. In the evening, the JAVA, which was to windward, bore up close with the BLENHEIM, both ships having the signal of distress flying. The BLENHEIM was observed by the officers of the HARRIER to have settled much lower in the water, and it was the general opinion that Capt Pigot, even in his own distress, had, while generously trying to save some, at least, of the unfortunate people on board the BLENHEIM, ran foul of her, and accelerated their destruction. As night came on, the HARRIER bore away for the Cape, where she arrived on the 28th of the same month. Such are the last and only accounts we have ever had of the BLENHEIM and the JAVA."

They are also the only accounts we have ever had of the death of James Morrison, one of the first Lewisman on record to have joined the navy voluntarily. In many of its aspects his career foreshadows the careers of thousands of Lewismen, who subsequently followed his example, making the navy their career, as regulars or as reservists, to say nothing of the anonymous hundreds, both before and after him, who sailed to their destiny, after being seized by the press gang. We can only conjecture his thoughts and feelings, on that final night, in the Indian Ocean, as the crew of the BLENHEIM struggled to transfer their passengers to the JAVA, knowing that, even if the passengers were saved, they themselves were inevitably doomed.

I think there can be little doubt that Troubridge's determination to sail in the BLENHEIM was influenced, largely, by his quarrel with Pellew. The Admiralty's bungling of the orders for the East Indian command, placing him in a subordinate position, was an affront. He was not prepared to slink off to his new command, flying his flag in an old Dutch frigate, or a brig. The offer of Pellew to give him whatever vessel he chose out of the whole fleet, although generously meant, could only have added to his grievance. The quarrel may also have influenced Pellew's decision, on hearing the HARRIER'S news, many weeks later, to send Troubridge's son to search for the missing BLENHEIM and JAVA, although it was clear beyond a shadow of doubt that the vessels had been lost and a search was useless.

Young Troubridge was now Capt of the GREYHOUND, a 32 gun ship, and he was ordered to proceed immediately to the Island of Roderique and then the Isle of France, and to send in a flag of truce to the French governor "for that information which, even in time of war, would not be refused by a generous enemy."

"On his arrival at the Isle of France, General de Caen sent him every information it had been in his power to collect from the different signal stations, together with a description of certain pieces of wreck which had been cast on shore; but there was nothing that could give the smallest clue to the fate of the BLENHEIM and the JAVA."

James Ralfe, in his massive naval biographies of the period, tries to justify Troubridge's decision to sail in an unseaworthy ship. Troubridge, he writes, "was jealous of fame, careless of safety, enamoured of glory, and 'ambitious to show that courage can triumph over fortune, and magnanimity over force; that nothing is invincible to the brave, or impregnable to the daring.' Was he then to be deterred from crossing the Indian ocean in company with two other vessels, because his own was defective?"

One can understand that Ralfe was anxious not to diminish the reputation of a great seaman - described by another authority as "the trusted friend, and almost the other self, of Nelson" - because of one error of judgment, into which, to an extent, he was provoked. Owen Rutter, however, in the introduction to the Golden Cockerel edition of Morrison's Journal, puts it differently:

"The officers warned the Admiral that she would be the coffin of all on board if he sailed in her even to the Cape, and urged him to sail in another ship. But he vowed that he would not leave her. 'I will go to the Cape with her,' he declared, 'or not go at all.' In this connection Lady Belcher refers to him admiringly as 'the intrepid Admiral'. Personally I can see nothing admirable in that gesture. It is true that he was one of the most brilliant officers of the Nelson period; and it may even be that his orders admitted of no delay. Yet his reasons for sailing in the BLENHEIM appear to have been personal, and, as I see it, no commander is entitled to risk the lives of his officers and men in a condemned ship to satisfy a whim. His purple patch might have been very well had it affected no lives but his own; as it was, he succeeded in drowning the whole ship's company... Thus did James Morrison, having nearly suffered hanging through the rancour of one commander, and drowning through the callousness of a second, finally meet his end through the sentimental recklessness of a third."

22

A REPRESENTATIVE ISLAND SEAMAN

The only description we have of James Morrison is that given by Bligh, when the navy was hunting him down after the mutiny on the BOUNTY. He was of medium height, sallow complexion, slender build, with long black hair. He had lost the use of the upper joint of the forefinger of his right hand and had a scar on one arm from a wound made by a musket ball. He was elaborately tattooed with the insignia of the star and garter. The star was tattooed on his left breast, and the garter, with the celebrated motto "Honi soit qui mal y pense", round the left leg.

Surviving muster rolls and pay books give us some glimpses of his domestic economy. The pay books of his first ship, the SUFFOLK, show that on 13th December, 1781, his full wages amounted to ú39:3:10 and his Neat (or as we would say now, his net) wages to ú29:2:0. It is not stated what period these wages covered, but they probably refer to his whole tour of duty on the SUFFOLK. In 1781 an able seaman's wage was 24 shillings per month, but the navy reckoned by the lunar month, so that the annual rate for an able seaman was slightly more than thirteen times 24 shillings. From that there were deductions to be made, and the net pay of an able seaman was reckoned to be ú14:12:6 per annum. Clearly the ú39:3:10 earned by Morrison, as captain's clerk, covered more than one year. It might be noted in passing that naval pay had not been increased for more than a hundred years: it was still the same as it had been in 1653. The pay of soldiers had risen considerably over the same period and one of the causes of mutiny in the Georgian navy was the discrepancy between the pay of sailors and soldiers travelling on the same ship.

The difference between Morrison's full pay and his "neat" pay is, in theory, accounted for by the following deductions: clothes 14/-; dead men's clothes ú6:16; beds 10/10; tobacco 9/6; Chatham Chest ú1:10 and hospital 10/6. The sums do not square. In fact the sums do not square in any of his pay books which I have examined. Whether there is some rational explanation for the discrepancies, or whether they are just due to slapdash book-keeping, I do not know. They do not, however, seem to be due to anyone "chiselling" the pay because, in this instance, Morrison would appear to have received 9/- more than he should, if we subtract the deductions from the gross pay.

The deduction for clothes is quite straight forward, but the deduction for dead men's clothes requires some explanation. When ship's were at sea, and clothes were difficult to come by, the effects of anyone who died were sold, generally I believe by auction. The entry "dead men's clothes" is often accompanied by the signature of the ship's surgeon, who had to certify that the deceased had not suffered from a contagious disease before his effects were disposed of. There are frequent references to dead men's clothes against Morrison's name, but it would require considerable research to establish whether or not he resorted more frequently than normal to this method of equipping himself. Even if he did, there is a further consideration. When clothes were sold in this way, the proceeds of the sale went to the dead man's widow, if he was married and in the habit of making remittances home. Often, if the dead man had been popular and his widow was believed to be in poverty, shipmates would bid up the price of his clothes, above their true value, to help her. It is impossible to establish whether the fairly frequent purchase of dead men's clothes by Morrison shows that he was prudently buying secondhand clothes because they were cheap, or trying to help the widows of deceased shipmates by paying more than he need for their husbands' effects. I think it might be fair to assume that some of his transactions, especially on his first voyage, when he moved from captain's clerk to midshipman, were purely to equip himself, but his conduct at the trial and after it suggests that some at least of these transactions had a charitable motive.

The purchase of tobacco is self explanatory but the item occurs in only one of the pay books which I have examined. Whether that means that he gave up smoking after his first voyage, or that my research is incomplete, I cannot say.

The Chatham Chest was a fund for distressed navymen to which they were obliged to contribute 1/- a month. Seamen were also obliged to contribute to Greenwich Hospital at the rate of 6d per month. This means that seamen in the Georgian navy had a primitive social security system supported by a levy on wages. The hospital deduction from Morrison's pay is considerably less than half the deduction for the Chatham Chest, and the entry in the pay book does not mention Greenwich, just "hospital". The SUFFOLK was based at Leith, and, at the end of the voyage, Morrison was admitted to Leith Hospital. This suggests the possibility that a different rate of deduction was made for vessels based at Leith and using the services of Leith Hospital, but that is speculation: I have no evidence for it.

A particularly interesting entry in the SUFFOLK's pay book reads "To James Morrison, Clerk of the Cutting House to this Office ú7:10s for bill dated 29th September 1782 for one quarter's house rent ending this day at ú30 per annum." This would seem to imply that, when Morrison was discharged from Leith Hospital, he went into private lodgings to convalesce and the navy met his expenses, although the house rent was considerably more than his gross wages. Although discipline was harsh, and bureaucracy rampant, the Georgian navy did try to look after its men.

The SUFFOLK pay book also shows that Morrison remitted wages from abroad, presumably to his parents, through a Mr Woodmeston, and, when he left the ship in Leith, his wages were paid to Jno John Richards, attorney, again, presumably, for onward transmission to his family. N.A.M. Rodger in "The Wooden World" makes a point about naval wages which is probably relevant to Morrison's motives in enlisting. "The wages earned by an able seaman are one obvious reason why boys should have wanted to go to sea, for in an age when a ploughman might earn ú3 or ú4 a year, an able seaman's pay was attractive. Even a landman's pay [that is a landman in the navy, who was two grades below an AB] was more than many countrymen might earn, specially in the poorer parts of the three kingdoms. Moreover, because all seamen's wages were paid at long intervals they often represented quite large sums when they came." And, of course, there was always the hope of prize money. Morrison, as Captain's clerk, then for a time midshipman, aspiring to commissioned rank, and finally as a master gunner, one of the most important warrant officers on a ship of the line, had very much better prospects than an AB and his share of any prize money was proportionately larger. His position as a gunner in the navy was probably as lucrative employment as the son of a merchant and tacksman in Lewis, in the late 18th century, could hope for.

Morrison seems to have relied on a number of attorney's to collect and transmit his wages. The name Hugh Stanger, attorney, appears on several occasions when he was on AMBUUSCADE and CULLODEN, but there was also a James Smith and a Dan Lowe, and others. In the AMBUSCADE pay book there is an entry against his name: "Ticket No 400 from 1st Sept. 1801 to 25th Sept 1802." This confirms my assumption that he was on the AMBUSCADE only temporarily, and was never a full member of her crew. Tickets, in lieu of pay, were issued to men who had been sent temporarily to another ship, or who were ashore in hospital. The ticket could only be cashed in the vessel's home port, when she paid off, and normally the recipient had to sell the ticket at a discount to an agent, who was always expensive, and often dishonest. The wages of seamen were always in arrears, deliberately, to discourage desertion, but it was possible to make an allowance to relatives ashore. The constant reference to attorneys in pay book entries relating to Morrison, suggest that he was making such remittances. I have found no evidence that he ever married. Equally I have no firm proof that he did not. There is a letter in the Seaforth Muniments, which I will refer to later and which indicates that the balance of probability is that he never married and that the remittances were made to his parents in Stornoway.

Because of the varying periods to which pay entries relate it is not possible to compare Morrison's earnings at different stages in his career, although clearly the amounts increased as he progressed to master gunner, and to larger ships. References in the pay books to "compensation for two servants" also mark his upward progress. The final entry in the pay books of the BLENHEIM is bleak and conclusive: No 1071 per warrant 2nd April 1805. James Morrison. Gunner. Discharged Dead." The entry seems to indicate that, although the BLENHEIM was lost in February 1807, Morrison's wages were paid until 13th Sept 1808. Presumably the ship was not definitely accepted as lost until young Capt Troubridge had completed his search, and reported back to the Admiralty.

We can only speculate how, and when, James Morison, the merchant in Stornoway, learned that his son, James Morrison, master gunner on HMS BLENHEIM, had been drowned at sea. The feared loss of Sir Thomas Troubridge would have been reported in Britain, as soon as the HARRIER'S despatches arrived from Cape Town. After all, he was one of the most famous admirals in the British navy. The news would have percolated down from the London to the Scottish press and would eventually have reached Stornoway. The newspapers may even have been anticipated by a passing ship. Stornoway heard of Nelson's death, in this way, long before newspapers reached the town with the news of Trafalgar.

Ten years after Morrison's death, on 18th March, 1817, the Factor in Lewis wrote a tantalising letter to the proprietor, Mrs Stewart Mackenzie of Seaforth, generally known as

Lady Hood Mackenzie: "Mr Jas Morison tells me that there had been ú300 remitted from the effects of his son to Mr William Mackenzie and that the two years rent would be paid from that firm."

The William Mackenzie is easily identified. He was for many years the Seaforth's family lawyer in Edinburgh: a man to whom a Stornoway merchant would readily turn if he required sound legal advice. But who was the son? Clearly he was someone who had died and whose identity and circumstances Mrs Mackenzie knew. A search has failed to locate any will or deed registered in Scotland around that time which would cast light on the transaction, although the records are well indexed. The inference is that William Mackenzie's services were invoked to pursue some tricky matter of legal business originating outside Scotland. It occurred to me that the transaction might relate to the prize money James Morrison accumulated on his fateful voyage to the East Indies. The other half of the story, I hoped, would be found among the Admiralty Records in Kew. I am advised, however, that the relevant papers for the year in question are missing, and we are left with nothing but conjecture.

The enquiries I have made suggest that the sum involved is not unreasonable for a master gunner on a ship of the line to have due to him, after a very successful voyage, in terms of prizes captured. I am also advised that ten years is not an unreasonable period for the negotiations for payment, especially in a case where there was no proof and death had to be assumed. The Lewis Estate papers provide some interesting evidence of the difficulty of negotiating a claim of that sort from a distant island, given the impenetrable red tape which surrounded the bureaucracy. From a period ten or fifteen years earlier than James Morrison's death, there survives a list of "John Macleod's expenses about getting up the pay due to his brother at Portsmouth." The expenses include a fee "for a search of the navy office books for what wages was due to Thos Macleod"; a fee for a "stampt power and letter of attorney"; a mysterious payment "at the Archbishop's Prerogative Court" in respect of letters of administration; another fee for a search of the pay books at Portsmouth, the first fee being presumably for a search at the navy Office in London; and finally a fee "paid to a broker or pettyfogging attorney at the navy Office for negotiating the money at Portsmouth where the BRISTOL'S books lay."

The term "pettifogging attorney" is not used in the derogatory sense which it almost inevitably carries for us today. It was the normal and correct description of "a legal practitioner of inferior status who gets up or conducts petty cases." The collection of wages due to a seaman, even when there was no dispute was, clearly, a complicated matter, and in Thos Macleod's case seems to have required a personal visit to London and Portsmouth by his brother. On the other hand, the fact that John Macleod thought it worth his while to go to Portsmouth suggests that fairly considerable sums could be involved in a seaman's estate. There is thus a possibility, even if one can put it no higher, that the Factor's letter about James Morison's affairs, does relate to prize money earned by his seafaring son in the East Indies.

The fact that the merchant in Stornoway spelt Morison with one "r", while the master gunner spelt Morrison with two "r's", might seem to argue against their identification as father and son. Anyone who knows the Islands, however, is familiar with the process by which the spelling Morison, which is much nearer the Irish origins of the name, has been ousted, even among Gaelic enthusiasts, by the English spelling. The change should, perhaps, be interpreted as evidence of the son's anxiety to lose, or conceal, or fudge, his Highland identity at a time when many people in places of authority still saw Jacobites under every bed, and the speaking of Gaelic was forbidden on His Majesty's ships.

In many ways a small group, differentiated by language, culture, or geography, but with open access to a dominant, neighbouring, social and economic structure, is more endangered than one which is overtly oppressed. Where movement is free between the minority and the majority groupings, the ambitious, the enterprising, the natural leaders and opinion formers, among the minority, are siphoned off and enrich the dominant structure, while those who remain behind lose faith even in the value of the language and culture they preserve by their immobility. From James Morrison's day down almost to the present moment, the Gaelic areas of Scotland have been subject to a debilitating process of leakage and leeching, against which the only protection was the crumbling wall of language. It is not without significance that, although the mutiny on the BOUNTY is generally regarded as an English affair, and the quarrel between Bligh and Fletcher Christian certainly was, Shetland, Orkney and the Western Isles were all represented in the crew of 46: a contribution far out of proportion to the population. In addition, the carpenter who built the vessel the RESOLUTION was a Highlander named Macintosh, who is generally described as a man from Shields, where his wife passed as Mrs Tosh, anglicising the family surname in much the same way as James Morrison had anglicised his. The benefits were not all on one side, of course. People would not have left the islands if they did not advantage themselves by doing so and the possibility that the ú300, which saved James Morison's Stornoway business from the threat of bankruptcy in 1817, came from the prize money won by James Morrison of the BLENHEIM, shows that something did feed back to the place of origin. The loss, however, was clearly greater than the gain.

James Morrison's death is not the end of his story. He is still the subject of debate and controversy nearly two centuries after his death. In fact the second trial of James Morrison is still in progress. His Journal is our main source for the case against Bligh and anyone who attempts to rehabilitate Bligh can only do so by denigrating Morrison. In recent years, in two of the best researched books on the BOUNTY we have, Gavin Kennedy has cleared Bligh of the grosser charges of physical brutality made against him, notably in the film in which Charles Laughton played the part of Bligh. His anxiety to exculpate Bligh has, however, led Kennedy to make some curious allegations against Morrison.

Referring to the local war, in which Morrison and some of his companions were caught up, Kennedy writes: "They embarked on the stratagem of taking round the island the boy king, Tu, accompanied by a Union Jack, and compelling the other chiefs and their subjects to show deference on pain of violence. That Morrison and company would have permitted the Union Jack to be used in this way says little for their sense of responsibility. By allowing the British symbol to be misused in a bloody fight between factions which had nothing to do with British interests, they put at severe risk future callers to the island who displayed the same symbol."

The facts are rather different from the gloss which Kennedy has put on them. The Union Jack was given to the Tahitians by Capt Cox of the brig MERCURY which visited Tahiti while the BOUNTY was still at Tubai. Morrison and his companions had nothing to do with it. Moreover it was not flown as a flag but was incorporated by the Tahitians into a symbol of their own, embellished with feathers, breast plates and tassels. Morrison was well aware of the fact that the Union Jack was interpreted as a symbol of British power but what was he to do about it? The group from the BOUNTY had no command structure. They had disintegrated into little factions of their own. Some had "gone native", and made no attempt to exercise the authority of their rank over other members of the crew; others were trouble-makers causing problems for their shipmates; Morrison, and his immediate companions, were living as guests of the Tahitians. They had just succeeded, with great diplomacy, in getting authority to fell timber to build the RESOLUTION and the assistance of a vast number of natives to launch the vessel when it was ready. In that situation how do you take from your hosts a flag given to them by someone else and to which they obviously attach the greatest importance?

Kennedy reinforces his charge against Morrison and his companions by prefacing it with a little homily on the damage they allegedly did to the demographic structure of the island by introducing European firepower into the civil wars, which, conducted with native weapons, kept the population nicely in balance. "The population," he writes "declined after this and their living standards collapsed; the mutineers must carry part of the responsibility for this process." As a comment on the whole course of European colonialism, what Kennedy says is admirable but, when he implies that Tahitian history would have been significantly different, if Morrison and his companions had not returned there after the mutiny, he loses all sense of proportion and contact with reality. The disintegration of the indigenous society began when the first British man-of-war, HMS DOLPHIN, visited Tahiti and an Irish member of the crew discovered that he could buy the favours of the local women for the price of an iron nail. In a short time there were so many nails in circulation, the Captain ordered the carpenter to check his stores for pilfering. The stores were in order, but the officers discovered that the men were sleeping on the deck because they had no nails to hold their hammocks up. A little later it was found that nails were being drawn from the cleats as well. When anyone tried to tie a rope, the cleat came away in his hand. Before the DOLPHIN sailed, she was beginning to fall apart. The date of the DOLPHIN's arrival in Tahiti was 19th June 1766, when James Morrison was about six years old. The process of disintegration in Tahiti was well under way long before the mutiny on the BOUNTY, a quarter of a century later.

Apart from the fantastic suggestion that Morrison and his companions were largely responsible for corrupting the people of Tahiti and destroying the balance of the population, Gavin Kennedy makes a number of more serious charges. More serious because they relate to Morrison's character, and lie within the bounds of credibility. He says Morrison displayed a sea lawyer's mind; that his defence was "a bit too clever" and that he was "a loud mouthed fool." These criticisms are made incidentally in an examination of the status of Morrison's Journal, and the validity of Morrison's evidence against Bligh.

There can be little doubt, I think, that Kennedy is right in his contention that Morrison's Journal was written after the event, and not day by day as the events unfolded. There is nothing to indicate that Morrison ever represented it as a contemporary account. Considering the harshness of Capt Edwards, it would be more than surprising if Morrison had access to writing materials when he was on board the PANDORA; or that he retained possession of any notes he had made while on the BOUNTY or in Tahiti. It is possible that, if he had notes, they were seized on his arrest, retained with the PANDORA'S papers, and so saved from the wreck, but there is nothing to support that supposition. The status of Morrison's Journal is very much the same as the status of the paper he wrote in his own defence, and which was read at his trial. It is based on his recollection, and was no doubt coloured by the threat which was hanging over him.

Kennedy examines in minute detail every statement Morrison made in relation to Bligh but these passages do not concern us here, except for what one, borrowing from the law, might call the writer's *obiter dicta* which reflect on Morrison himself. Of special interest is Kennedy's account of a correspondence Morrison had with Rev William Howell, the minister of St John's Chapel, Portsea, after he had been condemned to death but before his reprieve. Kennedy's suggestion is that Morrison was using Howell to disseminate in naval circles his charge that the mutiny took place because Bligh had so antagonised his officers none of them would lead an attempt to retake the ship, and his complaints that the treatment he had received from Capt Edwards, as a prisoner on the PANDORA, was so oppressive as to discredit the navy, despite the harsh disciplinary standards of the day. Kennedy shows that Howell was in a position to exercise considerable influence. He was in correspondence, for instance, with Capt Molesworth Phillips, who had sailed with Capt Cook on his last voyage and was with him when he was murdered. Even more importantly, Phillips was working for Sir Joseph Banks, on whose initiative the BOUNTY sailed. The suggestion that this correspondence may have had something to do with Morrison's reprieve is possibly correct, but, instead of marvelling that a boatswain's mate under sentence of death, should be able to mobilise such influential friends from his prison, Kennedy suggests that Morrison was attempting to blackmail the authorities, because the publication of his charges against Bligh and Edwards would almost certainly have led to their appearance before a court martial. The theory would seem to be that the King pardoned Morrison to keep his mouth shut, so that Sir Joseph Banks would not be embarrassed by his protégé Bligh appearing before a court martial. That seems a pretty untenable proposition. If Howell was prepared to disseminate Morrison's side of the story, it was not because Morrison was using him to blackmail the authorities, but because Howell had been impressed by Morrison as a man and with Morrison's case. Howell was a free man and his contact with the prisoner must have been on his initiative, not Morrison's. We have already seen that Morrison made a deep impression on the anonymous writer in the "Gentleman's Magazine", who was in all probabilty one of his judges at the Court Martial. It seems perverse to attribute to some Machiavellian scheming on Morrison's part, the creation of a lobby in his favour, which, however we regard it, is a remarkable tribute to the character, courage and general charisma of the man.

The charge that Morrison was "a loud mouthed fool" is based on the account of his altercation with Capt Edwards, when he was lashed down in the bottom of the PANDORA'S pinnace for daring to speak to MacIntosh, when they were at the oars together. "If he had argued back, as he claims he did in a ship in the Channel Fleet he would have been lucky to receive less than 500 lashes," comments Kennedy. It is difficult to see the relevance of that comment. Kennedy no doubt agrees that 500 lashes for a minor breach of discipline was a monstrous and sadistic penalty. It follows from that, inevitably, that any man of spirit would try to break free from the control of an overbearing officer whenever there was an opportunity to do so with some hope of impunity. Otherwise mankind would live under perpetual tyranny.

By chance, when I was writing this chapter, I received a copy of "Lewis and Harris Seamen - 1939-45" by John and Annie Morrison of North Tolsta. There I read this extract from the reminiscences of a Carloway seaman: "Another vivid recollection is of a Lochs shipmate who took great exception to an RN Petty Officer who was forever bullying the younger and less experienced seamen, despite the Lochsman's protests. Eventually his patience was exhausted and, in full view of the ship's officers, he took the law into his own hands. He advanced on the PO and knocked him out cold. Needless to say, he found himself in the "cooler" ashore for a period followed by the unofficial punishment of a draft to the Russian convoy route." Do we condemn the Lochsman for not protecting his own skin by obeying the rules, or do we commend him for protecting the weak from a bully? It seems to me there is an affinity between that story from the Second World War and Morrison's account of the incident in the PANDORA'S pinnace, although they are separated by a century and a half of naval history. Mutiny was endemic in the Georgian navy. Generally it was justified, sometimes it was effective, and almost invariably it was provoked by the inhuman harshness of the discipline. Mutinies are not made by conspiracies in the f'c'sle. They are generally provoked from the bridge.

The incident in the PANDORA'S pinnace raises another question to which, unfortunately, there is no answer. Morrison does not indicate the nature of the conversation with Macintosh which so provoked Capt Edwards's wrath. Is it possible they were having a quiet chat in Gaelic? Morrison nowhere in his Journal gives any indication that he was a Gaelic speaker, or indeed of his Island provenance, and I have suggested the reasons for this low profile, My speculation may be entirely wide of the mark, but, at least, it is consistent with what we know of Gaelic speakers, in similar situations, in other wars.

The old proverb tells us that a man is known by the company he keeps. Perhaps in a highly structured society like the Georgian navy we should say the company that keeps him. Our assessment of James Morrison rests on a much more solid base than the close textual scrutiny of the BOUNTY literature by people who are arguing the case between Bligh and Fletcher Christian. We can best define Morrison's position and status by taking bearings from those around him. Morrison was disliked by Capt Edwards of the PANDORA, who was manifestly a harsh tyrannical commander and by Capt Bligh who had a disagreeable nature and a vicious tongue, which alienated even his officers. On the other hand, Morrison had the confidence of Captain Stirling, who vouched for him in very specific terms at the Court Martial as a man responsive to discipline. He also had the confidence of Pellew, under whom he served in very difficult circumstances. Above all he was so highly regarded for his professional skill by Troubridge that he was sought out to be master gunner on his flagship. Charles Stirling had a distinguished career in the navy and rose to the rank of rear admiral. Pellew, who became Lord Exmouth, was one of the most influential men in the navy in his day. Troubridge was esteemed by his contemporaries as second only to Nelson. None of them would have tolerated "a loud mouthed fool".

There is a phrase in Professor Derick Thomson's "Introduction to Gaelic Poetry" which may give us the clue to Morrison's character. Dealing with the outspoken criticism of a degenerate laird in the poems of An Clarsair Dall, Thomson suggests the Harper was raising "the independent and fearless voice of the Lewisman." In standing up to Capt Bligh and Capt Edwards, and in his defence before the Court Martial, James Morrison, who was a great grandson of the Harper, was doing the same He was, in fact, a representative island seaman: skilled in the handling of boats; imperturbable in the face of danger; ready to be led by those he respected while utterly resistant to coercion. He was one of the pioneers of a great island tradition which reached its highest point in the Second World War.